EUROPE

pp.110–211

ICELAND
154
155
156
153

NORWAY
312
313
314

SWEDEN
311
308

FINLAND
310
306
307

ESTONIA
303
309

LATVIA

LITHUANIA

BELARUS

DENMARK
232
233

SCOTLAND
165
171 168
166 172
170
163 167 169
164

IRELAND
157
162 158–161

UNITED KINGDOM
178
176 181
173
WALES
174
ENGLAND
179 184 182
180 177 186–193
183 185

NETHERLANDS
230
229
231
248
228
BELGIUM

GERMANY
238
241–247

POLAND
288
287

UKRAINE

CZECH REPUBLIC
286

SLOVAKIA
285

MOLDOVA

FRANCE
211 213–221
225
241
240
209
194
212 235 236 237
222
210
211
223 224
226 227
SWITZERLAND
234
239
249
250
256
254
270
253
259
260
258
257

AUSTRIA
251–252
277
SLOVENIA
276
255

HUNGARY
283
289

ROMANIA
291

CROATIA
284
278
279
281
280
282

BOSNIA AND HERZEGOVINA

SERBIA

MONTE NEGRO
KOSOVO

BULGARIA
292
298

NORTH MACEDONIA

ALBANIA
290

ITALY
261–269
270–271 272
273
274
275

PORTUGAL
196
195

SPAIN
197
206
203
208
202
204 205
207
200
198 199 201

GREECE
293
296
294
295

TURKEY
299 301
302
300
297

THE
TRAVEL
BUCKET LIST

THE
TRAVEL
BUCKET LIST

Dream up your next
big adventure

CONTENTS

INTRODUCTION

○────────○

If you could go anywhere in the world tomorrow, where would it be? To Egypt to see the pyramids? To Japan for cherry blossom season? Perhaps to Brazil to party at Rio carnival? No doubt all three are on your bucket list—and they're on ours too.

But what about the travel dreams you never knew you had? You'll find exactly that within these pages. We've drawn on decades of travel expertise to create *The Travel Bucket List*, the ultimate collection of sights, cities, festivals, food—you name it—to enjoy in a lifetime. Because travel is one of life's greatest pleasures. It takes us to landscapes beyond our wildest imagination, transports us back in time to long-gone civilizations, and exposes us to different people and cultures—and you better be sure you'll always be left with a story to tell for years to come.

We'll help you write the first page. *The Travel Bucket List* takes you on a journey around the world, from the southern tip of South America to the northern reaches of Europe, and everywhere in between. Enjoy the perfect gelato on the streets of Florence, witness the roaring Victoria Falls of Zimbabwe, road trip down the Pacific Coast Highway—both big and small, bucket list adventures can be found around every corner.

After all, the thrill of discovering something and somewhere new is unmatched, and dreaming is just the beginning.

Previous page: China's mighty Li River flowing past the karst mountains of Guilin
This page: An evening sunset casting a golden glow over Horseshoe Bend in Arizona

NORTH AMERICA

Catch a wave and surf the waters of Hawaii

As the birthplace of modern surfing, the Aloha State is where dreams of riding the swells of the Pacific can come true—even for those new to this ancient Polynesian tradition. Make like the legendary surfer Duke Kahanamoku and start out with a longboard lesson in the gentle blue waves of Oʻahu's Waikīkī Beach. Ready to elevate your game? Join the salty dawn patrol of Oʻahu's windy North Shore, where you can take to the epic rollers of Haleʻiwa Beach Park. Only the most skilled can charge toward the renowned Banzai Pipeline over at ʻEhukai Beach Park, where thick, looming curls of water reach heights of up to 30 ft (9 m) and thunder back down to the ocean with such force that the sandy beach shudders underfoot. No matter your level, there really is nowhere quite like Hawaii to surf.

Good to know: Winter is when the North Shore waves reach their peak point, while the ocean calms in the summer months.

WHERE ELSE TO WATCH LAVA FLOW

MOUNT ETNA, SICILY, ITALY
Europe's highest and most active volcano, towering Mount Etna regularly emits oozing streams of lava from 10,990 ft (3,350 m).

KIRISHIMA-KINKOWAN NATIONAL PARK, JAPAN
Lava flows are rare in Japan, which makes the activity from the strata-volcano Sakurajima at this park even more impressive.

1

See lava glow at Hawaiʻi Volcanoes National Park

While journeying to the center of the Earth is off-limits, you can at least imagine you're halfway there with a visit to Hawaiʻi Volcanoes National Park. Located on Hawaiʻi (also known as the Big Island), a pair of majestic volcanoes make up this elemental attraction: Mauna Loa and Kīlauea, two of the most active volcanoes in the world. The park offers the chance to see lava spew into the ocean, walk across a hardened lava lake and watch steam rise from the ground. And while an eruption can cause devastation, there's life here too: old-growth koa and ʻohiʻa lehua rainforests, endemic birds such as the ʻelepaio and ʻapapane, and endless petroglyphs that speak of the island's earliest inhabitants. Two scenic routes provide easy ways of getting close to the action: the Crater Rim Drive, which skirts the edge of the Kīlauea caldera, and the Chain of Craters Road, which veers toward the coast. Drive both. A bubbling, bursting, restless Earth awaits.

Good to know: Check the official Hawaiʻi Volcanoes National Park website for updates on current lava sightings.

Discover the ancient landscapes of Kaua'i

No real dinosaurs ever roamed Hawaii's oldest island, but Steven Spielberg's animatronic creations in *Jurassic Park* didn't exactly look out of place here. That's because Kaua'i's landscape still feels pre-historic: fern-filled rainforests cloak ancient peaks and rushing waterfalls tumble into lush valleys. Much of this verdant landscape has changed little since it was first created. Take Kaua'i's spectacular Waimea Canyon, a world of plunging gorges formed millions of years ago by the Earth's shuddering tectonic plates. Or there's the Nāpali Coast State Wilderness Park, its spiky ancient cliffs mimicking the spine of a slumbering stegosaurus. Numerous hiking trails weave through the island, guaranteeing jaw-dropping views. You won't see any dinosaurs of course, but the slightest ripple of a puddle could still send a shiver down your spine.

Good to know: Be prepared—the weather can change from heavy rainstorm to bluebird-blue sky within an hour.

ALASKA, USA

Kayak through Denali National Park

Larger than the entire state of New Hampshire, Alaska's renowned national park promises nature on the grandest scale. And there's no better way to see it all than by kayak. Byers Lake, at the foothills of the rocky Kesugi Ridge, is the base for your paddling adventure. Here, you'll float across a translucent watery surface, silently slipping past the shore—with less chance of disturbing the local wildlife than if you were on foot. And this isn't the kind of wildlife you want to disturb: hulking grizzly bears, prowling wolves, and wandering moose can all be found within the vast wilderness of the park. In a kayak, you'll also be treated to two images of this painterly landscape. Reflected across the shimmering water is a blanket of multihued forest, overlooked by the snowy hulk of Mount Denali, North America's tallest peak. Take it all in while bobbing upon the tranquil waters of the lake, arms a little tired, but soul soothed.

Good to know: Kayak rentals (and guided tours) are available from Denali Southside River Guides at Byers Lake.

ALASKA, USA

See Mendenhall Glacier

Of Alaska's 616 named glaciers, Mendenhall is one of the most impressive and, fortunately, most accessible. This pale-blue river of ice oozes from the massive Juneau Icefield, creaking and cracking as it shifts. It measures a staggering 13 miles (21 km) long and ½ mile (0.8 km) wide and can, unlike many of Alaska's glaciers, be viewed without taking a cruise. Just pick one of the short walks that fan out from the visitor center and you'll soon find yourself rewarded with an unobstructed panorama of Mendenhall Lake (the glacier's terminus). Here, lonely icebergs float beneath the glistening glacial towers as more chunks break away—Mendenhall is, after all, in a state of retreat. Receding by more than 160 ft (50 m) per year, the glacier has revealed the remains of a once-smothered ancient forest. It's a remarkable scene, but it could very easily be a transient one. As this fragile natural wonder continues to retreat, it's fast becoming a once-in-a-lifetime experience to see it for yourself.

Good to know: The drive to the Mendenhall Glacier Visitor Center is just 12 miles (19 km) from downtown Juneau.

6

ALASKA, USA

Cruise the Inside Passage

Want to get away from it all? Set sail through the Inside Passage. Cut off from the rest of North America, this spectacular sea channel of islands is sandwiched between the fjordlands of the Pacific Northwest. Journeys by cruise ship usually start in Seattle or Vancouver, before winding their way past snow-tipped peaks, dense forested islands and open ocean. Small port towns dot the coastline, offering the occasional dose of reality, but most of the time you'll be surrounded by a landscape untouched by civilization. Here, wildlife rules. Grizzly and black bears stalk deserted isles while orcas and whales (best viewed from May to December) lay claim to the vast ocean depths. On a cruise ship, you'll see—and hear—it all: fall asleep to the sound of howling wolves along the shore and awaken to a chorus of seals. As you enter the chilly edges of Alaska, the grand finale awaits. Home to 11 tidewater glaciers, magnificent Glacier Bay feels more akin to Antarctica than America. Adrift in the ocean here, a wall of ice in front of you, you'll surely feel far away from it all.

Good to know: To cover the full route of the Inside Passage, you'll need to set aside around one week.

> Small port towns dot the coastline, offering the occasional dose of reality, but most of the time you'll be surrounded by a landscape untouched by civilization.

7

WASHINGTON, USA

Smell that teen spirit in Seattle

Seattle is one of the biggest cultural hubs in the northwest US. It's famous for being the home of Starbucks and TV sitcom radio host Frasier, but perhaps more than anything, grunge. In the early 1990s, bands like Nirvana, Soundgarden and Pearl Jam blasted onto the scene, defining a new musical movement. The guitar-heavy, metal-infused genre became the soul of Seattle Sound and remains much-loved in the city, drawing fans from around the world for musical pilgrimages. The Museum of Pop Culture is a great first stop, offering a deep dive into its history. You can retrace the steps of the greats at the Terminal Sales Building, home to the grunge record label Sub Pop, and Central Saloon, where many bands played early gigs. Over in Viretta Park, pay your respects to the Nirvana front man at the Kurt Cobain Bench. To literally walk in the footsteps of grunge's greats, simply stare out moodily at West Point Lighthouse—it shows up in several seminal music videos.

Good to know: If you're short on time, opt for one of the many organized music-themed tours from local operators.

8

MISSOURI TO OREGON, USA

Follow in the footsteps of Lewis and Clark

Imagine a time when traveling meant traversing unmapped territory. Those days may be behind us, but you can still embrace the spirit of discovery on this epic cross-country road trip. In 1804, Lewis and Clark led an expeditionary party—including civilians; enslaved people; and Sacagawea, a Shoshone interpreter—to establish an American presence in the region. The route they forged linked the muddy Mississippi River with the Pacific Ocean, and today you can drive its spectacular 4,900 miles (7,900 km). Start in St. Louis and head northwest through one scenic state and then another. Be sure to stop at Fort Clatsop, home to a replica Lewis and Clark camp. Even if a land has been traveled before, there is still wonder in discovering it for yourself—with the help of Google Maps, thank heavens.

Good to know: Stop at the trail's headquarters in Omaha to learn about the expedition and plan your journey.

9

MONTANA , USA

Hit Going-to-the-Sun Road

Twisting through Glacier National Park, Going-to-the-Sun Road climbs over the Continental Divide—expect gasp-worthy views that get bigger and better the higher you go. Despite being only 50 miles (80 km), this route encompasses some of the area's most spectacular alpine scenery. Yes, you could complete the drive in a couple of hours, but set aside a full day to take in the sights, which range from glacier-carved peaks to ancient forests. From West Glacier, the route spins along the flat shore of Lake McDonald before ascending a valley corridor squeezed by soaring peaks. Look out for wildlife, including mountain goats and bighorn sheep around Logan Pass. As you descend to the end point of turquoise St. Mary Lake, spot grizzly bears, regular visitors to the plains at Two Dog Flats on the mountain's eastern side. Short and sweet, Going-to-the-Sun Road remains a jam-packed drive.

Good to know: The road is usually open from July to October, but check for road closures as close to departing as you can.

10

MONTANA AND WYOMING, USA

Spy American bison

There are few images more representative of the American West than bison roaming on the open plains. The species nearly became extinct in the 19th century, but now number in their thousands. You can catch a glimpse of them in Wyoming's Yellowstone National Park, where thousands live freely in the wild; its 4,700-strong population is not only the world's largest herd but also the oldest in the country. These great beasts rove the park's forests and grasslands, occasionally making their way to the road, where they stop traffic and wander beside vehicles. Along with Yellowstone National Park, another great place to see bison in their natural habitat is at Flathead Valley's Bison Range in Montana. This famed bison conservation area is the place to see around 350 bison roam alongside abundant other wildlife: pronghorns, bears, and elk among them.

Good to know: Yellowstone's Hayden and Lamar Valleys are some of the best places in the park to see bison.

Raft in Grand Teton National Park

Another of Wyoming's extraordinary national parks, Grand Teton is a mere 30 miles (50 km) away from nearby Yellowstone. But in terms of what these two incredible parks offer, they couldn't be further apart. Grand Teton is home to some of the youngest mountains in the world, as well as spectacular stretches of wilderness. And the park's 485 sq miles (1,300 sq km) of plains and valleys are best seen from the water. Snake River, near the town of Jackson, offers a wealth of superb rafting in the area. There are whitewater options, but if you're keen to admire the landscape and spy wildlife—think black and grizzly bears, bison, elk, and bald eagles—then opt for scenic rafting instead. On a guided trip, you'll meander along the river in Jackson Hole Valley, passing spruce forests and wildflower-dusted plains. As you bob downriver, with snow-capped mountains rising above you, any thoughts of rival parks (no matter how close they are) will surely drift away.

Good to know: The town of Jackson makes a good base for exploring the park's southern reaches and top spots for rafting.

WYOMING, USA

Count the colors at Grand Prismatic Spring

Set atop a dormant supervolcano, Yellowstone National Park holds more than half the world's geysers and hydrothermal features, making it truly unique. Walk amid bubbling mud pots, hissing fumaroles and sizzling hot springs in a remarkable, otherworldly landscape that glows with seemingly unnatural hues. None impresses more than the technicolor Grand Prismatic, America's largest (and the world's third-largest) hot spring, and the star of the park's Midway Geyser Basin. Its deep blue pool is surrounded by bands of turquoise, yellow, orange and brown in an otherwise blasted volcanic landscape of mud and white ash. Plumes of steam rise dramatically from its boiling center and, with a diameter of around 370 ft (110 m), it's quite the spectacle. The basin's boardwalk snakes around a few other geothermal features, including the dormant Excelsior Geyser and the smaller, calmer Turquoise and Opal pools. Part of the bubbling, volcanic Firehole River Valley, the basin is especially magical in early evening, when hikers and bison herds are silhouetted against plumes of mineral spray and steam.

Good to know: For a bird's-eye view, walk ½ mile (1 km) from Fairy Falls Trailhead; the colors are best from May to September.

CALIFORNIA, USA

Drive along the Pacific Coast Highway

There's no denying that America is the home of the road trip, with many epic drives fighting for the title of country's finest. One worthy contender is the Pacific Coast Highway. Stretching out between San Diego and Seattle for some 1,650 miles (2,655 km), it really is the stuff of classic road-trip dreams. The journey from LA to San Francisco is enough for most: heading north, the glittering ocean opens up almost as soon as you leave the Hollywood hot spot. Stop at the likes of Santa Barbara for outdoor adventures and San Simeon to spot elephant seals. Farther north, you'll pass through Big Sur, the unquestionable highlight of the entire ride. Picture jagged-edged cliffs rising from the ocean and dense redwood forests reaching for the sky. What are you waiting for? Hop in a convertible and hit the road.

Good to know: Stop off at Piedras Blancas between Los Angeles and San Francisco to see huge elephant seals on the shores.

SOUTH DAKOTA, USA

Meet former presidents at Mount Rushmore

Ever met a president? How about four of them at once? Make your way to South Dakota's Mount Rushmore National Memorial and you'll find yourself face to face with just that. Memorialized in the mountain are George Washington, Thomas Jefferson, Theodore Roosevelt, and Abraham Lincoln, their huge, protruding faces looming over the valley below. Named *Shrine of Democracy*, the colossal sculpture was constructed from 1927 to 1941, with each of the presidents' faces standing 60 ft (18 m) tall. For the best vantage point, walk along the Avenue of Flags pedestrian mall to reach Grand View Terrace, which overlooks an amphitheater, a swathe of pine forest and Mount Rushmore beyond. The sculpture isn't without its controversy: the Black Hills are considered sacred by the Lakota Sioux people, who continue to demand the land's return. The Crazy Horse Memorial under construction in the Black Hills nearby seeks to remind visitors that for some Americans, there are other heroes worth recognizing too.

Good to know: The Presidential Trail leads to the Sculptor's Studio, where designer Gutzon Borglum lived and worked.

SAN FRANCISCO

Free-thinkin', flamboyant 'Frisco is alive and kicking. Visit this Californian gem
to discover those steep hills and painted houses you've seen in the movies, taste
fine food and drink made from a bounty of local fresh produce, and uncover the
stories that have quite literally inspired a nation.

15

Let inspiration strike at the SFMOMA

The dramatic San Francisco Museum of Modern
Art, known better as SFMOMA, is the heart of the
city's art scene. The iconic Modernist building is
impressive inside and out, housing more than 17,000
works of art in its 50,000 sq ft (4,600 sq m) of gallery
space, and offering a dynamic schedule of changing
exhibits from around the world. It's chock-full of
20th- and 21st-century art: you'll find everything
from Frida Kahlo's deceptively simple *Frida and
Diego Rivera* (1931) to Olafur Eliasson's bright
and immersive *One-way color tunnel* (2007) here.
Then there's the memorable gallery dedicated to
the dainty, abstract mobiles of sculptor Alexander
Calder. The institution also champions local artists,
who are involved in an ongoing project to cover one
gallery in murals, while the garden outside features
America's largest living wall, a vast green blanket
of 19,000 plants. Immerse yourself in the creativity
that imbues this space and let yourself feel inspired
by the art, old and new, around you.

Good to know: The San Francisco CityPASS offers a good
discount on entry to SFMOMA (plus three more attractions).

16

Walk across the Golden Gate Bridge

Standing on the Golden Gate Bridge, what hits the hardest is its sheer scale—it's not easy to gauge from pictures just how far you are from the icy waters below, not to mention the extraordinary length of the structure. A leisurely walk across the iconic Golden Gate can take anything from 30 minutes to an hour, depending on how much time you spend soaking in the views. Looking 220 ft (70 m) below, you can see and smell the briny tides of San Francisco Bay, as well as the ships and vessels that pass beneath it. Gaze up to appreciate the engineering prowess needed to build the bridge's towers, some 750 ft (230 m) above the water and painted in distinctive "International Orange." The views from the walkway are mesmerizing, encompassing Sausalito and Angel Island, Alcatraz and the skyscrapers of downtown San Francisco. If the city's famous fog lifts, you may even spy the rugged Farallon Islands far out in the Pacific. Not many bridges are worthy of travel bucket lists, but this one definitely lives up to the hype.

Good to know: To cross the bridge on foot, you'll need to use the East Sidewalk; check opening times before setting out.

MUST-SEE SIGHTS FOR SAN FRAN HISTORY

Haight-Ashbury Clock
A long-time reminder of the city's 1967 Summer of Love and hippie culture.

San Francisco Cable Car Museum
Discover the mysteries of the cable-car system.

Rainbow Honor Walk
This LGBTQ+ "Walk of Fame" honors the Castro's history of queer activism.

Chinatown
Take a tour of San Francisco's Chinatown, said to be the oldest in the country.

The Beat Museum
The spirit of the Beat generation lives on at this indie spot.

Alcatraz
Learn about the former residents of this iconic prison.

Painted Ladies
Oft-pictured, these pastel-colored houses are a reminder of the city of old.

17

Patrol Alcatraz

"The Rock" is only a short boat ride from the busy and touristy Fisherman's Wharf, but, when a cool fog drifts in, it's like arriving in another world. It's no wonder it was near impossible to escape: surrounded by the deadly currents and freezing waters of San Francisco Bay, the former prison looms above the waves, its granite cliffs and crags reinforced by thick brick walls and guard towers. Lying 3 miles (5 km) east of the Golden Gate, Alcatraz Island served as a maximum-security penitentiary from 1934 to 1963, housing some of America's most notorious criminals (Al Capone and "Machine Gun" Kelly among them). Today, it's a whole other story—the island is now part of the National Parks system and open to all for tours. You can walk around the main cell block, beneath which lie the remnants of a Civil War–era fortress known as the "dungeon." Exhibits also bring to life the extraordinary events of 1969, when the island was seized by members of the Native American Movement seeking to reclaim the land. For such a small island, it packs in a lot of history.

Good to know: Ferries crossing the bay and tours of Alcatraz quickly sell out, so make advance reservations.

18

CALIFORNIA TO WASHINGTON, USA

Take the Amtrak Coast Starlight train

Gorgeous train routes are not the easiest to come by in the US, which makes this rare example all the more appealing. Leaving LA, Amtrak's *Coast Starlight* travels some 1,370 miles (2,200 km), tracing the Pacific coastline before scooting north through Oregon and Washington to journey's end in Seattle. The service takes in some of America's most dazzling scenery: the snow-smothered peaks of the Cascade Range; lush redwood forests; and long, misty stretches of Pacific Ocean shoreline. In northern California, snow-capped volcanoes fill the horizon, among them the giant cone of Mount Shasta, which looms over pine woods, its white-streaked summit shimmering in the sunshine. As the journey continues, expect mirror lakes, twisting mountain passes and more volcanic peaks in Oregon and Washington. If you feel like splashing out on some comforts, the train's fancy Superliner bedrooms come with twin bunks and a private bathroom, plus onboard meals. But, even if you're riding coach, the views from your reclining seat are no less superb. On the final stretch, it feels like you're skimming Puget Sound as the skyscrapers of Seattle tower ahead. Who said the US can't do great train journeys?

Good to know: Book ahead to get the best prices; reclining coach seats are much cheaper than private sleeper rooms.

LOS ANGELES

All that glitters may not always be gold in Tinseltown, but at least you can count on dazzling sunshine most days. Warm rays illuminate every corner of this city and infuse it with a sense of ease as well as glamour. Whether strolling down a palm-lined beachfront or the Walk of Fame, this laid-back city is hard to miss.

19

Dive into film history in Hollywood

Getting déjà vu while checking out LA? It's probably because you're somewhere that you've seen on screen. Hollywood looms large here, with industry icons sprinkled all over town—and luckily for film fans, you can see many of them for free. Take a peek inside the Bradbury Building, which starred in *Blade Runner* and *Citizen Kane*. Stroll down Rodeo Drive like Julia Roberts in *Pretty Woman*. Or pretend you're at Harvard with Elle Woods at USC Campus (a filming location for *Legally Blonde*). If you'd rather check off a bunch of filming locations at once, head to a studio. Warner Bros Studio Tour offers one of the most famous backstage passes in the city, giving visitors a chance to see the *Friends* fountain and wander around the picture-perfect town of Stars Hollow from *Gilmore Girls*. Paramount Studios and Sony Pictures also offer fascinating tours of their back lots. Eager for more? The list of locations is endless. From the very birth of Hollywood, Tinseltown has provided a backdrop for hundreds of films and TV shows. You might not even realize when you're walking past a legendary location—and wait, was that who I think it was? Walking along Hollywood's streets, there's no telling which famous stars and places you might see along the way.

Good to know: You can apply ahead of time online to be part of the live audiences on shows like *America's Got Talent*.

20

See LA's alternative side in Venice Beach

The Venice Beach of your imagination can't actually be real, can it? Sweat-slicked bodybuilders testing their strength on the sand, super-tanned skateboarders whizzing along the boardwalk: LA's iconic beach resort has a famously eccentric reputation. And amazingly, it's all true. Muscle Beach, the birthplace of the US's fitness boom and former training ground of Arnold Schwarzenegger, still attracts tremendously toned locals. Meanwhile, the palm tree-lined boardwalk remains a rush of rollerbladers, street performers, and buzzing market stalls. LA's freewheeling neighborhood has long stayed true to its roots: it began as a party area in the 1910s with its rowdy dance hall before becoming a hub for the beatnik community in the 1950s. Today, it's a snapshot of the real LA, a haven for arty hippies, street performers, and kids with big dreams. Hands down, this is the city's best place to go people-watching. Grab a coffee from a local café and take a walk along the boardwalk, absorbing the colorful scenes that play out in front of you. Or better yet, strap on your rollerblades (as escapees Barbie and Ken do in Greta Gerwig's blockbuster hit) and take a ride beside the sands.

Good to know: Spring and fall are the best times to visit, with more bearable temperatures and fewer crowds.

MUST-SEE LA BEACHES

Venice Beach
Wander along the boardwalk to enjoy the eccentric atmosphere of this famous area.

Malibu Beach
Promising some of the city's best waves, Malibu Beach is LA's surfing hot spot. It's also famed for its wealthy residents—spot the mansions curving around the shore.

Zuma Beach
See dolphins and whales as you watch the sunset from this scenic swathe of sand. The water here is also the cleanest in the city.

South Beach Santa Monica
Escape the crowds of Venice Beach at this nearby area, loved by locals.

Paradise Cove
For a taste of glitz and glamour, rent a sunbed at this lovely sandy beach. Partly private, it's very well maintained.

Leo Carrillo State Park
You'll find one of the few beaches in LA that welcomes dogs in this coastal park.

21

Explore the famous sights of Griffith Park

Few sights in the States are as iconic as the huge Hollywood sign. And the swathes of greenery that surround it are LA's famed Griffith Park. The largest urban park in the US, this vast wilderness of rolling hills, gentle valleys, and flower-filled meadows is slap bang in the center of the city. You'd be forgiven for feeling cinematic when you walk around it—the park has been immortalized in a flurry of films, from the classic *Rebel Without a Cause* (1955) to musical extravaganza *La La Land* (2016). Standing beneath the looming letters (erected in 1923 to advertise the Hollywoodland housing development) is a must, but no visit to the park is complete without a trip to the iconic Griffith Observatory. Sporting a grand black and white exterior, the building houses astral exhibits, a huge public telescope, and a beloved planetarium, with the world's most advanced projector inside. It's perched high on the slopes of Mount Hollywood, too, meaning visitors can enjoy both staggering views of the stars and breathtaking panoramas of the downtown skyline below.

Good to know: Griffith Park is huge and one of the best ways to explore it is by bike—rent one from Spokes 'n Stuff.

CALIFORNIA, USA

Explore Yosemite National Park

The national parks are sometimes described as "America's best idea," and Yosemite was the light bulb that sparked the whole project. First protected in 1864 and designated a national park in 1890, this natural arena promises beauty in abundance. Waterfalls tumble down the cliffs, catching the light to create shimmering rainbows. Giant sequoias and redwoods rule the forests, casting shadows on the wild bears that roam here. Easily the park's most recognizable landmark, however, is Half Dome, a wavelike peak that has come to symbolize Yosemite's dramatic terrain. Still protected, the park draws millions of visitors a year, and it's one of the project's first success stories. There are 62 other parks in the National Park System, but if you're going to visit one, make it Yosemite.

Good to know: Reservations are required to drive through the park on some days between mid-April and late October.

24

CALIFORNIA, USA

See the tallest trees in Sequoia National Park

There's something inherently magical about a park named after the largest tree species in the world. The giant sequoia trees are the undeniable highlight, but Sequoia National Park doesn't stop there when it comes to colossal natural wonders. It also harbors a 10,000-year-old cave complex found deep underground and Mount Whitney, the highest peak in the Lower 48 states. Defining the landscape in the western half of the park are the world-renowned sequoias that give it its name. Among these is the General Sherman tree, which reaches a jaw-dropping, neck-cricking height of 275 ft (85 m). Thought to be well over 2,000 years old, General Sherman is also the largest known tree on earth, standing tall in the park's impressive Giant Forest. Fallen trees remain too: the Tunnel Log is famed for the large hole cut through its lower half, which cars can pass through, while Tharp's Log was hollowed out and made into the one-time home of the 19th-century pioneer Hale Tharp. Wherever you ramble through this park's roadless wilderness, nature's giants create a space of epic proportions.

Good to know: Shuttles run daily in summer, stopping at major attractions like the Sherman Tree and Giant Forest Museum.

23

CALIFORNIA, USA

Spy a California condor at Pinnacles National Park

Smaller and younger than other parks, the craggy Pinnacles National Park is not to be overlooked. There are trademark cliffs and hidden talus caves, but there's also something even rarer: the elusive California condor. With a wingspan up to 10 ft (3 m) wide, the California condor is the largest land bird in America. In the 1980s, it became extinct in the wild before being saved through captive breeding. Due to the endangered nature of these huge vultures (there are around 500 in the world today), you'll have to work hard to see one. But, once you do, watching them swerve past the volcanic outcroppings is truly breathtaking. Climb to the High Peaks viewing areas at dawn or dusk, when the birds will most likely take to the air. If you spot a large bird gliding smoothly through the air, you've found yourself a condor.

Good to know: Visit in the spring, when temperatures are best for walking and wildflowers are in bloom along the trails.

THE YUKON, CANADA

Competition over Canada's natural resources came to a head when a large gold nugget was found in the Klondike River in 1896. Head to this northwest territory to see the landscapes that kick-started the gold rush.

ALASKA, USA

Gold fever hit Alaska in the late 19th century. Visit towns such as Juneau, Skagway, and Nome to discover gold rush history or set off on the 35-mile (56-km) Chilkoot Trail, the most famous of several trails linking the coast with the Yukon goldfields.

WASHINGTON, USA

Seattle was the largest and closest US city to the gold fields of the Klondike, making it a primary outfitting and embarkation point. Visit the city's Klondike Gold Rush National Historical Park to find out more.

25

CALIFORNIA, USA

Explore gold rush history in Death Valley

The Golden State has long been a hopeful beacon of possibility, inspiring dreams of great success and prosperity. This identity dates back to the infamous gold rush of 1848, which saw Americans traipsing from east to west in the hopes of finding some of those precious gold specks in California's waterways. The journey was fraught with dangers along the way, none more so than in Death Valley, named after pioneers who perished there while traveling through. Today a national park, the broiling desert region is where the history of the gold rush really comes to life. Step back in time from one of the valley's bases for exploration, like The Oasis at Death Valley over in Furnace Creek, which also has a visitor center. The Skidoo town site is easy to get to, as is the ghost town of Rhyolite, preserved as a striking example of a gold rush boomtown. Among all the valley's unforgiving canyons, burning salt flats, and silken sand dunes, you'll really understand the trials and tribulations of the gold-hungry prospectors of the 19th century.

Good to know: The hot landscape of Death Valley can be relentless, so come prepared with ample water and supplies.

Lose yourself in Las Vegas

Ever imitated but never bettered, there's nowhere quite like Las Vegas. To visit this bright light city is to enter a bubble universe, one where neon reigns supreme and time seemingly stands still. One minute you're whiling away the evening in the casino, the next you're blinking into the bright daylight and grueling Nevada heat, unsure whether it's been four hours or 24. Along the Strip, that infamous 4-mile (6-km) road at the heart of the city, couples hotfoot it hand in hand to one of the Elvis-themed wedding chapels, passing sights that seem to belong elsewhere, like the replica Eiffel Tower outside the Paris Hotel. Among it all, some of the world's biggest stars, those identifiable by just one name— Adele, Elton, Britney—take to the stage with spectacular shows as part of their famous Las Vegas residencies. How you'll wish there were more than 24 hours in the day—it's hard to sleep a minute away in "Sin City."

Good to know: More than 40 million visitors head to Vegas's many hotels each year—plan ahead to ensure your stay.

NEVADA, USA

Let your hair down at Burning Man

Once a year, dedicated festival-goers travel to a remote Nevada desert and set up a makeshift city for a week. With no currency, no sponsorships and no programming, what happens is totally dependent on who shows up and what they bring to the table. While Burning Man is known as a place where you can let your freak flag fly, it's also an experiment in collaboration and goodwill, rooted in self-reliance, active participation, and getting nothing in return. Strange and beautiful art exhibits light up the desert, mutant art cars cruise the open "playa," and the city's "streets" are full of unique experiences to explore, entirely curated by those who attend. Free yoga classes, makeshift bars, educational seminars, all-night parties, pyrotechnics a plenty: this is what happens when creative people come together.

Good to know: Burning Man takes places the week leading up to and including Labor Day weekend.

UTAH, USA

Admire the red rocks of Zion National Park

Towering red cliffs, rock formations dating back millions of years, frozen sand dunes: Zion National Park is a desert playground for adventurers of all kinds. It centers on a sublime canyon, carved 2,640 ft (800 m) deep by the Virgin River. Venture into its heart, where cottonwoods crinkle in the wind and sandstone cliffs tower overhead. In the Narrows, follow the river as it squeezes between walls just 20 ft (6 m) apart. Splashing through the shallow waters, with striated rock all around, is an unforgettable experience. Having gazed up at the canyon, head to Angels Landing for a bird's-eye view over the gorge; to get there involves a hike along a narrow fin of rock, not ideal for the acrophobic. Fortunately the in-park lodge and a plethora of picnic tables provide a more relaxing vantage point.

Good to know: Rain in the desert can create dangerous flash floods, so always check the weather before canyon hiking.

ARIZONA, USA

Take in Canyon de Chelly National Monument

There might be many places in southwest USA to see relics of Indigenous life, but none are quite like Canyon De Chelly National Monument, an area that people have called home for more than 5,000 years. Located within the boundaries of the Navajo Nation, and still inhabited by several dozen families, the monument contains preserved cliff dwellings and rock art from the Ancestral Puebloans who lived here more than a thousand years ago. There is abundant natural beauty in the red rock canyons, towering rock spires, and working farms, all of which can be seen from overlooks on the canyon's rim. The real draw here is the chance to travel to the canyon floor with a Diné (Navajo) guide. Head down on foot, horseback, or even a 4WD, and feel the history within these sandstone walls.

Good to know: The White House Ruin trail is the only in-canyon route non-Navajo visitors can hike without a guide.

ARIZONA, USA

See the Grand Canyon at Horseshoe Bend

No matter how many pictures you've seen, nothing prepares you for the beauty of the Grand Canyon. Words like "magnificent" and "stupendous" pale in comparison to the scene that stretches as far as your eyes can see. One of the landscape's most incredible spots is Horseshoe Bend, where the dark-green Colorado river meanders around a huge column of sandstone. Take in the view from the East Rim of the Grand Canyon. Standing here, trying to absorb the sheer scale of the gorge, it's easy to understand why it's considered one of the seven natural wonders of the world. To make your experience even more memorable, stop off at the parking lot on Route 89 and follow the easy but dusty hike to the viewpoint around dusk, when the sinking sun turns the rocky desert of the Navajo Nation a rusty red.

Good to know: Visit at the weekend or before 10 a.m. or after 2 p.m. to try to avoid the (practically unavoidable) crowds.

COLORADO, USA

Sample a craft brew in Denver

Beer is a staple across much of the US, and the city of Denver is home to plenty of the good stuff. Robust stouts and jet-black porters. German-style wheat beers and pilsners. Fruit beers, pumpkin ales, and IPAs—a hoppy favorite perfected here and brewed at triple strength. Denver's beer revolution began in the late 1980s, when small-batch producers like Wynkoop Brewing opened in LoDo (Lower Downtown). It's not hard to see why the beer here is so good: the snow-topped Rockies are clearly visible from the city, their mountain springs providing the water for its many breweries. Today, the Denver Beer Trail encompasses a whopping 150 brewpubs, microbreweries, and taprooms. Most are small-scale affairs: think warehouse-like spaces with a handful of tables, a bar lined with taps, and current brews described and listed on wooden slats above. It's all pretty casual, with nightly food trucks providing the bar snacks, but you can usually bring your own too. Start with a flight of sample beers before grabbing a tall glass of your favorite brew—plus a four-pack to take home.

Good to know: Most Denver taprooms have happy hours when brews are discounted, usually daily Sunday to Wednesday.

NEW MEXICO, USA

Watch hot-air balloons rise across Albuquerque

One hot-air balloon, sailing silently across the sky, is enough to stop you in your tracks. Now imagine hundreds of them, dotting the sky in an endless canvas of abstract shapes and vivid colors. This is exactly what you'll see at the yearly Albuquerque International Balloon Fiesta, the largest convention of hot-air balloons in the world. Many of the balloons are unlike any you've seen before: the Artistic Vision display exhibits balloons vibrantly painted by local artists, for example, while the Special Shape Rodeo balloons are shaped like cows, people, cartoon characters, and anything else you can imagine. The balloons are akin to carnival floats, which suits the party atmosphere down on the ground. By day, music, dance shows, food trucks, and bars keep revelers busy as colorful orbs float above. Come nightfall, festival-goers stand in awe of the "Glowdeo," when hundreds of balloons on the ground are illuminated all at once from the glow of their burners.

Good to know: The fiesta starts on the first Saturday of October each year; it's best to book a shuttle to the grounds.

34

TEXAS, USA

Visit Bandera, the Cowboy Capital of the World

Stetsons, cowboy boots, and rodeos might be a bit of a Texas stereotype, but as a traveler, there are some stereotypes you secretly hope are grounded in truth. You can decide how accurate these are in Bandera, a southern Texas town that merrily embraces its image as the "Cowboy Capital of the World"—think a Wild West–style downtown, Saturday "gunfights" (actually safe reenactments), and horses hitched in front of modern saloons. But Bandera isn't just about observing cowboy culture; it's a chance to immerse yourself in it too. Tour a dude ranch, enjoying horse riding and cookouts as you get roped into Bandera life. The small town itself is dwarfed by the wide open spaces surrounding it, all gentle, rocky hills; windswept grasslands; and vast skies. Just like you imagined it would be.

Good to know: Mark your calendar for Memorial Day weekend (end of May), when Bandera's biggest rodeo comes to town.

33

TEXAS, USA

Help keep Austin weird

If the major cities of Texas are a family, Austin is undoubtedly the cool sibling. It's the sort of place where Tex-Mex taco trucks earn national renown, live music resounds every night of the week, and junk stores and dog bars thrive alongside tech startups. And it's the sort of place where locals get a kick out of, well, supporting local. The phrase "Keep Austin Weird" is more than just a marketing slogan—it's a way of life. Beneath the facade of strip malls, chain restaurants, and big businesses are monuments to independently owned brilliance. Food trucks? Too many to count. Live music venues? Austin is the live music capital of the world, don't you know. A cathedral of junk? Well, yes, you'll find that here too. So whether you visit Austin for the Tex-Mex or the BBQ, the outdoor beer gardens or the out-and-out good vibes, don't be surprised when it makes its way from bucket-list trip to repeat offender in your travel plans.

Good to know: Austin hosts the legendary SXSW festival, with more than 2,000 artists performing every year.

> Austin is a place where Tex-Mex taco trucks earn national renown, live music resounds every night of the week, and junk stores and dog bars thrive alongside tech startups.

NEW ORLEANS

Louisiana's unofficial motto is "Laissez les bons temps rouler" (let the good times roll), and, boy, does New Orleans know it. A zest for life runs deep in these parts, from infamous Mardi Gras celebrations to a vibrant music scene. Walking down the city's historical, song-filled streets, there's no escaping Louisiana's infectious energy.

Hear the sounds of historic Bourbon Street

Vibrant Mardi Gras celebrations may be this street's claim to fame, but the party goes on throughout the year here. That's all thanks to the passionate music houses that dot this street, all of which pay homage to the city's jazz heritage. It was in New Orleans that jazz originated in the late 19th and early 20th centuries, when the city's African American communities drew on ragtime and blues music. The city is still ground zero for some of the best jazz musicians, many of whom play around-the-clock live music along this legendary street in the French Quarter. At No 733, for instance, the intimate Fritzel's Jazz Club has attracted the best musicians since 1969. A few minutes away is Preservation Hall, which has helped preserve New Orleans jazz since 1961, and still hosts top-quality jazz night after night. This is also the heartland of the "go-cup" (most places will serve your drink in a plastic cup to go) so you can wander along, cocktail in hand, while the sultry sax tones, scat vocals, and melodic piano notes filter out of bars. With an atmosphere of revelry that is unmatched in the city, Bourbon Street is where New Orleans' passion for the good life is at its most obvious.

Good to know: The best time to hit the town is between February and May, when the weather is cooler and drier.

36

Sip a Sazerac
at sundown

A long tradition of good drinking is one of New Orleans' trademarks, and one of the city's most-loved cocktails, the Sazerac, was invented here in 1838. It's said that apothecary Antoine Peychaud invented the cocktail at his shop, naming it after his favorite French brandy, Sazerac-de-Forge et fils. By the 1850s, the first Sazerac cocktail house opened, and people came far and wide to sip the tipple, fast making it the city's favorite drink. The concoction originally featured cognac, a spirit that was imported from France at the time, but when this supply was cut off from Europe, rye whiskey made for a fast substitute. Indeed, like the jazz that the city is synonymous with, variations on the Sazerac have been improvised over the years. Today, this delicious elixir is made with rye whiskey, often in an absinthe-rinsed glass and combined with sugar and bitters, making it the perfect drink to cool down with on a balmy bayou day. Can't get enough? The Sazerac House has an entire museum dedicated to the cocktail, with tours and tastings to boot. Enjoy yours in the French Quarter, for old times' sake.

Good to know: There's no finer place to drink a Sazerac than at its namesake bar in the Roosevelt Hotel.

MUST-TRY
NEW
ORLEANS
DRINKS

Sazerac
This potent and fragrant cocktail dates from before the Civil War.

Mint Julep
Iconic in the American South, mint juleps are a fragrant mix of bourbon, mint, sugar, and water.

Ramos Gin Fizz
Also called New Orleans Fizz, this mixes gin, lemon, lime, egg white, cream, sugar, and orange-flower and soda waters.

Vieux Carré
This potent whiskey cocktail was first concocted in the Carousel Bar of the famous Hotel Monteleone.

Cajun Bloody Mary
Not just any old Bloody Mary will do—in New Orleans, hot sauce and horseradish are added to this classic cocktail.

Hurricane
This powerful sweet rum drink was invented at the French Quarter's Pat O'Brien's bar in the 1940s.

37

Catch a game at the
Caesars Superdome

Football is *the* ultimate US sport. And New Orleans' home stadium, the Caesars Superdome, is by far one of the best places in the country to enjoy it. A real masterpiece of engineering, it's the world's largest fixed-dome structure and has been a city icon ever since it first opened to crowds of fans back in 1975. Step inside and you're sure to see some high-level football played out within this stadium of epic proportions. The home team, the New Orleans Saints, won the Super Bowl back in 2009. Catch one of their games, and you'll be in for a full-day football bonanza. Games usually last several hours, with spectators fueled by classic pick-me-ups—like hot dogs washed down with soda—from one of the food and drink stalls. Outside, endless cars and trucks host tailgate parties, where trunks are opened up for food, drink, and watching the game on a small TV. Team spirit here is strong, so don some black and gold and let yourself get swept up in the pep of it all.

Good to know: To catch a football game here, make sure to visit during NFL season; it runs from September to January.

Chomp into a beignet

In a city so famous for its cuisine, it's hard to pick a hallmark dish. But a strong case can be made for the beignet. Akin to a doughnut, this square piece of fried dough dusted with powdered sugar is perfect in its simplicity. You can spot someone who's recently indulged in one by the tell-tale fluffy white powder on their chin. To join them, head to the iconic Café du Monde on Decatur Street in the French Quarter, recognizable for its open sides and green-and-white awnings. The menu at this spot is reassuringly slim: beignets, washed down with a drink of chocolate milk; orange juice; or strong, chicory-infused coffee. This earthy concoction is a classic New Orleans enlivener, which originated when a Civil War–era coffee shortage forced locals to improvise and incorporate the nutty, woody chicory root into their morning brew. Order one coupled with an order of beignets—they always come in threes—while you happily people-watch the hustle and bustle of the historic French Quarter.

Good to know: Café du Monde gets busy, so avoid weekends and arrive in time for opening to join a smaller line.

Party at Mardi Gras

If you only visit New Orleans once in your life, make sure to visit during Mardi Gras. It's when a vibrant party atmosphere descends across New Orleans during the two weeks leading up to Shrove Tuesday. "Mardi Gras," meaning "Fat Tuesday," is an apt name for this joyous blowout. There's a whole load of chowing down, drinking, and dancing before the start of the more restrained Lent period. Across the city, especially in the French Quarter, restaurants and food stalls offer up classic local foods like jambalaya (made with rice, shrimp, and andouille sausage), fried catfish, and king cake (a rainbow-hued cinnamon swirl filled with jam and cream cheese). Grab yourself a bite and head out to see the huge floats processing through the streets. Giant figures of skeletons, jesters, and celebrity caricatures, among others, tower above latticed iron balconies. But it's when the sun goes down that the party really kicks off. Some locals may retreat to exclusive ballrooms, but the raucous spirit of Mardi Gras reverberates through the city's street parties and bars, with revelers sipping ojen (an anise-flavored liqueur) while dancing the night away.

Good to know: Hotel rooms book up months in advance during Mardi Gras, so make sure to plan ahead.

40

KENTUCKY, USA

Try bourbon at its source

Kentucky, with its horse farms, green fields, and bluegrass bars, is one of the most characterful corners of the United States. For many visitors, though, there's no doubting the headline attraction: the chance to tour whiskey distilleries and try the state's famous bourbon. There are 46 distilleries along the Kentucky Bourbon Trail, which stretches all over the state and accounts for the bulk of the USA's booming spirit industry. Of these, one of the most atmospheric and historic is also the oldest and smallest: Woodford Reserve, housed in its original brick buildings from 1812. At the other end of the scale are beautiful modern facilities like those in Bardstown. Wherever you go, you'll be welcomed by the same famous Southern hospitality as you tour distilling facilities to learn how bourbon is made and what makes it unique. And here comes the good bit: you'll get the chance to try it, with guided tastings through the excellent rye, malt, twice-barreled, and wheat varieties, and many more. Don't miss the chance to try a mint julep too: bourbon mixed with fresh mint and sugar—the ultimate Kentucky cocktail.

Good to know: A range of public transportation options connect the distilleries, from buses to boats.

 41

FLORIDA, USA

Take an airboat tour through the Everglades

Up for speeding through a subtropical swamp on a propeller-powered boat? Florida's Everglades National Park is just the place to do it. It's not only the easiest way to explore the park's unique (and UNESCO-listed) landscapes, but also undoubtedly the most exciting. The airboats can zip along at up to 40 mph (65 kph) as they cut a course through the wetlands, powered by huge propellers that stand proud at the rear of the craft. Most of the time, though, you'll be taking it slow—all the better to take in the beautiful scenery and spot the wild and wonderful things that live here. Because did we mention the alligators? You'll likely see them, as well as turtles, raccoons, and hogs, as you cruise past tangled mangroves and swaying sedge. You might even have the chance to disembark for a walking tour through the jungle. Keep an eye out for the Everglades' most elusive plant, the ghost orchid—and for what lurks in the shadows ...

Good to know: For fewer mosquitoes and more temperate weather, visit in December to April.

42

FLORIDA, USA

Spot turtles at Dry Tortugas National Park

More than 99 percent water, Dry Tortugas is a national park like no other, comprising seven idyllic islands in the Gulf of Mexico. It's the ideal environment for the *tortugas* (turtles) that gave the islands the name of "Las Tortugas" back in 1513, when the Spanish explorer Juan Ponce de León came across an abundance of turtles living in the surrounding waters. The change to "Dry" came years later as a warning to other explorers that the islands were devoid of fresh water. Centuries on, the area is still a hot spot for hawksbill, green and loggerhead turtles, who nest on the beach, lounge on the water's surface, and swim alongside shipwrecks; more than 30 species of coral and dozens of species of fish. Spy them at a distance while sailing among the islands—it's always an exceptional thrill when one passes by.

Good to know: The park is only accessible by boat or seaplane, which drop you off at Garden Key, the second-largest island.

Whimsical, bold, fun, and jaunty, Miami's Art Deco is an aesthetic you'll rarely find in other cities.

43

FLORIDA, USA

Embrace Art Deco Miami

Whimsical, bold, fun, and jaunty, Miami's Art Deco is an aesthetic you'll rarely find in other cities. When Art Deco reached America from Europe in the 1930s, the thrilling new style was just what was needed to counteract the gloom of the Great Depression. Miami took this style and exuberantly ran with it, designing buildings with ice-cream colors, nautical features, and tropical motifs that birthed a unique "Tropical Deco" style. While many of these new structures were torn down after World War II, activist Barbara Baer Capitman fought a famous battle to preserve the buildings, resulting in the designation of the Miami Beach Art Deco District in 1979. Today, this part of South Beach is home to the world's largest concentration of Art Deco buildings—800, to be precise. The best of them line Ocean Drive, showing off their clean lines, bright colors, and neon lights, making the area feel like a chic outdoor design gallery. Miami is Florida's most glamorous city, after all.

Good to know: The Art Deco Welcome Center hosts daily walking tours, so you can see the best of South Beach.

TENNESSEE, USA

Jam to live music in Memphis

Memphis, Tennessee, is famous for a lot of things: its rich civil rights history, being the one-time home of Elvis Presley, and its lip-smacking barbecue joints, to name a few. But, above all that, Memphis is home to the blues. The genre sprung up all over the Deep South from the 1860s onward, but it was in this city that W. C. Handy released its first real hit, "Memphis Blues," in 1912. Ever since then, the many clubs of Memphis's famous Beale Street have been *the* place to come and enjoy the best of the blues. Some of the world's most famous singers and guitarists regularly grace the stage at historic venues like B. B. King's Blues Club and Alfred's. Gigs often unspool into full-out jam sessions, with some of the more musical spectators even being invited to join in. The magic lingers late into the night, and clubs maintain their original collaborative spirit; if you're a guitarist, be sure to pack a plectrum.

Good to know: On busy Fridays, Saturdays, and holidays, there is a small fee to enter historic Beale Street.

TENNESSEE, USA

Hit the honky-tonk bars of Nashville

Welcome to Nashville, the Music City where the stars of tomorrow come to chase their dreams. Country music is the golden thread connecting the city's best-loved venues, but other genres are available, from folksy singer-songwriters and raucous rockers to crowd-pleasing country-pop acts. The question is: where to start? The rootin'-tootin' honky-tonks of Broadway are the boisterous cowboy heart of the city, so they're a natural first stop—try Tootsie's Orchid Lounge, with its recognizable purple facade. Further afield, Bluebird Café and the Grand Ole Opry are two more iconic venues—Dolly Parton, Johnny Cash, and Taylor Swift all cut their teeth in these joints. Duck into virtually any downtown bar at any time of day and you'll find musicians bringing the house down, but to see Nashville at its liveliest, stick around after dark. This is when the bars really sing, with members of the audience being hauled on stage to belt out a country classic. Did someone say "Jolene"?

Good to know: Bars in America are only open to over-21s—they tend to ID everyone, regardless of age, so bring identification.

> The rootin'-tootin' honky-tonks of Broadway are the boisterous cowboy heart of the city, so they're a natural first stop.

TENNESSEE AND NORTH CAROLINA, USA

Explore the Great Smoky Mountains

Of all the US national parks, the Great Smoky Mountains draw the biggest crowds: more than 12 million people flock here each year. It could be that they're after the jaw-dropping landscapes, which are often sheathed in a hazy fog that gives the park its name. In fact, this is the most biodiverse of the national parks, with more than 19,000 species thriving within its dense forests—including many curious black bears. Others, though, may be drawn to its history. The area, spanning the border of Tennessee and North Carolina, is a hub of Appalachian culture and also offers insight into early mountain life at places like Cades Cove. For adventurers, the great hiking trails may just be the highlight. A trek up to Chimney Tops or Mount Le Conte rewards with sweeping views, and there's an off-the-grid lodge close by for those seeking a wilderness escape. But really, it's the combination of it all which makes its legacy and appeal so enduring. There's no other national park quite like it.

Good to know: Gatlinburg, a mountain town on the park's border, is a popular base camp for Smoky adventures.

46

TENNESSEE, USA

Pilgrimage to Graceland

Put on your blue suede shoes and shimmy on down to the former home-turned-museum of the King of Rock 'n' Roll, Elvis Presley. When Elvis's first single was released in 1954, it was revolutionary. His sound was inspired by traditional blues, and his hip-shaking dance moves and signature rhinestone jumpsuits sent crowds into a frenzy, changing the trajectory of rock 'n' roll forever. Throughout his 20-year career, his Memphis home was a safe haven, a place that he lived, played, and recorded in from 1957 until his death in 1977. Since then, Graceland has become a holy land for old and new fans—hundreds of thousands of people come to walk in his footsteps and pay their respects at his grave here annually. The mansion has remained largely untouched since Presley lived here, with stained-glass peacocks decorating the living room and a floor-to-ceiling shag carpet decking out the famed Jungle Room (his "man cave"), showcasing the theatrical flourishes that he adored. You can't help re-falling in love with Elvis while here.

Good to know: Visit the museum across the street to see more, like Elvis's private jet and three floors of his famed jumpsuits.

LOUISIANA TO TENNESSEE, USA

Drive the Blues Highway

Legend has it that blues star Robert Johnson met the devil at the crossroads of highways 61 and 49 and sold his soul for musical success. Whether true or not, he certainly became a shining light in the Delta blues style, along with many more from the humid, fertile plains of the Mississippi delta. It was here that the soul-stirring blues genre was born, rooted in the field hollers and chants of enslaved Africans, and Highway 61 has become its beat-ridden artery, a road that music greats have traveled and found inspiration along. Music still carries drivers from Memphis to Vicksburg, a section of the road known as the Blues Highway, and major stops include the Delta Blues Museum in Clarksdale and Malaco Records in Jackson. But this is as much about the region's ramshackle juke joints that shake with the sound of slide guitar, and its pint-size churches thrumming with gospel music. See where the sounds of blues, soul, gospel, and R&B take you—few road trips sound better than this one.

Good to know: The Mississippi Blues Trail app contains interactive maps and information to help plan your route.

LOUISIANA TO TENNESSEE, USA

Cruise along the Lower Mississippi River

In a land of great rivers, the Mississippi might be the most majestic of them all. Although not the longest river here, it snakes from north to south down almost the entire length of the USA, from glacial Lake Itasca in Minnesota all the way to the Gulf of Mexico in Louisiana. Steamboats were the preferred way to travel from north to south along the river in the 19th century, with the few remaining tiered decks still an iconic sight along its waters. They still ply the rivers today—although, this time, taking tourists along the way. Many routes start in New Orleans, where you can stop off to soak up some jazz and feast on Louisiana Creole cuisine, before jumping on a boat to head north. At Baton Rouge, disembark to learn more about Louisiana's French history at the magnificent Capitol building, while also discovering how country communities lived at the Louisiana Rural Life Museum. After that, there's no missing Memphis as you cruise into Tennessee—the best place to round off the day with a barbecue feast by this mighty river.

Good to know: April to June is the best time of year to cruise the Mississippi, before the heat and humidity of summer descend.

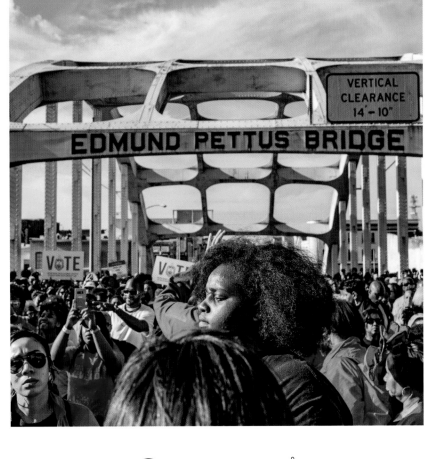

SOUTH CAROLINA, USA

Get to know Charleston

It goes without saying that you'll want to visit one of the oldest cities in the US for its history. This is where the first shot of the Civil War was fired, for starters, and walking along the cobblestone streets, past flickering lanterns and horse-drawn carriages, feels like stepping into a bygone era. But if history infiltrates anything in this city, it's certainly the food. "Lowcountry cuisine" has its roots in South Carolina, when enslaved Africans were forced into fields and kitchens in and around the city in its early days. They worked with products from the surrounding areas, including rice and seafood, and embellished these with foods brought over from West Africa and spices from the colonial trade. The resulting dishes blended Indigenous, African, and European flavors, and you'll still find the likes of she-crab soup, catfish stew, and shrimp and grits on menus here, paying tribute to the impact of past African communities. Between visiting plantations, Civil War sites, and antebellum mansions to get to grips with the city's tumultuous past of slavery and colonialism, be sure to fill your belly.

Good to know: Immerse yourself in Charleston's past on one of the many walking and bus tours, detailed on the tourist website.

50

USA

Follow in the footsteps of civil rights trailblazers

Political leaders. Ordinary citizens. Schoolchildren. All those who fought for equal rights in the 1950s and '60s made modern-day America possible, and their struggles, sacrifices, and triumphs are honored on the US Civil Rights Trail. Launched in 2017, the trail connects key sites in the campaign for Black Americans' equal rights, creating an inspiring pilgrimage through 15 states. See places where the world changed—like the bridge protesters marched across in Selma and the Woolworth counter where the first sit-ins occurred—and the sights where sparks were fanned—courthouses, churches, and schoolyards. Immersing yourself in this living history is a powerful reminder that small moments can build on each other to create momentous change, a principle that rings as true today as it did then.

> All those who fought for equal rights in the 1950s and '60s made modern-day America possible, and their struggles, sacrifices, and triumphs are honored on the US Civil Rights Trail.

Good to know: Plan your route so there's no rush at the stops on the trail, allowing time to process the experience.

ILLINOIS TO CALIFORNIA, USA

Get your kicks on Route 66

Few road trips are as iconic as Route 66. Stretching from Chicago to Los Angeles, America's "Mother Road" passes through eight states in its 2,400 miles (3,900 km) but—perhaps more potently—it also transports road-trippers back in time. Established in 1926, it was officially decommissioned in 1985, but its path can still be traced via a blend of county roads, interstate highways, and scenic byways. You don't drive this route just to see America, but to see Americana: kitsch motels, faded road signs, classic diners, and hulking fiberglass Muffler men punctuate the route. That said, it's also, quite simply, just a beautiful drive in places. You'll pass through wide-open farmland dotted with weathered red barns and roadside farm stalls in Oklahoma, and the otherworldly landscapes of Petrified Forest National Park glowing like flames in the Arizona sunset, before the road finally runs out at the dramatic Pacific coastline. Get behind the wheel in Illinois and let the adventure begin.

Good to know: Set aside two weeks to drive the route at a good pace, bedding down at historic motels along the way.

ILLINOIS, USA

Catch a baseball game

The windy city may be the birthplace of the great skyscraper and home to world-famous art, but there's another thing that defines Chicago: its love of baseball. Not one, but two Major League teams call it home, and there's no better way to celebrate this than by heading to Wrigley Field for a game. Grab a frosty malt drink, a local favorite, before settling in for some top-tier baseball. Opened in 1914, Wrigley Field is the second-oldest baseball stadium in the country—and looks it. The brick outfield wall is smothered in ivy, while the scoreboard is still hand operated. The number of fans has swelled since it opened, so the seating extends beyond the limits of the stadium and onto the Wrigley Rooftops, where spectators watch the batters swing from the tops of adjacent apartment buildings. The stadium itself is a classic, but it's the lively atmosphere that makes the experience. Catch a high-energy game between the crosstown rivals, the Chicago Cubs and White Sox, and you'll have really hit a home run.

Good to know: Outside of rowdy baseball days, non-game-day tours can take you behind the scenes and even onto the field.

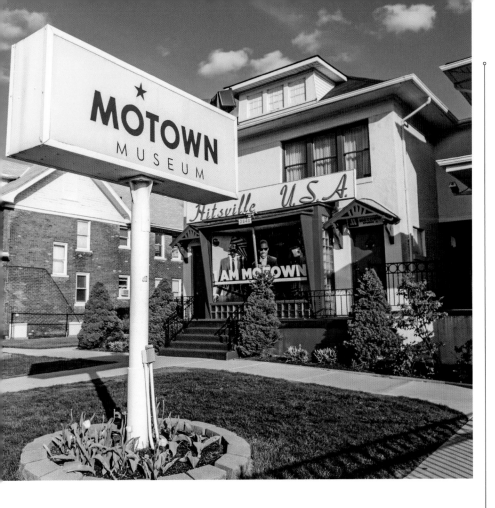

USA

Cycle along the Underground Railroad

This cycle trail takes you through a hugely important episode in US history. With slavery still legal in many states in the early 1800s, tens of thousands of enslaved people pursued liberation via the Underground Railroad, a clandestine network created to get them to freedom. The Underground Railroad Bicycle Route follows a strand of that network, linking the Gulf Coast with Ontario in an epic 2,000-mile (3,200-km) route. Beginning in Mobile, Alabama, you'll pedal past miles of cotton fields, through wetlands, and over hills, where the constellations were used as navigation aids. Along the way are historic towns, museums, plaques, and remnants of the old railroad stations and hidden maroon communities that offered refuge. Seven states later, journey's end is Ontario, Canada, the railroad's most northerly haven.

Good to know: The epic route can easily be broken up into more manageable sections, with spring bringing the best weather.

54

MICHIGAN, USA

Dive into Motown history

A warm, lilting bass still runs through the streets of Detroit, where Motown was born and music history was made. Hits of the 1960s came to life in this city, which lends its nickname to the genre. In the center, a house sporting a "Hitsville U.S.A." sign was once the first studio of Motown Records. The label played a pivotal role in launching Black artists into the mainstream, and the house is where artists like Marvin Gaye, the Temptations, and the Supremes once recorded. Today it's a museum where you can see displays of Motown memorabilia, visit founder Berry Gordy's studio apartment, and see some of the sound equipment used to record the nation's favorite tunes. And it's also here that Motown continues its legacy, offering workshops, after-school programs, and artist development for young people and budding artists in the community. Svelte tunes and soulful sounds, old and new, thrive at this unmissable cultural hub.

Good to know: The museum is only open from Wednesday to Sunday, so plan your visit accordingly.

> A warm, lilting bass still runs through the streets of Detroit, where Motown was born and music history was made.

Celebrate the Fourth of July

Sizzling backyard barbecues. Fireworks lighting up the night sky. And, importantly, red, white, and blue galore. The Fourth of July is one of the biggest holidays in the Land of Liberty. It marks the signing of the Declaration of Independence and, as a result, the birth of the United States of America (which, until then, was still largely a colony). The holiday is marked with gusto all over the country and is a highlight of the summer months for many. And while you can celebrate it anywhere, one of the best places to mark it is Washington, D.C. Surrounded by monuments to many of the Founding Fathers—like the towering Washington Memorial—there's a sense of history in the air, and fireworks light up the monuments on the Mall before a raucous concert kicks off. Another unmissable experience lies farther north, on New York's East River, where fireworks explode overhead for more than a mile. Wherever you are, you're guaranteed to find a full-on, all-American bash to mark the day.

Good to know: For the best views of the New York fireworks, book a spot on the Circle Line's Fourth of July Fireworks Cruise.

> Curving between West Virginia and Minnesota, the trail takes in everything from the pine forests of Mississippi to the prairies of Oklahoma and the salt flats of Utah.

Hit the TransAmerica Trail

By far the biggest motorcycle adventure in the US, the TransAmerica Trail is an epic ride. It's a route that takes riders across 5,000 miles (8,000 km) of amazing landscapes, where mountains, plains, and deserts await. Those who dare to brave the lone roads and tricky terrain will be rewarded with star-filled skies and rarely seen vistas over the 25-day journey. Curving between West Virginia and Minnesota, the trail takes in everything from the pine forests of Mississippi to the prairies of Oklahoma and the salt flats of Utah. Along the twisting roads are endless switchbacks that keep your attention, while the few soul food and barbecue joints en route keep you fueled. Small farming towns punctuate the journey, but often you'll be alone for miles, traveling down long, straight roads across the Great Plains, circling sapphire-blue lakes and climbing craggy peaks in the Rockies. It's a trip that requires fortitude—if you've got what it takes, grab a helmet and saddle up for the ride of a lifetime.

Good to know: Most of the trail is off-road, so you'll need a dual-sport motorcycle or a 4WD for the journey.

58

NEW ENGLAND, USA

Go leaf peeping in New England

Fall is a time of change, and New England sets the scene for the season's grand finale. It's when maple-themed treats start to appear; anticipation for cozy, cold-weather activities builds; and stunning, orange-covered trees take over the region. From mid-September to October, great forests of sugar maple, beech, and hemlock blaze with color—and not a leaf here goes unturned. The display is so remarkable that it has even inspired the phrase "leaf peeping" to describe the act of seeking out and photographing these vibrant scenes. Less-traveled roads reveal quiet woods that burst with deep crimson maples. Over in Vermont, you can mountain bike, hike, or even take cable-cars up the multicolored slopes of Mount Mansfield. And to see covered bridges framed by bright foliage, there's really no beating Montgomery. Among such natural beauty, it's hard to resist the pull of the new season.

Good to know: The peak leaf peeping period is usually early October in northern New England to late October in the south.

PENNSYLVANIA, USA

Walk through Gettysburg National Military Park

Quiet farmland, tree groves, and distant ridgelines make up Gettysburg National Military Park. But these pastoral landscapes belie some of the most turbulent parts of US history. Gettysburg was the site of the bloodiest battle and a key turning point of the American Civil War. These huge 6,000 acres (2,400 ha) of former battlefields have since been carefully restored to look as they did back in 1863, bringing history to life in this part of southern Pennsylvania. Civil War buffs will recognize sites like Little Round Top and Devil's Den, as well as the national cemetery made famous by Abraham Lincoln's 1863 Gettysburg Address. Though it could take days to tour the full battlefield, leave time to venture into the town of Gettysburg. Here, you can visit historic homes (some still with bullet holes in them) and enjoy a farm-to-table meal or some ice cream on a quaint square.

Good to know: It's possible to hire a licensed battlefield guide during your visit, offering a customized tour of the military park.

> Gettysburg was the site of the bloodiest battle and a key turning point of the American Civil War.

59

NEW ENGLAND, USA

Feast on lobster in New England

Head to any town in the East Coast region of New England, and you're bound to stumble upon a cozy joint serving up fresh lobster. It's a veritable seafood staple in these parts, but nowhere more so than in Maine—this state alone harvests more than 50,000 tons (44,600 metric tons) of the tasty crustacean each year. Cities like the lobster-fishing capital of Rockland teem with wholesalers, food trucks, fishing co-ops, and seafood shacks, all selling no-frills crustaceans by the pound. Shacks usually offer a dish of steamed whole lobster, more often than not with melted butter and a side of corn on the cob. To make it, the lobster is prepared in pots traditionally packed with seaweed gathered straight from the ocean, helping to steam the lobster and adding some natural salt. Lobster rolls are even more popular, and much easier to eat. The best way to enjoy either variety is to tuck in on the wooden trestles outside a shack, with the chilly waters of the Atlantic coast in sight.

Good to know: Most lobster shacks in the region are open between mid-April and mid-October.

GEORGIA TO MAINE, USA

Hike the Appalachian Trail

The longest hiking-only footpath in the world, the gargantuan Appalachian Trail runs over 2,190 miles (3,530 km) between leafy Springer Mountain in Georgia and Mount Katahdin in Maine. Heading out on the trail may be a mammoth challenge, but it's not all hard going. Charming Boiling Springs, North Carolina, is a real favorite among hikers passing through, its bubbling thermal waters and spas perfect for soothing well-worked muscles. There are plenty of historic places along the way too; in West Virginia, the legacy of antislavery activist John Brown is preserved within the 19th-century town of Harpers Ferry. But undoubtedly, it's the embarrassment of natural riches that draw people in droves: the Blue Ridge vistas in Shenandoah National Park, the clapboard villages surrounded by fiery maples in New England, the soaring peaks and misty valleys in the Great Smoky Mountains. Even if you decide to just tackle a short section, you'll find yourself in the middle of awe-inspiring landscapes in no time.

Good to know: Hikers often start in Georgia in March, following the warm weather as it creeps north up until mid-October.

NEW YORK CITY

There's a reason why this place never sleeps: when you've got epic skyscrapers to marvel at, great food to enjoy on every corner, famous shopping streets to stroll down, and some of the greatest museums on the planet to explore, why would you rest? In the Big Apple, you'll always find something to keep you busy.

62

Stop off in Times Square and Broadway

This world-famous landmark needs no introduction. At the mention of its name, images of colossal video screens, 24-hour news tickers, and thronging crowds come to mind, whether you've visited this iconic spot or not. This is the "Crossroads of the World," New York's most famous intersection, where its moniker "The City That Never Sleeps" springs vividly to life. But Times Square is more than New York's buzzy center—it's also the junction that leads to the Broadway Theater District, the heart of the modern musical. In this pocket of the city, ovation-worthy performances of the likes of *The Phantom of the Opera* and *The Lion King* have been staged for decades, with raucous audiences applauding the major stars that headline every season. Can't decide what to see? Head to the Richard Rodgers Theatre to see *Hamilton*, which won a whopping 11 Tony Awards, then wind down at the St. Cloud Rooftop in Times Square, watching the city's epicenter hum and sparkle till dawn below. As they say, if you can make it in New York, you can make it anywhere— and that tells you everything you need to know about how world-class its live scene is.

Good to know: Line up for heavily discounted Broadway tickets at the Times Square TKTS booth on 47th St.

63

Visit the Metropolitan Museum of Art

It would take weeks to see everything this iconic museum has to offer. The Met is home to one of the most prestigious collections in the world, and has been a fixture on the edge of Central Park since 1880, a decade after a group of artists and philanthropists dreamed of opening an American art institution to rival those found in Europe. And they succeeded, with artifacts and artworks dating from prehistoric times to the present, spanning 5,000 years of culture. When the museum opened, it held only three European collections and 174 paintings; since then, the Gothic Revival building has been expanded many times and the present holdings number more than two million, including 2,500 European paintings, one of the largest collections of Egyptian art outside Cairo, and celebrated works by Pablo Picasso and Andy Warhol. Haven't got the luxury of two weeks to see everything? Seek out unmissable works like Claude Monet's *Bridge Over a Pond of Water Lilies*, Duccio's *Madonna and Child*, and Cézanne's *The Card Players*. Few museums can compete with the Met's gargantuan collection of global art.

Good to know: Save time by booking advance tickets, and visit in the mornings, which tend to be less busy than afternoons.

MUST-SEE NEW YORK CITY MUSEUMS

American Museum of Natural History
Expect fossils, taxidermy, and skeletons galore at this museum.

Museum of Modern Art (MoMA)
Home to some of the world's most iconic modern artworks.

The Guggenheim
Famous for its stunning building as much as for the modern art inside, this is a must-stop for art buffs.

Brooklyn Museum
A one-stop-shop of artifacts from around the world, displayed across five floors.

The Metropolitan Museum of Art
An impressive space to house an impressive collection of more than two million artworks.

Ellis Island Immigration Museum
This museum pays homage to the 20th-century wave of immigration.

64

Take in the views of the Empire State Building

King Kong clung to it. Buddy the Elf worked inside it. And aliens vaporized it. Playing a starring role in many a film, the Empire State Building is iconic. It soars high above midtown Manhattan and, beyond the silver screen, it's provided a blueprint for tall structures since 1931. The iconic Art Deco design coupled with its distinctive antenna make it one of the most elegant skyscrapers in a city of looming towers. Famed for its exterior, the inside impresses too: the lobby has marble floors, gleaming murals, and a brass vault ceiling, while exhibitions on the 2nd and 80th floors chronicle the building's history. But the real highlight remains the stellar views from the 86th-floor observatory, some 1,050 ft (320 m) above ground. To the north of this panorama lies the green rectangle of Central Park, peeping out between the spires and towers of "Billionaire's Row"; to the south is the Statue of Liberty and the hazy expanse of the Atlantic beyond. It's *the* iconic view in an iconic city.

Good to know: To avoid long waits to enter the building, book advance tickets online.

65

Gawk at the Statue of Liberty

Lady Liberty, Mother of Freedom, the Green Goddess. She's known by many names but one thing is certain: the Statue of Liberty is just about the most famous statue in the world. Perched proudly on Liberty Island, just off Manhattan's southern tip, Liberty Enlightening the World (to give her official name) has been a beacon of hope for centuries. The statue was a gift from France, and was said to depict the Roman goddess of Freedom holding an iron tablet inscribed with the US's date of independence. For the millions of immigrants who arrived in New York in the 19th and 20th centuries, she represented that and more: freedom, a warm welcome, and a fresh start. To get a glimpse yourself, cross the waves of the Hudson aboard a ferry and disembark for a closer look. Venture inside to explore and take in the views from the crown, of course, but, honestly, this is a statue best admired from the outside. She's the embodiment of the American dream, after all.

Good to know: The Statue Cruises Ferry crosses from Battery Park to Liberty Island every 20 to 30 minutes most days.

> Lady Liberty, Mother of Freedom, the Green Goddess. She's known by many names but one thing is certain: the Statue of Liberty is just about the most famous statue in the world.

66

Hop aboard the Staten Island ferry

It's New York's biggest bargain—a free ferry ride in one of the world's most expensive cities. Sailing between Whitehall Terminal and Staten Island 24 hours a day, these unassuming vessels offer a free trip to the city's southernmost borough—plus priceless views along the way. Jump aboard any time and grab your preferred space on the outside deck, camera at the ready. Departing Manhattan, the back of the boat provides sweeping views of the Financial District, with skyscrapers soaring up from the water and boats puttering around Battery Park, while the front reveals the low hills of Staten Island. It's the right side of the boat that most photographers cherish, though—from here you'll glimpse the emotive Statue of Liberty, the pale green giant brandishing her torch high above the harbor as the ferry slips by.

Good to know: Aim to avoid the ferries during rush hour (normally 6–9:30 a.m. and 4–8 p.m.).

See Rockefeller Center

This Art Deco complex has dominated New York's midtown since the 1930s. Comprising several commercial buildings, it's world famous for its winter ice rink and *that* Christmas tree. And while winter is inevitably the ideal time to make a bucket-list trip here, there's plenty to enjoy out of season too. Outside the building of television network NBC, you'll find crowds hoping for a chance to be in the live audience for shows like *Saturday Night Live* and *The Tonight Show Starring Jimmy Fallon*. The NBC Studio Tour reveals more about it all, but the biggest draw is actually on the roof—literally, the Top of the Rock. Here, there's an observation deck with "The Beam," a homage to the heart-racing 1932 photo of ironworkers nonchalantly eating their lunch on a steel beam high above Manhattan. This beam really hovers over the edge of the building, giving the illusion, at least, of floating high above the city streets.

Good to know: Winter skating is usually on a first-come-first-served basis, so arrive early to avoid a long wait.

Get festive at Radio City Music Hall

It's a New York tradition—the "Radio City Christmas Spectacular." Since it first began in 1932, this beloved show at Radio City Music Hall has become a rite of passage for New Yorkers. The performance features numerous elements, but the stars have always been—and will always be—the Rockettes, an American dance company famed for their kick-line (synchronized kicking). Clad in dazzling costumes, toes always pointed, and kicks incredibly in sync, these high-energy dancers can shake the Christmas spirit out of any grumbling Scrooge. Seeing their annual show also gives visitors a chance to experience Radio City Music Hall in all its festive cheer. Adorned with Christmas trees, giant baubles, and an array of twinkling lights, the so-called "Showplace of the Nation" is almost as magical as the show itself. Almost.

Good to know: You can meet one of the high-kicking Rockettes on a Christmas tour.

Get lost in Central Park

Is a trip to New York really complete without a stroll through its leafy lungs? Stretching for 51 skyscraper-studded blocks in the middle of Manhattan, this urban oasis is no ordinary park. Within its phenomenal sprawl are boating lakes, dense woodland, numerous monuments, and vast grassy lawns. And those aren't even the best bits: catch a Shakespeare play at the open-air theater; walk hand-in-hand over romantic Bow Bridge; or gaze at the fairytale Belvedere Castle, an inconceivable folly in the heart of the park. Whatever the season, there's something to do here. Flocks of migrating birds arrive in the spring, while sunbathers take over the sweeping lawns in the summer. Fall, meanwhile, promises a blanket of gold, amber, and red foliage, and in winter, the park delights with huge ice rinks and snowy slopes ideal for sledding. A playground for millions of New Yorkers, this world-famous park really does have it all. Of course, you won't be able to check everything off in one day, but that just gives you yet another excuse to come back.

Good to know: To get free Shakespeare in the Park tickets, arrive at the park's Delacorte Theater early (before 9 a.m.).

69

Groove to gospel music in Harlem

The sound builds as the choir moves rhythmically from side to side, hands reaching for the sky. The organ player rocks in their chair, while worshippers clap, shout, and dance; the whole city, it seems, is singing along. Named after the historical term for Ethiopia, the Abyssinian Baptist Church in Harlem is New York's most famous gospel church and its choir—the Inspirational Voices of Abyssinian—is one of the best. Attending a service here is a true Harlem experience. Attendees are dressed to the nines (all elegant hats and billowy frocks, dress suits and bow ties), while the choir are resplendent in wine-colored robes and golden collars. The Sunday finery might seem like the star of the show at first, but then the singing starts. Accompanied by a brilliant live band, the Inspirational Voices of Abyssinian belt out traditional and contemporary gospel songs. An assured medley of voices, they cheer in support of the soloists and move together to the music. A simple service here feels like a ticket-worthy show, and to think: the congregation gets to experience this every Sunday.

Good to know: To secure a spot on Sundays, line up at the "Tourist Entry Point" (West 138th St and Powell Blvd) before 9 a.m.

> A simple service here feels like a ticket-worthy show, and to think: the congregation gets to experience this every Sunday.

Window-shop along Fifth Avenue

The strip of Fifth Avenue, New York's best-known boulevard, between 42nd and 59th streets has been a haven for luxury since 1883. This is when the first of the palatial residences here sprung up, and the high-end retailers followed soon after. The resulting air of sophistication continues today: you'll find the city's crème de la crème milling about the luxury fashion boutiques, elegant hotels, and converted Beaux-Arts mansions. For visitors, a walk among the shops lining Fifth Avenue is the simplest way to get a taste of the high life. Among the most iconic is the jeweler Tiffany & Co, made famous by the 1961 film starring Audrey Hepburn. Today, you can enjoy breakfast (or brunch) at Tiffany's stylish Blue Box Café. Other beloved department stores, including Bergdorf Goodman and Saks, have flagship branches here, where the upper echelons of the retail world continue to symbolize and define wealth and social standing to many.

Good to know: Shops, including Saks and Cartier, put on spectacular light shows and window displays each winter.

71

Catch a ballet at Lincoln Center

Lincoln Center in Manhattan is a New York institution, and has been since it opened in 1962. Housing the likes of the New York Philharmonic, the School of American Ballet, and the Metropolitan Opera, there is endless creativity within the walls of its 20 venues. Some of the world's most talented dancers can be seen in the David H. Koch Theater, home to the New York City Ballet. Here, you can reliably expect a multi-sensory affair full of stunning costumes and famous set pieces. And, come wintertime, the quintessential holiday ballet *The Nutcracker* fills this stage with dancers who embody toy soldiers, magical mice, and sugar plum fairies, all set to the familiar, foot-tapping score by Pyotr Ilyich Tchaikovsky. No matter the season or performance, this iconic dance venue sets the bar (or barre) high every time.

Good to know: The American Ballet Theatre offers discounted orchestra on-the-day tickets online for all performances.

Cross Brooklyn Bridge

With its arched brick towers, web of cables, and characterful wooden walkways, New York's most iconic bridge soars across the East River. Completed in 1883, it was once the largest suspension bridge in the world and the first to be made of steel. Locals, however, weren't initially convinced that the bridge was safe, so in 1884 twenty-one elephants were marched across the wooden walkway to show that it was, in fact, very sturdy. Today, cars, cyclists, pedestrians, and their pups share this famous crossing between Manhattan and Brooklyn. For locals, it's a scenic commute. For tourists, it's a chance to see some of New York's breathtaking views. Start on the Brooklyn side and you'll see all of Manhattan laid out before you. To the right, the Empire State Building and the lofty towers of Midtown. To the left, the huddle of Financial District skyscrapers—dominated by One World Trade Center—and the old sailing ships at South Street Seaport. These skyline views have changed dramatically since the 1880s, but the bridge is still as awe-inspiring (and safe) as ever.

Good to know: Early morning is the best time to cross the bridge from the Brooklyn side, with the sun behind you.

Grand Central Terminal

Another New York icon and mainstay on the movie screen, Grand Central Terminal is one of the world's most storied stations. In practical terms, this enormous terminal is a hub for subway and commuter services. Yet the beauty of Grand Central is that it's not all practical. The largest Tiffany clock in the world gleams above its entrance while another four-sided clock (estimated to be worth nearly $20 million) sits at the center of its main hall. This central concourse is most famous for its celestial ceiling: a wash of turquoise dusted with gold-leaf constellations—beautiful, but mistakenly painted backward. Tucked away below the main concourse, the beloved Oyster Bar serves up delicious Manhattan Clam Chowder and Blue Point oysters, while the Campbell, an elegant bar set in the former private office of a 1920s banker, offers old-school cocktails. As train stations go, this one's pretty fabulous.

Good to know: Take a 1½-hour guided tour to learn the secrets and stories of the terminal.

> This central concourse is most famous for its celestial ceiling: a wash of turquoise dusted with gold-leaf constellations—beautiful, but mistakenly painted backward.

74

MASSACHUSETTS, USA

Cheer on the runners in the Boston Marathon

First come the elite runners, pounding the asphalt in clusters, faces gripped with concentration. Then, gradually, some 30,000 people follow, their diverse ranks containing supermen and wonder women, wheelchair athletes, Sesame Street characters, local students, sprightly retirees, dinosaurs, unicorns, and even the occasional barefoot hero. The Boston Marathon isn't only the oldest annual marathon in the world (held since 1897), it's also one of the most fun to watch. It gained a layer of poignancy after 2013, when "Boston Strong" became a rallying cry after a devastating terror attack that year. The race has come to represent a spirit of resilience and defiant joy, its atmosphere maintained by those roaring crowds, often 500,000-strong, lining the 26-mile (42-km) route from rural Hopkinton to Downtown Boston. The crowds get especially raucous near the halfway mark, at the notorious Wellesley College "scream tunnel." The volume rises again near the finish, where the cheers spur the runners on for one last desperate push.

Good to know: Top spots to watch include just off the Boston College stop on the Green line B subway and Kenmore Square.

WASHINGTON, D.C., USA

Explore the National Mall

Monuments, rose gardens, vast museums, and the seat of US government—the National Mall is an impressive spot. The main east–west thoroughfare is a 2-mile (3.5-km) swathe of manicured lawn, along which are some of the country's key buildings. On one end, there's the Capitol, where Congress is based, as well as the tranquil Lincoln Memorial, with its giant statue of the celebrated Civil War president. In the middle stands the Washington Memorial, a 555-ft (169-m) marble and granite obelisk that remains the tallest structure in the city. On the east side are many famous museums, like the National Museum of American History, the National Air and Space Museum, and the National Gallery of Art. The poignant memorials to Vietnam and Korean War veterans, Martin Luther King Jr., and many others can be seen to the west. Behind lawns and security barriers, though, looms the most important building of them all: the iconic White House, home to the US President.

Good to know: All Smithsonian museums in D.C. are free to enter, as are the monuments.

USA AND CANADA

Witness Niagara Falls

Any list of natural wonders to see in a lifetime would be incomplete without the astounding Niagara Falls. The waterfall to end all others, it's made of not one but three falls. Though nowhere near the world's tallest, their sheer volume and force is unparalleled. Day in, day out, more than 8,500 bathtubs of water tumble down every second, creating great plumes of icy mist. Despite the cold, rarely do the falls freeze and stop all together (and when they do, it usually makes international headlines). Originally formed when melting glaciers created the Great Lakes around 12,000 years ago, today the falls are receding at a rate of approximately 1 ft (0.3 m) every year. See them at their best before it's too late: viewing points like Bridal Veil Falls on the US side and Horseshoe Falls on the Canadian side offer great vantage points.

Good to know: With the Niagara Falls Adventure Classic Pass, you'll have access to the Falls from multiple viewpoints.

USA TO ARGENTINA

Drive the Pan-American Highway

The Pan-American Highway is, quite simply, the greatest road trip on Earth. Spanning the length of the Americas, it stretches from Alaska in the north to Tierra del Fuego all the way down in the south. The whole route passes through at least 14 different countries, crossing the equator while on the way to cities as diverse as Los Angeles, Medellín, Lima, and Buenos Aires. Alongside a host of wonders old and new—including the ancient pyramids of Teotihuacan in Mexico and the Panama Canal—it takes in jaw-dropping landscapes. Remarkably, only two sections of the 19,000-mile (30,000-km) route are not drivable: the mountainous jungle of the Darién Gap, between Panama and Colombia, and the Strait of Magellan must be bypassed by boat or plane and car ferry, respectively. Driving along the Pan-American Highway requires a lot of time and commitment—completing the entire route takes anything from nine months to two years—but the rewards are immense.

Good to know: While roads in the north are generally good, conditions in the far south can be challenging.

79

CANADA

Canoe the Yukon River

When it comes to the great outdoors, there are few places that beat Canada. So how about a trip down the Yukon River? Canoe and kayak expeditions along this legendary waterway are the stuff of true adventuring dreams. Traveling upstream, immerse yourself in the vast and sparsely populated landscape where wildlife roams free and tranquility reigns. From the city of Whitehorse, a popular starting point, there are many paddling trips to choose from, each one tailored to different skill levels and destinations. Whether you opt for a leisurely half-day excursion or a more challenging multi-day expedition over to peaceful Carmacks or Dawson City, the Yukon River promises rewarding views along the way. Seeking the ultimate Yukon escapade? Then test your skill and endurance on the great Yukon River Quest. Known as the world's premier canoe and kayak race, this event covers the classic 460-mile (740-km) route from Whitehorse to Dawson City, drawing serious paddlers from around the globe to the river.

Good to know: Take a travel buddy—self-guided canoe excursions require a minimum of two people.

CANADA

Try poutine in Quebec

There's no better way to end a night of merriment in Quebec than by ducking into a late-night poutine joint. Created in Canada's French-speaking Quebec, poutine—a base of steaming French fries topped with melting, squeaky cheese curds and hot, rich gravy—is one of those warm, comforting, and immensely satisfying dishes you never knew you wanted. OK, it doesn't sound like much but this is Quebec's, heck, Canada's beloved national dish. It first emerged during the 1950s and '60s, and has been quelling rumbling stomachs ever since. In Montreal, you can grab a bite almost anywhere, but the most legendary poutine joint by far is buzzing La Banquise. The 24/7 retro-style restaurant, known for its weekend 4 a.m. rushes, serves up traditional poutine as well as variations topped with everything from bacon strips to corn dogs, guacamole to grilled onions. Over in Quebec City, the fast food chain Chez Ashton is a beloved maker of the legendary dish. Bad day? Hungover? Just hungry? Whenever you have a hankering, this is the dish for you.

Good to know: Poutine can be enjoyed on its own, but is often served up alongside a burger or a milkshake.

80

CANADA

Visit Montreal

One of Canada's busiest and most storied cities, Montreal defies obvious definition. The city's history goes back thousands of years, when Indigenous people knew the area as a rich source for hornfels, a rock used for crafting arrowheads. The city was founded in 1642 by the French, who left behind a legacy of 17th-century cobblestone streets, bilingual residents, and delicious food. The blend of cultures is still palpable today, and a walk here will take you past endless patisseries and brasseries, buzzing neighborhoods like Little Maghreb and Chinatown, and grand museums. The Montreal Museum of Fine Arts, in particular, is full of Canadian art, from early Indigenous to contemporary local works. With all this and more, there's no telling where Montreal will take you.

Good to know: Summer is a great time to visit, but with winter come magical ice-skating rinks and light installations.

CANADA

Skate the world's largest ice rink

Ontario's Rideau Canal is a great connector, linking the Canadian capital with the nearby city of Kingston since the 19th century. And, every winter, the section passing through Ottawa undergoes an enchanting transformation. The waterway becomes the Rideau Canal Skateway, the world's largest ice skating rink which stretches for almost 5 miles (8 km) through the city. The coldest months of the year (typically January to early March) see thousands of skaters glide up and down it for leisure and even as part of their commutes, passing historic architecture and snow-topped trees along the way. The canal is always abuzz with activity: fast-paced hockey face-offs unfurl, youngsters make wobbly first strides on the ice, and stalls serve hot drinks to those in need of warming up. Skating here offers some of the best views of the city too, with the stunning Gothic Revival sandstone Parliament Buildings and the glamorous 20th-century Château Laurier hotel in full view. Sightseeing a major city by skate? Now there's an experience you'll struggle to find elsewhere.

Good to know: For the best events, hit the ice during Ottawa-Gatineau's annual Winterlude festival in February.

CANADA

Whale-watching in the Canadian Maritimes

Many people have whale-watching on their bucket lists, and the chilly Maritimes region of Canada is one of the best places to do so. It's along this 125,000-mile (200,000-km) coastline that more than 30 species weave their way around the eastern provinces of New Brunswick, Nova Scotia, and Prince Edward Island. Whether or not a sighting takes place depends on luck, but there are few other regions where your chances are higher. Many species pass through, from majestic humpbacks, launching upward in epic breaches, to the endangered North Atlantic right whale, of which only some 350 exist. Colossal blue whales, the largest creatures on earth, also call these waters home, as do minkes, known for their playful, twisting water acrobatics. Viewing hot spots range from the Hudson Bay to the forested Cape Breton Highlands, among others. Inflatable dinghy, kayak, and snorkel tours offer small groups intimate encounters with these magnificent creatures around the region. There really is no shortage of ways to spot these gentle giants of the seas here.

Good to know: Plan to go during the peak whale migration season, usually from mid-July to mid-September each year.

WHERE ELSE TO GO WHALE-WATCHING

ALASKA, USA
Whales of all sizes can be found in Alaska's cold Pacific waters. Look for belugas at Turnagain Arm, or follow humpbacks and orcas through the Gulf of Alaska.

SOUTHWEST AUSTRALIA
Spring is whale-watching season in Australia. Albany's King George Sound welcomes resting humpbacks from June to August, then southern rights arrive to breed until October.

84

CANADA

Witness a Canadian ice hockey match

Glide right to the heart of what it means to be Canadian by hitting an ice hockey match. Whether catching a small play at the local rink or sitting arena-side for a professional match, ice hockey is a local pastime that anyone—and almost everyone here—enjoys. Canada's national sport takes its origins from Indigenous stick-and-ball games, and today leads to action-packed and easy-to-follow matches. Despite the icy temperatures and vigorous gameplay, a jovial atmosphere and much post-match merriment is a part of the ice hockey experience. Depending which fan you ask, the ultimate match could be a Montreal Canadiens vs Toronto Maple Leafs showdown (they're Canada's national rivals), or perhaps seeing players from these teams and more come together as Team Canada for an international playoff. Sitting in the bleachers for a match, don't be surprised if you find yourself cheering, hugging, and chatting with the locals—it's easy to get swept up in the atmosphere of it all.

Good to know: The sport is played all year round, but the top National Hockey League games are held from October to April.

85

CANADA

Try maple syrup

The maple leaf is Canada's uncontested emblem, its distinctive shape forming the center of the national flag. But it's not just the tree's foliage that the country has become known for: it's also the world's biggest producer of maple syrup. But how did this "liquid gold" come about? French explorer Jacques Cartier wrote about the sugar maple tree in the 1530s, after he encountered the Iroquois people extracting the sap. Fast forward to today, and Quebec yields two-thirds of the world's production—and it's the best place to sample this sweet treat. The syrup is categorized into different grades depending on the color: the richer the hue, the stronger the flavor. A typical tasting involves an entire meal, where maple notes shine through in steaming bowls of pea soup, baked beans, and *Quebecois tourtières* (meat pies), among other dishes. The maple-flavored finale comes in the form of taffy, which is made by drizzling hot syrup on another Canadian classic: snow.

Good to know: The best time for a tasting is from February to April, during harvest time.

CANADA

Hike around Emerald Lake

Emerald Lake is one of the most majestic of British Columbia's many bodies of water. It sits at 4,000 ft (1,200 m) above sea level, surrounded by groves of mature hemlock, pine trees, and—rising behind them—the Canadian Rockies. The surrounds are breathtaking, but so too is the lake itself, named for the blue-green hue of its waters. The deep, almost opaque color of Emerald Lake is a result of its "glacial flour," the finely ground mineral created by glacial erosion. The hue is at its most vibrant on bright summer days, which is also the best time to hike around the lake. The easiest route is the Emerald Lake Loop, which runs for around 3 miles (5 km). You'll pass through dense forests and over streams, with captivating views over the lake and up into the mountains. For a more challenging hike, add on a two-hour loop up to the glacier that created the lake's memorable color.

Good to know: The lake usually freezes over from November to June, so visit outside of these months to see it at its brightest.

CANADA

Take a train through the Canadian Rockies

Ride the rails through the remarkable landscapes of western Canada, taking in views of the iconic Rockies mountain range along the way. The legendary *Rocky Mountaineer* train offers three routes through the region's remote and scenic expanses. With some glass-domed carriages throughout the train, it's easy to take in the landscape and spot wildlife as you trundle out of Vancouver, where each route begins. The First Passage to the West route is one of the most popular, with visits to hot springs and gondola trips in Banff included. The Journey Through the Clouds, meanwhile, is all about stunning, tranquil nature, coursing across the Athabasca Glacier and to the highest peaks of the Rockies. If stops in historical mountain towns is what you're after, then the Rainforest to Gold Rush route, which passes through Whistler and Jasper, will be ideal. No matter the two-day route you choose, endless stunning landscapes are a given.

Good to know: To nab a seat in the train's iconic glass-domed carriage, book either the "SilverLeaf" or "GoldLeaf" services.

CANADA

Visit Toronto

The most populous city in Canada, Toronto is also one of the most multicultural in the world, so much so that "diversity is our strength" is the local motto. Nowhere is this strength more palpable than in the city's tempting food scene. Among its neighborhoods there are the "towns"—Koreatown, Greektown, and Chinatowns (yes, plural)—and the "littles"—Little Italy and Little Portugal, to name just a couple. In keeping with the blend of cultures here, fusion food is the order of the day: expect to find jerk chicken poutine, sushi burritos, kung pao chicken tacos, and kottu roti pizza during your foodie explorations. The delicious bites make for perfect fuel before taking in the city's other highlights: the tall modern structures set among red brick buildings, the pinnacle of which is the iconic 1,814-ft (553-m) spire of the CN Tower.

Good to know: Arrive in the fall, when Toronto's trees turn and the streets and islands are at their most scenic.

CANADA

Drive through Banff National Park

It's impossible to travel through Banff National Park and not feel awestruck. After all, it was the dramatic scenery and the discovery of natural hot springs in the town of Banff that inspired the government to create Canada's first national park here in 1885. More than a century later, the park is still home to some of the most spectacular scenery in the country, where the sublime Rocky Mountains soar over glimmering glaciers, evergreen forests, swift rivers flowing through lush valleys, and some of the bluest lakes on Earth. The best way to take it all in is cruising on the Icefields Parkway (Highway 93), a 143-mile (230-km) scenic mountain road that twists and turns through some of the tallest, most jagged spines of the Rocky Mountains, while offering a chance of seeing grizzly bears and mountain goats along the way. As the road climbs through high passes, from the famous Lake Louise to the neighboring Jasper National Park, every turn offers yet another inspiring view.

Good to know: Bow Summit is the highest point on the highway; take a side road to get to the gorgeous Peyto Lake viewpoint.

90

CANADA

See the salmon run in British Columbia

One of nature's most astonishing spectacles can be seen in the wild rivers of Canada's British Columbia province. In the fall months, the region's streams fill with thousands of large salmon, splashing urgently in the water and all heading in one direction: upstream. Standing along any of these banks, you'll bear witness to an immense feat of nature, one where the fish take up most of the space in the waterways—in some parts so densely grouped that it looks more like a stream of salmon rather than water—as they defy the odds. The journey from ocean to their spawning grounds is one that many won't finish: as the fish swim, they are under constant threat from hungry, sharp-eyed bald eagles, the quick swipe of bear claws, and the jaws of hunting wolves along the way. If they survive their predators, they'll have to battle whitewater rapids, strong currents, and the many miles from ocean to gravel beds—and all without feeding. The few salmon that end up making it are tasked with bringing to life the next generation in the protected shallows. Seeing this natural spectacle is truly one of life's privileges.

Good to know: Pitch up riverside from September to October for your best chances of catching this natural phenomenon.

91

CANADA

Channel your inner athlete at Whistler Ski Resort

Whistler initially rose to fame when it hosted the cross-country, ski jumping, and biathlon events during Vancouver's 2010 Winter Olympic Games. For winter-sports enthusiasts though, the expansive tree-lined slopes of the Whistler-Blackcomb peaks had it placed firmly on the map long before the Olympic torch arrived in town. In fact, this alpine village routinely tops the charts as one of the best ski resorts in the world. Situated just a 90-minute drive from Vancouver, it has 125 miles (200 km) of smooth slopes, beside luxury chalets, high-end restaurants, and après-ski haunts. The town's idyllic pedestrianized village and lively cultural agenda— not to mention a party circuit so wild that it featured on MTV—help round off this North American destination as a must-visit. If subzero temperatures aren't your thing, fear not: there are burgeoning BMX and paddleboarding scenes in the summer too. And for a dose of sporting competition worthy of its athletic heritage, head to the original Olympic Park. It'll give you inspiration to hit the slopes—not that you'll need it.

Good to know: See Whistler's mountain culture at its best during the town's World Ski & Snowboard Festival every April.

93

MEXICO

Tuck into fresh tacos from a *taquería*

You can't think of Mexico and not think of tacos—they're, arguably, the most popular food in the country. While Mexican street-food culture is thought to date back to 15th-century Tenochtitlán, the history of tacos is murky. They've been linked to 18th-century silver miners, and to Aztec emperor Montezuma's use of tortillas as a spoon. Either way, they're enjoyed morning, noon, and night around Mexico, with recipes varying from region to region. Some of the best fish and shrimp are found in La Paz, while daring souls can try tacos filled with scorpion in Mexico City. Like the best cuisines, tacos are, at their core, surprisingly simple. A soft corn or wheat tortilla, no larger than the palm of your hand, is folded and filled with tasty ingredients like marinated meat, fresh cilantro, finely chopped onions, and, of course, salsa. Grab a bite from one of the estimated 50,000 taco stands set up around Mexico—no cutlery is required, but a napkin or two won't go amiss.

Good to know: *Taquerías*—street vendors, food carts, or taco restaurants—can be reliably found throughout Mexico.

92

ARCTIC OCEAN

Stand on the North Pole

The North Pole can feel more like an idea than a real place—the end of the world, a perpetually frozen land of stark white and pure blue, harsh and beautiful. But for two months each year, this legendary spot becomes somewhere you can visit. The geographic North Pole is an enigma—a permanent physical place only on the seabed. Yet, 2½ miles (4 km) above it, on a thick layer of sea ice, it's possible to stand in perfect alignment with the Earth's northernmost point. The journey here makes the once-in-a-lifetime experience even more memorable. In June and July, expedition ships make the trip through fields of ice floes, passing walruses, seals, whales, and polar bears. After navigating north, you'll disembark onto the frozen sea, join hands with fellow passengers, and count yourself among very few people who can say that—technically—they have walked around the entire world in just a few minutes.

Good to know: Most expedition cruises to the North Pole depart from Svalbard, Norway, and last two to three weeks.

MEXICO

Witness the monarch butterfly migration

Just a couple of hours from the capital, one of the most remarkable natural events in Mexico takes place. Each November, more than 140 million monarch butterflies descend upon the Sierra Madre Mountains after a journey of more than 2,500 miles (4,000 km) from Canada and the northern US. These elegant insects cover the tree trunks and branches of the firs and pines so thickly that their collective weight often bends the boughs, creating cascades of butterflies. As the temperature rises with the sun each day, they become more active and flutter throughout the forest, briefly alighting on plants and people alike before flying off to their next perch. Many people find the experience moving, even spiritual—according to local Indigenous beliefs monarch butterflies embody the spirit of the forest and carry the souls of the ancestors on their wings. Whatever you believe, standing there as the delicate, colorful insects flutter around you is an amazing experience—and one you can only have here.

Good to know: For fluttering action, visit during the warmer months between late January and the end of March.

MEXICO

Take in Teotihuacán

Nothing can prepare you for the wonder that is the city of Teotihuacán. The name means "the place where the gods were created," and, on witnessing it for the first time, it's easy to see why the Aztecs believed this to be the center of the universe. Once a thriving metropolis that was home to around 100,000 people, today this ancient Mesoamerican city is a sprawling archaeological complex, and one of the largest in the world too. Much of the history of Teotihuacán's ruins remains shrouded in mystery. Construction is said to have taken place between 400 BCE and 300 CE, but little is known about its inhabitants, their rulers, or indeed why the city fell into ruin. Some of the most impressive buildings are the enormous Pirámides del Sol y de la Luna—one of two pyramids here—and the Templo de Quetzalcoatl, named after the Mesoamerican Feathered Serpent which adorns the temple's exterior. Remnants of a long-gone civilization, the structures throughout Teotihuacán nevertheless retain their grandeur and scale, true to their name.

Good to know: The site is an hour away from Mexico City, and usually takes about three to four hours to explore.

MEXICO

Marvel at Chichén Itzá

An icon of the Mesoamerican era, the Mayan city-state of Chichén Itzá in Yucatán was once among the most sacred sites in the region. And it retains an air of sanctity today, even as tourist groups mill through the grounds. At its heart lies the impressive Temple of Kukulcán (also known as El Castillo), the most renowned structure in Chichén Itzá. The pyramid is thought to have been built according to the principles of astronomy and has 365 steps that run down the middle of each side, one for each day of the Mayan solar calendar. The 79-ft- (24-m-) tall structure is the centerpiece of what was once a thriving city of around 35,000 people. Beyond it lie other structures, like the evocative Temple of the Warriors, an intriguing Caracol observatory, and one of the largest ball courts in Mesoamerica. While Chichén Itzá later fell into ruin, it's still easy to imagine it in its heyday as you wander through.

Good to know: Aim to visit Chichén Itzá as soon as it opens in the morning, before the crowds arrive.

MEXICO

Celebrate the Day of the Dead

Among all the world's diverse ways to honor the dead, Mexico's is undoubtedly among the liveliest: Día de los Muertos, or Day of the Dead. According to Mexican tradition, which in fact dates back to the Mesoamerican era, every year the dead have divine permission to visit their loved ones. Families begin preparing weeks ahead of the fiesta's culmination on November 1 and 2. They fill altars (ofrendas) with edible offerings for their ancestors, adding candles to keep vigil and fragrant, bright marigold arrangements, said to guide spirits back with their pungent scent. Colorful and sometimes even comical images of skeletons make light of the great unknown; snatches of songs, lively and mournful, drift on the breeze as mariachi bands play. As night approaches, families file into local cemeteries and gather around the graves they've lovingly cleaned and decorated. There is a moment of stillness as all await the spirits' arrival, and then the celebration resumes, this time with the entire family—living and dead—in attendance. It is a feast at once sensuous and spiritual, and the dead are the guests of honor.

Good to know: Aguascalientes' capital hosts the Festival de las Calaveras (Festival of Skulls), one of the longer celebrations.

MEXICO CITY

There's no better introduction to Mexico than its capital, Mexico City. One of the oldest cities in North America, it has many layers of history and culture. A walk past its ornate churches and museums will take you through a rich past, where ancient traditions thrive and cultures collide.

98

Watch Mexico City's Alebrijes Parade

Every October, the streets of Mexico City fill with brightly colored creatures, real and fantastical. These are the sights of the Alebrijes Parade, or Desfile de Alebrijes, a carnival-like procession created in 2007 that pays homage to Mexico's wildly varied folk arts and handicrafts. Most of the carnival's floats are *alebrijes*: dazzlingly colorful models of fantastical creatures, mostly made with a papier-mâché-like technique called *cartonería*. Their origins date back to 1936, when local artist Pedro Linares apparently had fever dreams of the bizarre-looking beasts, and subsequently sought to re-create them, resulting in the *alebrijes* figures. It's terrifically trippy to watch hundreds of these whimsical beings marching en masse around the city's main historic square, known as the Zócalo, as hundreds of thousands of excited onlookers gather around to see them. There are many other idiosyncratic elements to the parade too, including the presence of *catrinas*—drawings, models, and masks of skeletons—that hint at the forthcoming Day of the Dead celebrations. Together, all combine to create a distinctly Mexico City event: outlandish, and outstanding.

Good to know: Treat yourself with a stay at the luxurious Gran Hotel Ciudad de México.

Delve into the world of Frida Kahlo

One of the most iconic artists of the 20th century, Frida Kahlo evokes images of Mexico like few others. Her deep connection to her home country is clear through her powerful and symbol-laden paintings, how she dressed and presented herself, and even her art-filled home in tranquil Coyoacán. Casa Azul, named for the bright-blue walls that line most of the space, was both Kahlo's birthplace and where she lived during her long and tumultuous marriage to Mexican muralist Diego Rivera. Walking through, it gives a glimpse into the lives of these two era-defining artists: the space is full of their art, personal effects, and creatively arranged furnishings. It's like entering an artwork, one made up of colorful paintings and sculptures, exquisite pre-Hispanic ceramics, and—of course—Kahlo's vibrant folk dresses. She's often wearing them in her self-portraits, which she used to portray her interior world and explore issues of personal suffering, race, gender, and class both in Mexico and beyond. Her easel is still set up, with her wheelchair placed in front—as if she might soon appear from another room and take up her brush again.

Good to know: The museum's Fridabus runs to the nearby Museo Anahuacalli, designed by Diego Rivera, on weekends.

MUST-SEE MEXICO CITY MUSEUMS

Museo de Arte Moderno
Full of 20th-century Mexican art, with works by Diego Rivera, Rufino Tamayo, and Frida Kahlo on show.

Museo Nacional de Arte
Discover one of the best collections Mexican art dating back more than 400 years.

Museo Jumex
A private collection with works by some of the biggest artists of the 20th and 21st centuries.

Palacio de Bellas Artes
A grand Art Nouveau cultural center that hosts temporary exhibitions.

Museo Franz Mayer
This former hospital show-cases decorative arts from the 16th to 19th centuries.

Museo Nacional de Antropología
The largest museum in Latin America, housing many objects from pre-Hispanic Mexico.

Enjoy a mezcal tasting

Oaxaca: home to tropical beaches, Baroque churches, and thriving Indigenous culture and, of course, mezcal. This potent spirit's name derives from "mexcalli," a Nahuatl term meaning "oven-cooked agave." Today, the world's widest variety of agave plants are grown in Oaxaca—the heartland of this classic Mexican spirit. It's no surprise, then, that you can try some truly eclectic and surprising bottlings in Oaxaca City's many highly regarded *mezcalerias*. These mezcal tasting rooms treat the drink with the respect it deserves—meaning you don't knock a glass back quickly, but rather savor it like you would a top-notch Scotch. Tastings are connoisseurs' occasions, pulling from the *mezcaleria*'s collection to highlight small-batch producers from across the state, each one showcasing the unique flavors of its region. To get an even deeper insight into this Oaxacan drink, head to the source in key production center Santiago Matatlán, an hour's drive southeast of the region's capital city.

Good to know: Oaxaca City's Mezcaloteca offers *dégustations*, where you can sample three or five different styles of mezcal.

MEXICO

Dive into Cenote Dos Ojos

The beginnings of the stunning Cenotes Dos Ojos
near Tulum are out of this world, literally—this kind
of sinkhole was formed around 66 million years ago,
when an asteroid struck the Yucatán peninsula. The
impact shattered the region's limestone bedrock,
creating thousands of sinkholes known as *cenotes*.
These became central to the culture of the ancient
Maya, who considered them sacred entrances to the
underworld, and tributes like gold and jade, as well
as the remains of human sacrifices have been found.
The stunning Cenotes Dos Ojos today is a jaw-
dropping place to dive in and explore. While you
may not be lucky enough to find Mayan treasures,
slipping into the turquoise, crystal-clear waters
of this flooded cave system will transport you into
another realm, illuminated by shards of sunlight
and blessed with high underwater visibility. Guided
tours here allow you to explore its precipitous
depths: under the waters, you'll see multitudes of
stalactites and stalagmites, encountering a variety
of creatures, from jellyfish to bats, along the way.

Good to know: Snorkeling equipment can easily be rented at
the site, while tours are offered from many Yucatán agencies.

102

MEXICO

Relax on Tulum's beaches

White sandy bays, clear waters and palm trees swaying in the wind: this is the stuff of beach-vacation dreams. Tulum, located on Mexico's Yucatán peninsula, is a place where the pace is slow and the warm Caribbean Sea is always waiting. Sprawling and pristine, the positively paradisial Playa Paraíso lives up to its name. Solitary palms reach sideways above sun-kissed shores—it's a scene aching for laid-back beach-going. This stretch of beach is hugely popular, with yoga sessions to beach bars full of visitors most days. For a more secluded experience, there's no beating nearby Playa Las Palmas. It's the best place to set off on adventures like snorkeling, kiteboarding, or diving head-first into *cenotes* (sinkholes), common in the area. Tulum is not all sea, sand, and sun, though. It's also where some of Mexico's best-preserved Mayan ruins can be found, in the Tulum Archaeological Zone. Among such scenes, it's no wonder the Mayans pitched up on these shores—these are some of the most stunning beaches in the world.

Good to know: Visit between December and April to ensure mild weather and avoid the sea turtle nesting season.

103

MEXICO

Party in Cancún

Buzzing beach parties along moonlit shores, world-class clubs hosting top DJs, and exclusive VIP events—few places in the world party harder than Cancún. This beach town perfectly blends tropical beauty with an exuberant nightlife, drawing many revelers from all over the world. With its endless fiestas and reliably lively atmosphere, Cancún is the ultimate destination for an unforgettable party experience—and one located right in the heart of the Caribbean. The "party zone" (yes, it's really a thing) runs 365 days a year, with clubs catering to a whole range of music tastes: reggaeton, house, electronic, and rock all make an appearance. At any of the famous clubs here, you can expect to find all manner of entertainment: from the epic gravity-defying acrobatic performances over at Coco Bongo to an actual water slide at Señor Frog's (taking you from the bar all the way to nearby Nichupte Lagoon). Expect to rub shoulders with (or, at least, catch a glimpse of) A-listers as you dance the night away under the beams of an accompanying laser show.

Good to know: Most clubs close at 3 a.m., but you'll always find an after party on the beach that will see you through to sunrise.

CENTRAL AND SOUTH AMERICA

105

BELIZE

Dive in the Great Blue Hole

While a bird's-eye view of the Great Blue Hole showcases the striking contrast between its cerulean hue and the turquoise waters that surround it, to really appreciate its magnitude you need to get inside it. Located at the center of the Lighthouse Reef, 62 miles (100 km) off the coast of Belize, this giant sinkhole brims with electrifying creatures—lemon sharks, reef sharks, great barracudas, goliath groupers, and schools of parrotfish among them. As you enter deeper, marine life dissipates, but huge stalactites take their place, proving just as fascinating to explore. These ancient formations, which can reach more than 30 ft (10 m), reveal the Great Blue Hole's origins as a dry cave during the last Ice Age. Here's the bad news: with sand pouring into the hole each day, scientists predict that it won't be around forever. Lucky for you, there's still enough time to visit one of the world's best dive sites.

Good to know: Only those that have completed at least 24 dives are allowed to dive the extensive cave system.

104

GUATEMALA

Wake up with the jungle in Tikal

With the piercing call of a macaw and the roar of a howler monkey, the day has officially begun at Tikal National Park. The trappings of modern life are nowhere to be seen at this former Mayan metropolis, where an overnight stay brings you closer to the primal rhythms of nature. This complex of more than 3,000 ruins, some of which date to the 4th century BCE, was once a booming center of power and sophistication; today, it's at the mercy of the wilderness, the ruined stone monuments encased by dense jungle. Aside from the flitting parrots and prowling jaguars who make themselves known at around 4:30 a.m., the ancient site is almost empty in the early hours of the morning, the perfect time to run your hands across thousand-year-old temple hieroglyphs in quiet reflection. Tikal is a firm reminder that there is no king of the jungle; rather, the jungle reigns supreme.

Good to know: There are three hotels in the park, but renting a tent or hammock at the Tikal campground is a cheaper option.

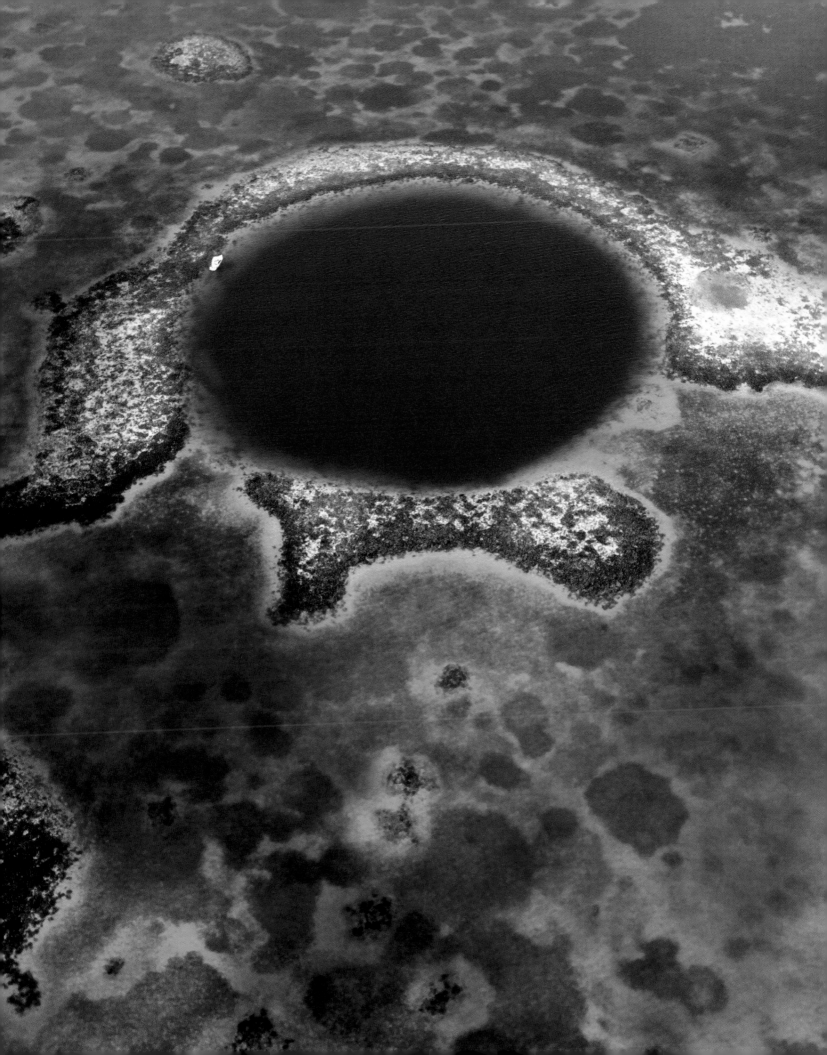

CUBA

Relish the rural bliss of Valle de Viñales

With its rust-red tobacco fields and towering royal palms, the Viñales Valley is home to Cuba's most quintessential scenery. But in this strip of land, tucked into the Sierra de los Órganos mountain range, the most spectacular features are the *mogotes*. These karst formations are all that remain of what was once a limestone plateau here; over millions of years, erosion collapsed the softer stone, forming the hollow pinnacles that rise up from the valley's plains today. A few other regions are studded with these iconic karst formations, but the Viñales Valley in western Cuba has the greatest concentration, with many hollowed out by internal caves. Aside from being gorgeous to photograph, these monoliths dutifully keep watch over one of the country's few working rural landscapes, where tobacco is cultivated and farmers till much of the land with oxen. So once you've stood in awe before the ancient *mogotes*, chat with the farmers to discover how cigars are made. You're in Cuba, after all.

Good to know: For the best view of the valley, look out from the hilltop Hotel Horizontes Los Jazmines.

107

CUBA

Sip a rum cocktail

Bacardi and Havana Club. The daiquiri and the mojito. Cuba Libre and El Presidente. You might have sipped these spirits and cocktails before, but nothing trumps tasting them in their birthplace. Ever since sugar cane reached Cuba in the 16th century, the nation has been known for its rum, spawning spirit brands and more internationally renowned drinks than most countries can shake a cocktail at. In Cuba, drinking a cocktail is as much a cultural experience as it is an indulgence. Top of the quaffs to try is the Havana-created mojito, made with white rum, lime juice, sugar, club soda, and a garnish of Cuban-grown mint, *Mentha x villosa*, which has sweeter leaves that are perfect for the drink. Then there's the daiquiri, supposedly heralding from the namesake village outside Santiago de Cuba and cobbled together with white rum, lime juice, and a lime peel twist. Even within the rum-rich Caribbean, Cuba's versions of the spirit has set production standards, so no matter what drink you go for, your highball will always be high-quality.

Good to know: Visit Havana's El Floridita bar to try a daiquiri in the place that popularized the cocktail.

108

CUBA

Drive a vintage car through Havana

You can hardly visit Cuba and not hit the road in a vintage convertible. The country is a classic-car-lover's dream, where one in every six cars predates the Revolution despite the decades of embargoes imposed by the US government. What's more, Cuba's roads were made for a leisurely road trip, especially the animated capital of Havana, where streets are studded with striking buildings that range in style from Art Nouveau to Art Deco. To make your road trip dream come true, pick up a Buick or Chevrolet in Havana's center, then join the rainbow parade of motors zipping east along the seafront promenade, the Malecón. Drive past the powder-soft sands before skirting through the center again, where iconic monuments like the cupola-topped National Capitol Building and Plaza de la Revolución come into view. If you'd rather soak it all up from the back seat, opt for a classic car tour instead—taking the slow road has never been so cool.

Good to know: Vehicles are in short supply, especially in high season, so reserve your desired car well in advance.

WHERE ELSE TO HAVE A CLASSIC CAR ADVENTURE

NAPIER, NEW ZEALAND
The Art Deco capital of the world, as it's known, Napier is all about vintage charm. Be chauffeured in a vintage Chevrolet or Packard and explore the architectural prowess of Napier.

KRAKÓW, POLAND
The district of Nowa Huta is famed for being the home of the Trabant, manufactured during the 1940s communist era and one of the most common cars in Central and Eastern Europe during the Cold War. Rent one in Nowa Huta and learn more about the area's history.

PROVENCE, FRANCE
Picture this: you're winding through lavender fields in a classic Citroën, the Mediterranean sun beaming down on you. This is pure French elegance, and an experience best had from the village of Eygalières.

109

CUBA

Take an architecture tour of Trinidad

The hillside settlement of Trinidad is a living, breathing museum. Here, cobbled streets are lined with pastel-colored houses, plazas are overlooked by 18th-century mansions, and the yellow tower of the Iglesia y Convento de San Francisco looks out on it all. As appealing as it is to wander the streets, what makes this place so important is the insight it gives us into the past. Founded in the 16th century by conquistador Diego Velázquez, Trinidad generated enormous wealth as a result of the forced labor of West African enslaved people, brought to the region to work on sugar mills. When slavery was abolished in 1866, major landowners left Trinidad behind, along with the huge mansions they built from sugar profits. After that, the city remained isolated until 1919, when Cuba's railroad was extended to Trinidad. It's a result of this isolation that the center has preserved its historic atmosphere, an appealing one at that.

Good to know: Take a locally guided architecture tour to learn more about the city's history.

110

CUBA

Explore Santiago de Cuba

It's often said that Santiago de Cuba is the most passionate city in Cuba, and its vibrant energy is certainly contagious. It was here that the country's quest for independence began, with Fidel Castro launching the struggle against Batista's dictatorship by attacking the Moncada Barracks in 1953. By 1959, Castro's efforts had paid off, and Santiago officially became the birthplace of the Revolution. The city is still high on this freedom today, with a colorful Afro-Cuban culture, vivacious nightlife, and the country's liveliest carnival in July celebrated with fervor. But it wasn't just the Revolution that Santiago spawned: many Cuban rhythms were born here, including salsa, bolero, and mambo. It's these infectious sounds that you'll hear pulsating from open windows and street corners while you explore the old town, where architectural wonders like the Parque Céspedes square lie. Havana might hog the travel headlines, but Santiago is where you'll really get under the skin of this spirited nation.

Good to know: Find out what's going on in the city by consulting the Noticias de Santiago de Cuba, a weekly cultural calendar.

BAHAMAS

Be inspired by the islands of the Bahamas

When you close your eyes and picture the perfect island paradise, chances are it's all pristine sandy beaches, turquoise waters, and endless sunshine. That's the Bahamas in a nutshell, an archipelago in the Atlantic Ocean that consists of 700 islands and more than 2,000 cays. The undisputed jewels of the Bahamas are the Exumas, home to 365 idyllic tropical islands and cays sprinkled across 120 miles (200 km) of sea. Much of this paradise lies within the protected waters of two national parks, best explored on a catamaran cruise when days are spent snorkeling and languishing in the sun. Then there are the famous blush-pink sands of Eleuthera island, made even more striking by electric-blue waters lapping at the beach edge. Wherever you live out your island escape, it'll be better than your imagination could even conjure.

Good to know: Transit options differ between the islands; most are connected by flight paths and ferries, but plan ahead.

112

BAHAMAS

Swim with pigs

On the Bahamas' Exuma Islands, the Caribbean idyll never gets "boar-ing." Here, you can ditch your fellow travelers and take a dunk with water-loving hogs instead by boarding a boat to the beach on Big Major Cay. As you approach, a herd of pigs paddle through the shallows, beckoning you to join them. What ensues is a surreal and side-splittingly comical swim with the swine. You're allowed to pet the pigs and feed them while they are in the water (fruit and vegetables are best), which elicit snorts of sheer delight from your new pig pals, and maybe some from you too. Theories about how the pigs arrived here vary: shipwreck survivors; beasts stashed by sailors as a future food source; founding livestock for an island farm that never took off. But if one thing's for sure, it's that you're not supporting a cruel tourist venture by diving in—far from it. The feral herd has been here for decades and make a hearty living off tourist tidbits, so don't miss out on saying hello. It's the bucket list dream you never knew you had.

Good to know: Stay at nearby Staniel Cay Yacht Club, which organizes tours to see the swimming pigs.

On the Bahamas' Exuma Islands, the Caribbean idyll never gets "boar-ing." Here, you can ditch your fellow travelers and take a dunk with water-loving hogs instead.

113

Listen to reggae

Reggae, the musical expression of Rastafarianism, originated on Jamaica in the 1960s, and when Bob Marley started to sing of future hopes for peace, the genre soon went global. A logical way to get into the rhythm is with a visit to Kingston's Bob Marley Museum, dedicated to the life and music of one of the world's favorite performers. Here, you can tour the clapboard house where the icon lived and recorded in his personal studio. The museum is also home to the legendary Tuff Gong, the Caribbean's most famous recording space, where you can learn everything about the Tuff Gong music label founded by Bob Marley and the Wailers, and the entire record-making process, Caribbean style. Better yet, top reggae tunes ring out as you go. But that's enough for reggae education—to really get to know the music, you need to join the locals and toe-tap to its infectious syncopated beat, which rings out from buses, beaches, and bars all over the country. Take heed from the icon himself: get together and you'll feel alright.

Good to know: Visit Jamaica in July, when the week-long Sumfest puts on memorable live reggae.

115

CARIBBEAN

Cruise the Caribbean

Stretching from the pink-sand beaches of the Bahamas to the wind-whipped shores of Aruba, the Caribbean spans a vast realm of isle-studded seas. Little wonder, then, that it's the world's top place for cruising. With more than two dozen Caribbean cruise lines operating in winter (December through April), the choice of ship is as varied as the islands, with itineraries that are often divided by region: western islands such as Nassau and Turks and Caicos, eastern ports like Puerto Rico and St. Barts, and southern stops including Martinique and Grenada. So, how to choose? Go for a cruise line that's actively attempting to lower its carbon emissions; the industry is planning to be net-zero by 2050, and you'll feel good helping it reach that goal while you set sail on the azure seas.

Good to know: Look for operators that are testing biofuels and liquid natural gas (a cleaner fossil fuel), like Royal Caribbean.

114

DOMINICAN REPUBLIC

Explore the Dominican Republic

Bountiful beaches? Check. Historic architecture? Check. Natural wonders and wildlife galore? Check and check. Often nicknamed the "Pearl of the Antilles," the Dominican Republic checks every box for the perfect Caribbean trip. Occupying the eastern two-thirds of the island of Hispaniola, the Caribbean's second-biggest country has plenty to shout about. It's home to both its tallest mountain, Pico Duarte, and its lowest point, Lake Enriquillo, not to mention the most-visited all-inclusive resort area along the coast around Punta Cana. But pride is also to be found in the country's intangible heritage. It's there in the national music forms, the *bachata* and *merengue*, twin and twangy genres that have locals dancing in bars across the country. And it's present in the baseball scene, best seen inside the stadiums of the six league teams. Then there's the capital, Santo Domingo, home to the Caribbean's oldest architecture. And that's barely scratching the surface of what this country offers.

Good to know: The dry season, November through April, is the most pleasant time to visit, with temperatures moderate.

WHERE ELSE TO TOUR A COFFEE PLANTATION

SIDAMO, ETHIOPIA
Ethiopia is the birthplace of coffee, and the Yirgacheffe region produces some of the world's finest thanks to its high elevation and rich soil. Visit during harvest time, November to February, to experience a coffee ceremony.

KONA, HAWAII
With its tropical rain and volcanic soil, Hawaii is able to produce mild, fruity coffee in its small farms. The Kona Coffee Cultural Festival celebrates the end of the harvest in November, where you can meet farmers (and sip a great brew).

WEST JAVA, INDONESIA
Located between mountains and the equator, Indonesia is able to produce top java. This region is home to the country's first coffee plantation, where you can learn about handpicking and how to sort quality beans.

 116

NICARAGUA

Taste Nicaragua's coffee

To produce top-notch coffee, you need perfect growing conditions and quality beans, two things that Nicaragua has in spades. Courtesy of the Ruta de Café (Coffee Route), which meanders through coffee-growing departments Matagalpa, Jinotega, Estelí, Madriz, and Nueva Segovia, you can experience Nicaragua's most important export being cultivated firsthand. If you only have time for one stop, make it Matagalpa. Some of the country's most gourmet coffees have been developed here, with java almost all shade-grown at high altitudes. The result? Beans that mature more slowly and acquire a fruity, chocolaty juiciness. Sitting pretty among the lake-dotted Matagalpa forest is Selva Negra, one of Central America's longest-established coffee plantations and a world leader in sustainable growing. Here, you can find out about regional production on an estate tour and lodge in bucolic luxury before waking up to smell the coffee.

Good to know: Book into Selva Negra's eco-lodge, where you'll take a coffee and farm tour after a restful sleep.

117

GRENADINES

Island-hop in the Grenadines

Isles with white sands and turquoise waters fill practically every horizon of the Caribbean, but this archipelago—shared between St. Vincent and the Grenadines and Grenada—comes closer than most islands to perfection. Cruising between the 30-odd isles in the chain, ideally under your own steam or as part of a charter, is the best way to see this dreamy region. Stop off at superlative beaches such as Macaroni Beach on Mustique for white sands backed by palms and greenery-clad hills. Or give some of the Caribbean's best diving and snorkeling a try around the tranquil Tobago Cays, flanked by a curling coral reef that provides a sanctuary for green sea turtles. Perhaps still more precious than any one envy-inducing vista is the blissful under-development compared to much of the Caribbean. Here, it really is possible to play out desert island fantasies, perhaps embellished by a hearty helping of archipelago staple callaloo soup or some locally made Sunset Rum.

Good to know: Horizon Yacht Charters offers luxury crewed sailboat charters in the Grenadines.

118

VIRGIN ISLANDS

Sail around the British Virgin Islands

Some Caribbean islands are made for basking on beaches, some for touring picturesque architecture and some—in the Virgin Islands' case—for standout yachting. This is one of the world's great sailing destinations, made so by generally calm seas and consistent trade winds that keep the oomph in your sails. Heaven for yachties is the British Virgin Islands (BVI), the part of the island chain with the best charters, where ideal line-of-sight sailing within the liberal scattering of 50-something isles is another major draw. Cast off from Tortola, BVI's largest island, chartering or bringing your own vessel to explore the archipelago. Stopping off where you wish and at your own pace is the way to go in a place where the most beautiful bits are scattered across many isles, only some of which are served by public boat. Think of mooring up alongside dream-worthy beach scenes such as those Red gets to see when finally free in *The Shawshank Redemption*, the end of which was filmed on these islands. The BVIs are film-set-worthy, that's for sure.

Good to know: BVI Yacht Charters has luxury yachts for charter at Wickhams Cay 2 in Tortola.

119

PUERTO RICO

Explore San Juan

If San Juan's cobbled streets, timeworn buildings, and bulky defenses could talk, they'd tell stories of naval invasions and piratical raids. This is the second-oldest city in the Americas, harking back to 1521, and its history feels palpable at every turn. The city's most epic fortification, Castillo San Felipe El Morro, was constructed over 250 years from 1539 to 1790, and welcomes visitors who cruise into San Juan. Behind this colonial backdrop, though, is a city that embraces the present as much as it cradles its past. Standout museums, world-class street art, and inventing the piña colada have allowed San Juan to write a new story. And oh, the beaches! Stretching for mile upon golden mile from Condado out to Isla Verde, these sandy shores are so splendid few cities in the Caribbean can come close. This is Puerto Rico at its finest, a delightful merging of old and new.

Good to know: Check into San Juan's Caribe Hilton, home to the bar where the piña colada was purportedly created.

121

COSTA RICA

Look out for rare birds

Birders, this one's for you. One of the most biodiverse places on Earth, Costa Rica occupies just 0.03 percent of the world's landmass, but accounts for a staggering 5 percent of all its living species. It's particularly rich in birdlife, home to around 900 avian species (roughly the same number as in the whole of Europe), many of which are found nowhere else on the planet. In rainforests and wetlands, mangroves and cloud forests, everything from tiny scintillant hummingbirds to giant king vultures fly around. But it's seeing a rare and endangered species that leaves a lasting memory, like the scarlet macaw that often perches in the south Osa peninsula, or the resplendent quetzal that calls the Parque Nacional Los Quetzales home. The best chance to see the country's bucket-list birds? Let them come to you.

Good to know: To spot the most elusive birds, join a tour with a company like Eagle-Eye Tours.

120

COSTA RICA

Catch a wave off Playa Negra

Lapped on either side by the Caribbean Sea and the Pacific Ocean, and with epic waves found at world-class spots like Santa Rosa, Tamarindo, and Dominical, Costa Rica is up there with some of the finest surfing spots in the Americas. For many boarders, destination numero uno is the dark-sand beach of Playa Negra near Los Pargos, which catapulted into surfing stardom thanks to the iconic 1994 surf movie *Endless Summer II*. Playa Negra is known for its feisty right-hand barrel that surges over a shallow rocky bottom, perfect for experienced surfers at high tide. Prevailing easterly trade winds and ceaselessly working Pacific swells give Playa Negra more or less year-round appeal. Better yet, the fact that there's only really room for a dozen-odd surfers here enhances its sought-after status, and makes for a laid-back session. While you're waiting to chase the waves, soak up the shoreline surrounds, an almighty tangle of tropical dry forest harboring howler monkeys, raccoon-like coatis, and regional wildcats called jaguarundis.

Good to know: The main break isn't beginner-friendly, so take a lesson in town before hitting the boards.

MINDO CLOUDFOREST, ECUADOR
The tiny town of Mindo is hidden among the clouds in Ecuador, where trails through the forest lead to waterfalls and the famed cock-of-the-rock makes an appearance at dawn and dusk.

BWINDI IMPENETRABLE FOREST, UGANDA
Home to half of the world's mountain gorillas, this forest in southwestern Uganda is the ideal spot for gorilla trekking. Be sure to go with a reputable safari company, since these gorillas are an endangered species.

COBÁN, GUATEMALA
The high humidity and high altitude of Cobán not only allows plants to thrive but offers the ideal conditions for producing coffee. Look for orchids on the forest floor and take a tour of the Chicoj Plantation.

COSTA RICA

Walk through the Monteverde Cloud Forest

Rolling mist, tree trunks blanketed with moss, and a chorus of birdsong: Monteverde is like something out of a fantasy novel. Named for the ephemeral mists that envelop them, Costa Rica's cloud forests are typically found at elevations of 3,300 ft (1,000 m) above sea level, and account for more than half of the country's terrain. Covering the slopes of the northwest, the Monteverde Cloud Forest Biological Reserve is the most famous of them all, and is extraordinarily biodiverse, home to an astounding 448 species of bird, 126 species of mammal, and more than 2,500 species of plant. While you can spot plenty of flora and fauna during the day (a network of well-marked trails make it easy to explore independently), the cloud forest comes alive after dark, when its most fascinating creatures spring into life. Grab a flashlight and join a guided night walk through the reserve, keeping your eyes peeled for sloths, tarantulas, pit vipers, and kinkajous. You'll have a story to tell for years.

Good to know: Daily visitor numbers are capped, so book your entry ticket in advance.

ECUADOR

Spot unique wildlife on the Galápagos Islands

They might be remote and minuscule, but these 19 islands couldn't be more momentous. Lying 620 miles (1,000 km) off the coast of Ecuador, the Galápagos are synonymous with naturalist Charles Darwin, who journeyed here in 1835 to observe characteristics in the endemic wildlife, which influenced his groundbreaking evolutionary theories. The wildlife is just as inspiring today. One of the world's best-preserved ecosystems, the islands protect a cast of creatures great and small: land and marine iguanas; flightless cormorants; seals and sea lions; equatorial penguins; and the long-living, slow-moving Galápagos giant tortoise. A range of vessels, from intimate yachts to 100-berth cruisers, offer trips around the islands, each with their own itinerary, so you might find yourself visiting the Charles Darwin Research Station or exploring the volcanic landscapes of Isabela, all the while on the look-out for unique wildlife. But of all the adventures you'll have, it'll likely be the snorkeling you'll remember the most: it's an underwater window into this remarkable world.

Good to know: A tourist card is required to visit the islands; find out more on the Governing Council of Galapagos website.

Journey to the Black Christ Festival

For many, it starts with a three-day trek from Panama City to reach the city of Portobelo, where tens of thousands of people honor the life-size statue of a brown-skinned Christ every October. This is the Festival del Cristo Negro, and it's more than your average event; it's both a celebration of Afro-Panamanian identity and an act of collective prayer against racial oppression and colonialism. Legend says a fisherman discovered El Nazareno, the statue that the festival centers around, on Portobelo's shores in the 17th century, and solemn ceremonies, such as changing El Nazareno's robes, and moving acts of penance mark the day's emotional depth. After mass at the Iglesia de San Felipe, a carnivalesque energy takes over, with a four-hour-long upbeat procession seeing food, beer, and craft vendors lining the streets and celebrants quickstepping to lively music. As the historic site of the first successful slavery rebellion in the Americas, Portobelo is the perfect backdrop for such a vital celebration.

Good to know: Mass begins at 6 p.m.; arrive at least two hours early if you want to get inside.

COLOMBIA

Make the pilgrimage to Ciudad Perdida

Spanish for "Lost City," Ciudad Perdida's story is almost as epic as a trek here. This northern Colombian archaeological site was established around 800 CE, and was likely the Tayrona people's capital city. In the 16th century, these people were largely driven out by Spanish conquistadors, their city abandoned and lost for centuries until it was serendipitously rediscovered in 1972. Though no longer lost, it's certainly isolated, perched within the UNESCO biosphere of Sierra Nevada de Santa Marta. To wade through this swathe of thickly forested mountains, rough paths and dense jungle foliage requires a grueling four-day, 37-mile (60-km) out-and-back hike, traversing the territory of the Kogui, Wiwa, Arhuaco and Kankuamo communities. Only an estimated 30–40 percent of the ruins in this jungle have been excavated, so who knows what more there is to uncover here.

Good to know: G Adventures offers a seven-day package to Colombia with the Ciudad Perdida trek as the focus.

GUYANA

Marvel at Kaieteur Falls

As tea-hued water plunges over the Potaro River, the roar is like nothing you've ever heard. At 741 ft (226 m) high, Guyana's showpiece is the world's largest single-drop waterfall, and its power is undeniable. With no roads leading to its remote location in Kaieteur National Park, deep in Guyana's interior, seeing this force of nature requires a multi-day trek or a flight on a small plane from the coastal capital of Georgetown. Once you're here, you'll feel like you're at the edge of the Earth, the water dropping at an exhilarating velocity from a vertical rock face where only the cocks-of-the-rock and swifts nest. Plus, with visitor facilities amounting to a ranger station and a rustic guesthouse, the sparse natural setting is a rare treat. Adding to the falls' mystique is the legend behind their name: according to Patamona legend, Chief Kai saved his people from war by paddling over the precipice in an act of self-sacrifice to appease the spirit Makonaima. Rest assured the only thing you'll spot diving over the edge today are birds taking the flight of their lives.

Good to know: There are daily return flights from Georgetown to Kaieteur Falls, but spaces are limited, so book ahead.

Lençóis is Portuguese for bedsheets, an aptly poetic name for this dreamy landscape stretching along Brazil's northern coast.

BRAZIL

Admire the dunes at Lençóis Maranhenses

Lençóis is Portuguese for bedsheets, an aptly poetic name for this dreamy landscape stretching along Brazil's northern coast. Indeed, at the Parque Nacional dos Lençóis Maranhenses, windswept sand dunes interspersed with turquoise rainwater lagoons read to the imagination as fresh linen billowing against a perfect sky. Getting to this surreal oasis, one of the country's most far-flung destinations, requires an off-road adventure tour in 4WDs that bounce, creep, and splash along paths leading to the dunes and lagoons. Up close, crystal-clear watery expanses of the likes of the Lagoa Azul and Lagoa Bonita are true relaxation havens—you can take a dip in them. Above the water, stand atop one of the *lençóis* dunes to catch the entire winding reverie of blue water and bleached sand. You'll be pinching yourself to make sure you're not dreaming.

Good to know: May to September is the best time to visit, to avoid heavy rains but still enjoy the season's lagoons.

BRAZIL

Spot spectacular wildlife in the Amazon Rainforest

Few places capture the imagination quite like the mystical Amazon Rainforest, the most important tropical forest on Earth. You could spend years exploring it; spread some 2.5 million sq miles (7 million sq km) across eight nations, it supports billions of trees, around 15 percent of the planet's bird and butterfly species, and many more types of mammal than exist in the entirety of Europe. More than half of the emerald forest is located in Brazil, and the Amazonian metropolis Manaus is the perfect launchpad for voyaging upriver into the jungle. From a dugout canoe on the murky waters, you'll clock a Noah's Ark's worth of animal sightings: pink river dolphins cruising the currents, caimans on the banks, and several monkey species cavorting through the canopy above. Alternatively, head off from the city of Santarém to venture deeper into primary jungle, where you might be so lucky as to spot the king of the Amazon, the elusive jaguar. Welcome to the jungle.

Good to know: Tour availability, facilities, and itineraries vary, so do your research.

RIO DE JANEIRO

When a city is blessed with year-round sunshine, endless beaches, and one of the world's greatest parties, why wouldn't you add it to your bucket list? Brazil's mammoth capital fizzes with an infectious energy and zest for life, where it's all too easy to let your hair down with a *caipirinha* in hand.

Party for days at Rio Carnival

Feathers and sequins glitter in the spotlights. Loudspeaker-laden floats rumble through the streets. Dancers twist and shake to a samba beat. This isn't your ordinary party, this is a Brazilian Carnival, and nowhere goes bigger than Rio. Being here during this time—from the Friday before Ash Wednesday to the following Thursday—is an unforgettable experience, with the city shutting down for five days and millions of people descending on endless street parties, live shows and epic balls. Spontaneous parades cruise the streets, swelling in size and raucousness as they pick up whimsically dressed revelers along the way. These vivacious and informal processions are at the heart of the celebrations and one of the best ways to embrace the Carnival spirit, but the iconic face of Carnival is the procession of Grupo Especial schools known as the Desfile. This spectacular competition between samba schools takes place in the 90,000-seat Sambadrome Marquês de Sapucaí, where towering floats pass through and as many as 4,000 dancers and musicians can be part of a single performance. There's no escaping the carousing, so lean in and join the world's greatest street party.

Good to know: Book any events in advance online—you can only see certain parades with tickets, and lines can be long.

130

See Christ the Redeemer statue

Holding its arms wide to the city, the Christ the Redeemer statue is as synonymous with Rio de Janeiro as its famous beaches. At 2,300 ft (710 m) above sea level, it stands at the top of Mount Corcovado, from where it watches over Guanabara Bay, Sugar Loaf Mountain, Copacabana, and Ipanema beaches, and the Atlantic Forest down below. But it's not just a watchful eye over Rio. The statue ties in to the abolition of slavery, its outstretched arms and gentle countenance symbolizing peace. In 1888, Princess Isabela outlawed slavery in Brazil, freeing hundreds of thousands of people and prompting many to suggest a statue in her honor. Instead, she proposed a statue of Christ, declaring him to be the "true redeemer of humankind," and the landmark was officially inaugurated in 1931. The journey to Christ's feet—a hike that threads through the Parque Nacional da Tijuca, or a 20-minute train ride up—is as rewarding as the panorama from the summit. Once you reach the top and look up at the colossal structure, you'll feel pretty humbled.

Good to know: It's typical to queue for up to three hours for train tickets, so book yours in advance online.

MUST-SEE RIO BEACHES

Ipanema
Play beach volleyball or relax on a sun lounger at this famed stretch of sand.

Copacabana
The king of city beaches, this broad stretch is perfect for sunbathing.

Barra da Tijuca
Rio's largest beach is a surfing and windsurfing paradise.

Flamengo
Pearl-white sand beach affording wonderful views of the bay and the Sugar Loaf.

Vermelha
Enclosed volcanic beach with reddish sand and often tranquil waters.

São Conrado
This sandy beach is lined with fancy mansions and modern architecture.

Grumari
A peaceful escape that's rarely busy, perfect for relaxing strolls and cycling.

131

Wander down Ipanema beach

Every evening, as the sun goes down behind the twin peaks of Dois Irmãos, residents toast "the best sunset in Rio." They could just as easily toast the best beach in Rio, heck, perhaps even the best city beach in the world. Nestled into the outer edge of Rio's affluent Ipanema district, the 1½-mile (2.5-km) arc of white sand has been the go-to hangout for those wanting to see and be seen since the 1960s. That's in part thanks to the bossa nova hit, "The Girl from Ipanema," which took the world by storm in 1964 and propelled Ipanema into the spotlight. And that spotlight hasn't dimmed a day since. Along the Praia de Arpoador stretch, skilled surfers tackle the mighty waves that give Ipanema its name—the area was first named Y-panema or "rough water" by the Tupi-Guarani people. Over on Praia Farme, an LGBTQ+ scene thrives. In between them, beachgoers frolic in the shallow surf and cyclists ride alongside the sands. And at the end of it all, a stunning sunset is a promise.

Good to know: Cool off with a caipirinha—a Brazilian cocktail made with cachaça, citrus juice, sugar, and ice—at a beach bar.

WHERE ELSE TO EXPERIENCE INCA PERU

PISAC
High above the Sacred Valley, the beguiling ruins of Pisac sit at the foot of a hill, and are still remarkably intact. Walk through the remains of temples, residential quarters, tombs, and ceremonial baths, as well as terraced fields.

QHAPAQ ÑAN
The Royal Highway covers a 25,000-mile (40,000-km) network of stone roads that criss-crossed the Inca Empire. Travel up stone stairways and through glorious scenery to get your fill of ancient ruins on the wonderfully preserved section from Castillo to Huánuco Pampa.

Q'ESWACHAKA ROPE BRIDGE
This is the last surviving example of an Incan rope bridge, spanning the raging Apurímac River. Take a tour from Cusco to Q'eswachaka to marvel at the imposing structure.

132

PERU

Roam the storied ruins of Machu Picchu

Clinging onto a precipitous ridge, the mist-cloaked lost city of the Incas is arguably the most famous sight in all of South America. The Inca Empire left behind many ancient treasures throughout the Andes, but this 15th-century citadel was never sacked by the Spanish, who failed to find it; instead, it was abandoned and left to nature to reclaim until 1911. Built of rock at an altitude of 7,710 ft (2,350 m), it's a fine display of Inca mastery; no other civilization has managed to assemble so many colossal stone blocks so seamlessly. Houses, temples, fountains, plazas, and agricultural terraces are linked by scores of stairs and paths, the exquisite stonework visible at every turn. Little wonder it's Peru's ultimate draw.

Good to know: Reach Machu Picchu from Cusco via train or the Inca Trail, and book an entry ticket six months in advance.

133
PERU

Lace up your boots for the Inca Trail

One of the world's most famous hikes, the four-day, 24-mile (39-km) Inca Trail is full of pre-Columbian pomp. While other hikes likewise lead to the most iconic of Peru's ancient ruins, Machu Picchu, none match the Inca Trail for theater. The Incas cut this route connecting the Sacred Valley with the superlative ridgetop ruined city high above the Río Urubamba. They then festooned it with myriad still-visible constructions like Llactapata, a ceremonial center and series of terraces for food cultivation near the trail's beginning, and the striking buildings and tumbling terraces at Wiñay Wayna toward journey's end. With preserved Inca paving and an Inca tunnel, you have a ramble that would be riveting for its history alone without even mentioning the scenery it traverses, which is just as mesmerizing. Scale three lofty mountain passes in view of Andean peaks and spot ruins straddling precipitous slopes along the way: what a prelude to Machu Picchu this is.

Good to know: Book your Inca Trail (guide obligatory) with Cusco agencies months in advance: limited places fill up fast.

134
PERU

Walk among the wildlife of Manú National Park

Out of the cloud-draped Andes you descend on a long, winding road, passing through cloud forest that supports some of South America's finest birdlife. After the better part of a day, you finally arrive at a river port, from where you'll likely spend another day traveling by boat to the edge of Manú National Park. Before you've even entered this rainforest domain, you've had some remarkable adventures—and they're about to get even more exhilarating. Manú is the best-protected tract of virgin Amazon jungle, covering an impressive 7,700 sq miles (20,000 sq km). More than 80 percent, however, lies in the "intangible zone," the abode of Indigenous peoples who have almost no contact with the outside world, and where travelers are prohibited. As for the other 20 percent, it's the domain of woolly monkeys roaming the forests, capybaras dipping in the shores, and horned screamers flitting around oxbow lakes. Set off on steep trails, along canopy platforms and towers, and you'll quickly be transported into a world where wildlife reigns supreme.

Good to know: You must be on a guided tour for a Manú adventure: try a company like Bonanza Tours.

Hike Rainbow Mountain

There's no trippier picture to share of your sojourn in South America than that of Rainbow Mountain, also known as Vinicunca ("mountain of colors"). Here, bands of some 14 different-colored minerals give the surrounding slopes the appearance of a rainbow, a kaleidoscopic glory that was only revealed a decade ago—up until 2013, the mountain was glacier-covered. It's a tough journey out to behold this phenomenon, starting with a 3½-hour drive southeast of Cusco near the village of Pitumarca. It's not the 6-mile (1-km) out-and-back distance that tests trekkers, though, but the breath-sapping elevations in excess of 16,400 ft (5,000 m). And yet the rewards are rich: stark, rolling *altiplano* (upland plains) dotted with alpacas and vicuñas, snow-bedaubed views of southern Peru's highest mountain country, and, of course, those surreal stripy rocks swooping up to Rainbow Mountain's 17,060-ft- (5,200-m-) high summit. It's nature's finest painting.

Good to know: Climate change has impacted Vinicunca, so follow responsible travel and "leave no trace" principles here.

135

PERU

See the heart of the Inca empire in Cusco

Legend says that when sun god Inti sent his son Manco Cápac to Earth to found the Inca civilization, his guidance was clear: wherever Manco could plunge a golden rod into the ground with a single thrust should be the place. That spot was Cusco, which became capital of the Inca world from the 13th to 16th centuries and has remained the historic hub of Andean Peru ever since. Though best known as the base for launching a trip to Machu Picchu, Cusco has so much more to give. Among steep labyrinthine streets that retain their original Inca paving are spectacles like Qoricancha, once the empire's most lavish temple, and the cathedral with its Cusco School artwork. Then there are the museums, which champion Inca culture; Machu Picchu finds; and even the national tipple, Pisco—where better to toast to the Incas?

Good to know: Cusco is high above sea level and altitude sickness is not uncommon, so take it easy for the first 24 hours.

137

PERU

Watch condors fly over Cañón de Colca

Andean condors are the planet's largest birds of prey, a whopping 4 ft (1.2 m) long with a wingspan of 10 ft (3 m). Suffice to say, seeing these birds glide on thermal currents and swoop over a steep-sided ravine is pretty impactful, and that's what you're in for at Colca Canyon, *the* place to see Peru's national bird. It takes some effort for a close encounter to happen, starting with a visit to the Cruz del Cóndor, a remote viewpoint positioned between the canyon settlements of Chivay and Cabanaconde. Timing also plays a huge part, since the condors that call this rocky place home do not always perform. For instance, you're unlikely to spot them in the wet season, they tend to prefer mornings for a glide, and tour bus commotion can keep them out of sight at any hour of the day. But with some luck you'll bear witness to these birds soaring against rock walls that drop a dizzying 3,940 ft (1,200 m) to the canyon floor. Pay attention to the remarkable canyon while you're here too: it's nearly twice the depth of the Grand Canyon.

Good to know: Almost all adventure operators in Arequipa organize trips to the canyon, including a stop at Cruz del Cóndor.

138

PERU

Travel aboard the Belmond Andean Explorer

Train journeys in South America are increasingly scarce, which makes this luxurious sleeper train all the more special. Linking up Cusco, Puno on the shores of Lake Titicaca, and the city of Arequipa, this high-altitude and slow-speed ride takes you through stellar Andean landscapes over a period of three dreamy days. As the midnight-blue train trundles out of Cusco, roads and rooftops are replaced by scenes of wild natural beauty, framed by rows of wide windows. One moment, you're curling around the bank of a thunderous river; the next, you're rumbling across a sweeping valley plain where wild vicuña nibble. You'll trundle along some of the highest tracks of any regularly used passenger train in the world; disembark at the world's loftiest navigable large lake, Titicaca; and have a chance to tour Arequipa's otherworldly rock-art-peppered caves at Cuevas de Sumbay. And you'll see it all in style from sumptuous train cars that are fit for the Inca emperor himself, where cocktails, fine dining, and an onboard spa await. This locomotive goes high up without dispensing with the high-end.

Good to know: Once-weekly trains depart between March and December, and tickets must be booked online.

139

PERU

Tuck into a bowl of ceviche

On a hot afternoon in Lima, capital of Peru, there's one meal guaranteed to cool you down, and that's ceviche. Peru's national dish, this seafood delight comprises chunks of raw fish marinated in lime juice, onions, and chiles, and is the perfect fusion of Indigenous and conquistador-introduced cuisine. The *corvinas* (sea bass) plying Peru's coastal waters have long been harvested by pre-Columbian peoples; Incas first preserved the fish with *chicha* (corn-fermented beer) as the marinade. The lime for the marinade that "cooks" the *corvina*, plus the red onions and cilantro that bestow on the dish its nuanced color and texture, are Spanish imports. Head to a cool neighborhood restaurant called a *cebichería* (dedicated ceviche spot) and ask for a glass of *leche de tigre*, the citrusy juices the dish is cooked in, to quaff alongside your zesty serving of ceviche.

Good to know: Find great ceviche spots along Lima's La Mar Avenue, also known as the "ceviche neighborhood."

140

PERU

Contemplate the complex Nazca Lines

"How did they do that?" It's a question that's never far from thought when exploring South America's incredible ancient sites, and nowhere more so than at the Nazca Lines. This collection of geoglyphs, dispersed on a high desert plateau between the towns of Nazca and Palpa, comprises more than 10,000 lines and more than 70 human figures and stylized animals. They're thought to have been etched into the plains between 500 BCE and 500 CE, and were first noticed from the air in 1927; since it never rains on the Peruvian coast, the lines have managed to survive so many centuries. Though attributed to the Nazca and Paracas cultures, these enigmatic lines remain one of the world's greatest archaeological mysteries. Were they a giant astronomical calendar? Perhaps an alien landing strip? Theorize for yourself on a flight over them, watching for a curly-tailed lizard, striking whale, and an enormous hummingbird.

Good to know: Many companies offer flights over portions of the Nazca Lines, such as Aeroparacas.

WHERE ELSE TO WITNESS AMAZING CARVINGS

UFFINGTON WHITE HORSE, ENGLAND
This huge chalk horse, measuring 350 ft (100 m) from nose to tail, is believed to be Britain's oldest hillside carving. Some say it was cut by the Saxon leader Hengist (whose name means "stallion" in German).

ATACAMA GIANT, CHILE
This geoglyph, 283 ft (86 m) tall, is the world's largest image of a human being. It rests on the west slope of Cerro Unitas hill, 9 miles (14 km) east of the town of Huara.

ROCK EAGLE EFFIGY MOUND, GEORGIA, USA
This huge stone effigy is shaped like a prone bird, and consists entirely of milky quartz rocks. It's thought to have been created 2,000 years ago by Indigenous peoples for religious or ceremonial purposes.

PERU

Homestay at Lake Titicaca

The highest navigable lake in the world, Lake Titicaca shimmers an unreal blue against a balmy spread of Andean agricultural land and mountains. The expanse of water stretches out for 120 miles (194 km) across Peru and Bolivia, reaching a whopping elevation of 12,500 ft (3,800 m). It's where, according to Inca mythology, the son of the sun god Manco Cápac first appeared, heralding the return of light after a time of darkness and the birth of the Inca civilization. Today, on the numerous islands sprinkled across the lake, inhabitants live traditionally, with life centered around fishing, farming, and weaving, and increasingly supplemented by homestay tourism. With no hotels on the lake, villagers on the islands, including Taquile, Amantaní and Chucuito, happily share their homes, welcoming visitors as well as encouraging them to get acquainted with ancient Indigenous culture. In return, you'll help with everyday tasks such as harvesting, minding cattle, and building houses. It's lake living, Peru style.

Good to know: Book a homestay in Puno either by visiting the community tour operators or the iPerú office.

142

BOLIVIA

Be mesmerized by the Salar de Uyuni salt flat

A mind-bending landscape, the Salar de Uyuni is the planet's biggest salt flat, but it hardly feels like it's on this planet at all. Located in southwestern Bolivia, this high-altitude, pancake-flat white expanse sprawls some 4,600 sq miles (12,000 sq km). Making up its surface are 11 billion tons (10 billion metric tons) of large halite (common salt) crystals, which form after the evaporation of water from the sea or saltwater lakes. The result of this natural phenomenon is a mesmerizing pattern of pentagons and hexagons, broken only by the occasional cacti-covered island in the region. It's a sight that's even more magical during the rainy season between November and March, when the Salar floods and transforms into a giant mirror, creating a perfect reflection of the sky on the ground; at this time, it's hard to see where the ground stops and the sky begins. Around the Salar's shoreline, you'll find centuries-old cave tombs and tiny villages of salt harvesters, where you can learn about salt extraction and even bed down in a salt hostel (yes, it's a thing). This is truly an experience like no other.

Good to know: Jeep trips from the nearby town of Uyuni traverse the salt flat.

WHERE ELSE TO SEE STONE HEAD STATUES

TÜRKIYE
Often labeled "Turkey's Easter Island," Nemrut Dağı's towering peak is home to a set of giant statues with heads that are around 6 ft (2 m) high.

COLOMBIA
South America's largest collection of ancient mega-lithic sculptures and religious monuments, including many stone heads, is found in the San Augustín Archaeological Park.

INDONESIA
Bada Valley on the island of Sulawesi is studded with around 400 ancient megalithic statues, which have minimalistic designs and were made around 5,000 years ago.

BOLIVIA
Near Lake Titicaca, the ruined capital of the pre-Inca Tiwanaku harbors a subterranean temple covered with unique limestone heads.

143

CHILE

See the stone heads of Rapa Nui

A tiny speck of land adrift in the Pacific, more than 2,175 miles (3,500 km) west of the Chilean mainland, Easter Island is one of the most remote inhabited places on Earth. Known locally by its Polynesian name, Rapa Nui, it was settled between 800 and 1200 CE by navigators who sailed vast distances. They created a flourishing society, famously carving stone statues known as *moai*, which were built from tuff (compacted volcanic ash), range from 6 ft (1 m) to 65 ft (20 m) in height, and represent revered ancestors. A whopping 1,000 *moai* remain on Easter Island today, with most originating in the grassy crater of Rano Raraku, dotted with some 400 statues in varying states of completion. That first glimpse of the 220-ton (200-metric ton) Te Tokanga, the largest *moai* ever carved, makes the lengthy trip to get here more than worthwhile.

Good to know: You'll need to take a 4½-hour flight from Santiago to reach Easter Island.

144

CHILE

Trek in Torres del Paine National Park

Few countries can compare with Chile when it comes to hiking, and few national parks can compete with the trekking options at Parque Nacional Torres del Paine. Named after the snow-streaked, blue-gray granite towers that rise 9,200 ft (2,800 m) in its center, Torres del Paine showcases Patagonia at its most ruggedly spectacular. It's a landscape that encompasses creaking glaciers, iceberg-strewn lakes, sweeping steppe, subpolar forests, and, of course, forbidding mountains—spellbinding terrain for a multitude of trails. The most renowned hikes here are the 44-mile (71-km) "W" (named after the shape it traces on the map) and the epic 70-mile (112-km) "O" circuit. Whichever trail you tread, you can expect scenery that casts a spell, be it turquoise shores and beech forests of the "W" or lumbering glaciers and granite peaks along the "O."

Good to know: You need to be reasonably fit to tackle these multi-day routes, and it's wise to go with a guide.

ARGENTINA

Explore Patagonia

Adventurers, explorers, and visionaries have been setting sail to Patagonia for centuries, lured by the excitement of seeing what exists at the bottom of the world. It's a thrill that remains today, where a vast wilderness of glistening lakes, giant glaciers, and native forest welcome those who venture this far south. Roughly the size of Mexico, the region spans southern Chile and Argentina, with the latter section filled with some of South America's greatest natural wonders. On the northeast coast, the Península Valdés marine reserve is a vital breeding ground for southern right whales, sea lions, and elephant seals, while around 150,000 Magellanic penguins find a home at nearby Punta Tombo. To the southwest, Los Glaciares National Park offers up a complete change of scene, encompassing a huge chunk of the Southern Patagonian Ice Field, one of the biggest of its kind outside the poles. In between it all are isolated towns and cities and intriguing ancient sites—perfect fodder for an adventure at the edge of the Earth.

Good to know: Spring (September to November) and fall (March to May) are generally the best times to visit.

CHILE

Venture into the Atacama Desert

Is there life on Mars? There certainly is in this huge northern portion of Chile, where the world's highest and driest desert is the next best thing to visiting the red planet—even NASA has deemed it the perfect analogue to Mars on Earth. In this psychedelic land, herds of skittish llamas wander sweeping sand dunes, flocks of candy-pink flamingos gather in salt flats, and geothermic fields rumble among hulking volcanic peaks. There's even the aptly named Valle de la Luna (Valley of the Moon), where wind and water have carved jagged rock formations. By day, explore the region on foot, bike, horseback, or jeep, embarking on adventures from sandboarding to scaling mountains, or calmer pursuits like lounging in a hot spring and visiting ancient ruined fortresses. Then, as the sun sets over the arid landscape, witness a celestial panorama of stars, planets, and galaxies reveal itself against an inky night sky.

Good to know: Set off from the inland hub of San Pedro de Atacama, and avoid the extreme heat of January to March.

PARIS, FRANCE
Tango dancing on the Seine is one of the city's most popular events— the city was the first in Europe to adopt the Argentine dance, after all. Show up with a pair of comfy shoes, grab a partner from the crowd, and be prepared to swing and dip until midnight.

BARCELONA, SPAIN
Hot on Paris's heels for the keenest adopter of tango in the early 20th century, Barcelona is home to schools and dance halls galore where you can master your technique on a Saturday night.

BELGRADE, SERBIA
From summer tango marathons to monthly performances, Belgrade offers up one of Europe's most exciting tango scenes. Sit back and let the pros do their thing at one of the city's many venues.

147

ARGENTINA

Experience Buenos Aires

If any capital city encapsulates the vibrancy of South America, it's Buenos Aires. It's there in the colorful architecture of La Boca and the ornate *fileteado* artwork decorating shops and cafés. It drifts in the smoke of roasting meat at a *parrilla* (steak house) and shimmers in a glass of malbec, Argentina's renowned wine. And it's in the intensity of the tango, the iconic dance at the heart of the Argentinian psyche, which has its roots in the bars and *bordellos* that sprung up around Buenos Aires at the turn of the 20th century. Truthfully, though, Buenos Aires refuses to be defined by one thing; rather, it's a place to let your passion guide you. Maybe it will lead you toward joining the roiling crowds at a fiercely contested soccer match, dancing a sultry tango at a late night *milonga* club or touring the eclectic architecture along tree-lined boulevards. This is a city to experience, not just see.

Good to know: Avoid the city when it's uncomfortably hot and visit in September to December or March to April.

148

ARGENTINA

Witness the Iguazú Falls

Before these mighty waterfalls even come into view, their rumbling roar and great clouds of spray hint at the spectacle beyond. A set of cataracts straddling the frontier between Argentina and Brazil, the Iguazú (or Iguaçu in Portuguese) Falls take their name from the Tupi-Guarani term for "great water," and they certainly live up to the billing. Protected by national parks on either side of the border, Iguazú consists of more than 250 waterfalls and extends for more than 1.6 miles (2.7 km). A visit to both sections is more than worthwhile, but if you've only got time to see one side, go for Argentina. While the Brazilian portion is best for panoramic views, including one of the powerful Devil's Throat, it's easier to get closer to the main cataracts and feel the spray from the forest trails on the Argentinian side. It's an awesome display of the power of nature (and pretty refreshing too).

Good to know: To visit both sides of the waterfalls, you'll need to have your passport stamped when you cross the border.

ARGENTINA

Hike the Andes

If hiking part of the longest mountain chain in the world sounds like your kind of adventure, lace up your boots and head to Argentina. Stretching from the high-altitude Bolivian border in the far north to the frigid shores of the Beagle Channel in the extreme south, Argentina's Andes are veined with incredible hiking trails. Some trace old trading routes used by the ancient Incas, others cut through pristine landscapes, and the finest routes lie in the far south. The rustic frontier town of El Chaltén is the gateway to the northern part of Parque Nacional Los Glaciares, Argentina's trekking capital, with well-marked trails and campsites. Trek to lagoons dotted with mini icebergs through dense subantarctic forests, and to epic viewpoints overlooking the jagged Monte Fitz Roy. On a clear, sunny day, this mountain is perfectly reflected in the below lake's blue-green waters, an image of heart-stopping beauty.

Good to know: Spring (September to November) and fall (March to May) are the best times to hike relatively crowd-free.

151
URUGUAY

Soak up seaside luxury in Punta del Este

Stretching on either side of a long peninsula, with more than 18 miles (30 km) of sandy Atlantic beaches, Punta del Este oozes glamour. Known as the "St. Tropez of South America," it's the place to mingle among well-heeled vacationers while getting in some blissful beach time. Its shores have something for every sun-, sand-, and surf-seeker, but highlights are Playa Bikini, a haven for party-goers, and Playa Pinares, perfect for a more relaxed vibe. Should you need a break from the beaming sun, you can still dabble in luxury at one of the award-winning spa resorts backing onto Punta del Este, where massages and saunas await. As the day comes to a close, sensational restaurants come to life as does a nightlife scene few Latin American cities can rival. The party can begin as early as late afternoon, flowing into cocktail-fueled dinners and exploding into dancing that lasts well beyond sunrise. Sleep a little, then repeat.

Good to know: For an indulgent stay, check into the Grand Hotel Punta del Este.

150
ARGENTINA

Head down to Ushuaia

On the edge of the Beagle Channel, backed by snow-streaked Andean peaks, Ushuaia is the biggest city in Tierra del Fuego, the southernmost tip of South America. At the southern end of the Pan-American Highway, this far-flung outpost lies barely 620 miles (1,000 km) north of Antarctica and is the main embarkation point for cruises to the continent, as well as for skiing and snowboarding in the nearby mountains. Ushuaia also has a tumultuous history. Founded in an area originally occupied by Yagán communities, it has been, in turn, a missionary base, a gold rush hub, and a notorious penal colony dubbed the "Siberia of the South." For an insight into the city's past, head to the Museo Marítimo y del Presidio, a fascinating museum dramatically housed in the former prison, and take a ride on the inmate-built *Tren del Fin del Mundo* (End of the World Train), which provides a snapshot of the region's history while immersing you in captivating scenery.

Good to know: The weather is best during the summer season (December to February); July is the peak winter sports month.

> **Stretching on either side of a long peninsula, with more than 18 miles (30 km) of sandy Atlantic beaches, Punta del Este oozes glamour.**

ANTARCTICA

Glimpse the Antarctic from an expedition ship

Nothing can prepare you for your first sight of the Antarctic Peninsula. Rising up from the cobalt sea like a giant avant-garde structure, it's a beautiful beast—a place so wild it sends a chill down your spine even before you've stepped outside. Every moment in the presence of nature's icy creation is a privilege, from walking among thousands of molting penguins to watching colossal icebergs float by. Kinder to this fragile landscape than traditional cruise ships, small expedition ships are also bigger on experience: there's no time wasted in lines, and the smaller passenger cohort has a way of fast-tracking new friendships. Your itinerary may take you along the western coast of the peninsula, where snow-capped mountains pierce the sky, or around its eastern tip and into the iceberg-filled Weddell Sea. With an itinerary guided by nature, every day at sea is an adventure. So go on, take the (polar) plunge.

Good to know: The main Antarctic expeditions run October to March, and most ships depart from Ushuaia or Punta Arenas.

EUROPE

153

ICELAND

Explore the Golden Circle

Iceland is Mother Nature at her most elemental, a land of fire and ice where volcanoes spew great fields of lava and tectonic plates tear the Earth apart. The Golden Circle, a 190-mile (300-km) circular route, is home to some of her most astronomical creations—not just in Iceland, but in the whole of Europe. Departing Reykjavík, your first stop is often Þingvellir, a remarkable rift valley marking the point where the North American and Eurasian tectonic plates meet and one of the only places on Earth that you can walk between them. Further down the road, the Geysir geothermal area puts on a spectacular show of steam and water, thrown dozens of yards into the air every 10 minutes or so by the geyser Strokkur. The best, as they say, is saved till last: the mighty Gullfoss waterfall at the route's eastern end, where vast columns of water plunge 105 ft (32 m) into the misty canyon below.

Good to know: Book your day tour with a reputable operator, like G Adventures or Arctic Adventures.

154

ICELAND

Drive Iceland's Ring Road

Only completed in 1974, Route 1, better known as the Ring Road (Hringvegur), is Iceland's major highway, circling the country for 828 miles (1,332 km) and taking in everything bar the Westfjords and the Snæfellsnes Peninsula. The drive can be completed in as little as a few days but stretching it out over a week or more is recommended to really explore some of the country's most famous sights. Walk behind the waterfall at Seljalandsfoss. Laze on a black-sand beach at Vík. Marvel at the icebergs of Jökulsárlón Glacier Lagoon. Or hike along the photogenic shores of Lake Mývatn. In between all these gasp-worthy sights you'll come across the country's most charming towns and villages, including Akureyri, Iceland's "second city" and home to laid-back bars and modernist churches, as well as the perfumed walkways of Lystigarðurinn, the world's most northerly botanical garden. "Are we there yet?" is not a question you'll hear as you drive along this epic road.

Good to know: You'll need winter tires between November and April, and snow chains should be used when necessary.

ICELAND

Take a dip in the Blue Lagoon

For somewhere so hyped, the Blue Lagoon still manages to live up to the highest of expectations. Iceland's most famous attraction is an otherworldly sight: a milky blue pool of geothermal seawater, its steam rising over the barren lava landscape of the Reykjanes Peninsula and its electric blue color the result of the rich deposits of the mineral silica. The lagoon started forming in 1976, when geothermal seawater flowing out of the Svartsengi Geothermal Power Station collected in the surrounding lava field. Locals were soon bathing in the pool, and the water's array of minerals were found to have beneficial effects on the skin. In 1987, the first public facilities were opened, and today, the lagoon includes not just the famed pools but also two hotels, three restaurants, a café, a subterranean spa, and a shop selling a range of skin products. You can spend as long as you like in the water, which hovers around a toasty 100°F (38°C). Order a drink at the wade-up bar, lather your face in a white silica mud mask, and relax.

Good to know: Volcanic eruptions in the region have caused the Blue Lagoon to close, so always check ahead.

ICELAND

Spend time in Reykjavík

Iceland might conjure up images of wild and dramatic landscapes, but this country also does small charm exceptionally well, and nowhere better than in Reykjavík. With its technicolor street murals and colorfully painted houses offsetting the often gray skies, Reykjavík feels more like a tiny town than the world's northernmost capital. And where better to get to know it than at the Aðalstræti Settlement Museum, where immersive exhibits put you in the shoes of the hardy souls who first settled Iceland, right here in Reykjavík in 870 BCE. Brilliant art galleries keep you busy too, like the Hafnarhús, which explores the vibrant world of Icelandic pop artist Erró. Culturally sated, head to a traditional restaurant to try some Icelandic delicacies before experiencing Reykjavík's thriving nightlife scene, which punches well above its weight for a city its size. Reykjavík makes an excellent base for exploring much of Iceland, but when you're all natural wonder-ed out, its pretty streets are the perfect remedy.

Good to know: Visit in summer for the best weather and the liveliest nightlife, when you can party under the midnight sun.

WHERE ELSE TO RELAX IN AN ICELANDIC LAGOON

SECRET LAGOON
It might not be much of a secret any more, but this beautifully sited thermal pool near Flúðir in Iceland is still a wonderful place to take a dip. The water remains at a very pleasant 100–104°F (38–40°C) all year.

HVAMMSVÍK
Enjoy eight different hot pools and beautiful views on the shoreline of scenic Hvalfjörður fjord. Ocean swims and Wim Hof breathing sessions are on offer, and a restaurant serves up delicious seafood soup. If you're lucky and visit in the evening, you might even witness the Northern Lights.

SKY LAGOON
Kópavogur's lagoon is hot on the heels of the Blue Lagoon, with breathtaking views overlooking the sea. The seven-step ritual is the highlight here, and includes everything from taking a cold plunge to relaxing in a sauna.

IRELAND

Take in Newgrange

There are ancient, mythological sites all around Ireland, but none is as sacred as Newgrange. This Neolithic passage tomb was built around 3200 BCE, which means it predates both the Great Pyramids in Egypt and Stonehenge in England. Viewed from the outside, the huge dome looks like something from *The Lord of the Rings*, complete with a slope covered in bright green grass. But take a walk inside this passage tomb, with its megalithic spirals carved into the rock, and you're transported to a world from thousands of years ago. It's not the only monument here, either—it's part of Brú na Bóinne, a World Heritage Site that incorporates Newgrange, Knowth, and Dowth. Newgrange is the only one you can enter, though, and it's at its most magical on the winter solstice, when the dawn light aligns perfectly, entering the tomb and illuminating the chamber. If you're lucky enough to get a ticket, it's a once-in-a-lifetime experience.

Good to know: The annual lottery for solstice tickets is held at the end of September, with winners announced in mid-October.

IRELAND

DUBLIN

If ever there was a city to charm your socks off, it's Dublin. This is quite possibly the most sociable city in Europe, where the world is put to rights over a pint and there's nothing a jolly trad session can't fix. Add to that impressive museums, vibrant street art, and great shops, and you've got a city you'll never want to leave.

Join in the St. Patrick's Day celebrations

Think of Ireland, and the lively St. Patrick's Day festivities likely come to mind. After all, this national holiday is a celebration of all things Irish, a day that honors the country's patron saint and the culture of Ireland as a whole. But while celebrations around the world can get a little raucous, in Ireland it's not quite the party you might expect—in the best way. Sure, the pubs are in full swing and there's no shortage of parties to be found wherever you are in the country. But it's more than just a booze-filled revelry. There are cultural events like traditional music sessions and Irish dancing, festivals dedicated to poetry and theater, and parades in every town around the country. The biggest parade takes place in Dublin and is attended by half a million people, who line the streets to watch the floats and marching bands go by, wearing their green hats and mingling with a pint as they navigate Dublin's lanes. Wherever you are, throw on something green, grab a bunch of shamrocks to wear in your buttonhole, and soak up the spirit of Ireland.

Good to know: Head to the end of the parade by St. Patrick's Cathedral, where the crowds are less busy.

Sip a pint of Guinness at the source

Many say that a pint of Guinness tastes better when you drink it in Ireland. But if you really want to try the best pint of your life, you need to go right to the source. The Guinness Storehouse is in the heart of Dublin's historic distilling district, right by the brewery where the stout is made. But this experience is about more than just the beer—there are seven floors of multimedia displays and installations, where you can learn all about the history of the brewing process and the famous advertisements that have become cult viewing over the decades. The real highlight comes at the end of the tour, up in the Gravity Bar. This panoramic glass and steel bar (designed to look like the heads of two pints of Guinness) offers 360-degree views of the city, from the nearby rooftops of the Liberties neighborhood to the Dublin Mountains in the distance. Here, you can sip on a perfectly poured pint and take in the views of Dublin, old and new.

Good to know: Learn how to pour the perfect pint yourself with the Guinness Academy Experience upgrade.

MUST-DO DUBLIN EVENTS

Temple Bar TradFest
A joyful celebration every January of traditional music and culture.

St. Patrick's Day
Five days in March are filled with parades, concerts, céilí dances, and fireworks.

Colors Boat Race
Trinity and University College Dublin compete in the age-old rivalry of a rowing race along the Liffey every March.

Dublin Pride
A ten-day-long celebration for the LGBTQ+ community in June.

Dublin Fringe Festival
Every September, the biggest performing arts festival in the country takes center stage.

Dublin New Year's Festival
Outdoor performances and celebrations in January mark the start of the New Year.

Listen to a lively trad session

Whether you catch a full-on céilí in a bustling pub, or a pared-back moment with just a few musicians, there's nothing like an Irish trad session. It's a moving experience, with musicians sitting around a table at the pub—a breeding ground for impromptu sessions—with their instruments, lost in the sounds of songs that have been played on this island for hundreds of years. Usually, you can expect to hear the fiddle; the tin whistle; and the bodhrán, an Irish drum that's played so fast you can barely see the beater (drumstick) moving as the beat picks up. Despite the Irish love of a sing-song, a trad session isn't a communal experience—only the best musicians take part, those with a mastery of the undulating melodies of ancient tunes. The music can get the crowd tapping their toes or sitting in hushed silence as a sean-nós singer performs. Dublin is packed with pubs that host trad sessions, so take your pick, sit back, and get swept up in the music.

Good to know: The Cobblestone in the Smithfield area is one of the best for trad, and puts on music every night.

DUBLIN

161

Peer into the Book of Kells at Trinity College

There are books, and then there is the *Book of Kells*. This ancient manuscript dates back to the 9th century and is a handwritten, illustrated copy of the four gospels of the New Testament, kept in the Old Library of Ireland's most prestigious university, Trinity College Dublin. The most richly decorated medieval Irish manuscript, it's embellished with intricate spirals and figures, and has been housed at Trinity since the 17th century. While you can't flick through the book yourself, you can see two intricately designed pages of the open manuscript, as well as explore an immersive interactive exhibition that brings the pages to life. And if you think the Book of Kells is impressive, wait until you see its setting. Step into the Long Room at the Library of Trinity College and you'll find yourself under a giant, barrel-vaulted ceiling, made from a glossy, dark oak. To each side are hundreds of shelves lined with heavy, leather-bound books, with towering wooden ladders leaning against the ledges. Bibliophiles, this one's for you.

Good to know: The Old Library is undergoing restoration work, so check on progress when planning your visit.

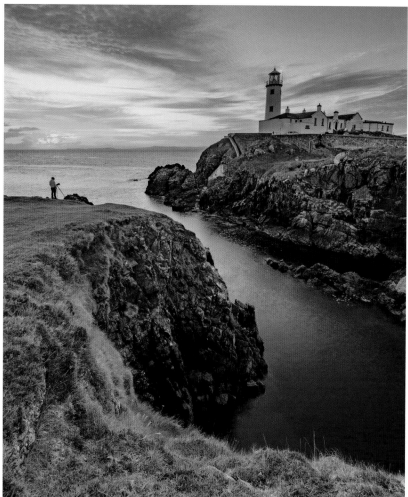

IRELAND

Hit the road and drive the Wild Atlantic Way

Snaking down the western coast of Ireland, the 1,500-mile (2,400-km) Wild Atlantic Way passes all the sights that make the Irish shores so magical. There are sea stacks off the coast of Donegal, where birds flit between the cliffs. There are blowholes in Mayo, where the Atlantic smashes through ancient rock formations. And there are endless stretches of pristine beaches, like the gleaming white sand and dazzling waters of Dog's Bay and Achill Island. You might be tempted to drive the whole thing in one epic trip, but it's best seen in shorter sections: Sligo to Donegal, Galway to Mayo, or Kerry to Cork. That way, you can allow time for diversions. After all, if you chat with a local who tells you about the best wild swimming spot, you'll want to make time for a spontaneous dip. This is a place to slow down and breathe in the wild, dramatic landscapes of Ireland at its finest.

Good to know: The road is at its busiest in July and August, so plan your drive for spring or fall.

163

NORTHERN IRELAND

Walk across a land of legend at Giant's Causeway

The Giant's Causeway seems to appear out of nowhere, with the kind of mind-boggling visuals that make it seem otherworldly. On the tip of the Antrim Coast, this ancient rock formation is made up of 40,000 hexagonal gray basalt columns, which jut out of the wild and swirling sea and morph into colors of amber and orange when the sun hits. Depending on who you're talking to, the formation is either the result of a volcanic eruption almost 60 million years ago, or the work of local giant Finn McCool, who is said to have created the causeway in order to cross the Irish Sea to reach his Scottish nemesis, Benandonner. Whether you take in the view from the rocks themselves or get a bird's-eye perspective from the cliffs above, it's an impressive sight: geometric towers rising in ethereal yet meticulous order, creating a natural staircase over the sea. It's also the only place in the world where you can see rocks from the Paleogene period formed in such a way, which makes it as unique as it is awe-inspiring.

Good to know: Be prepared for all weathers and be careful climbing the rocks—rogue waves can appear out of nowhere.

> The Giant's Causeway seems to appear out of nowhere, with the kind of mind-boggling visuals that make it seem otherworldly.

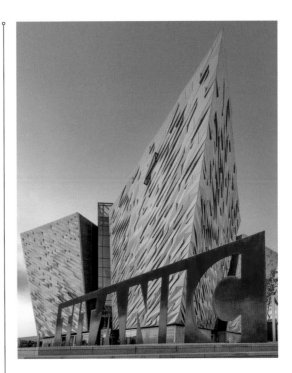

164

NORTHERN IRELAND

Feel the buzz of Belfast

Its history is emotive. Its people are great craic. Its foodie scene is one of Europe's best. Often overlooked, Belfast is filled with character (and characters). While the Troubles and the decline of heavy industry had a huge impact on Northern Ireland's capital, the peace process and a burst of regeneration projects have revitalized this handsome, friendly city into one of Europe's most exciting places. On its distinctive red-brick walls, political murals recall the Troubles, a time when street art played a conspicuous role in proclaiming the loyalties of two intransigent communities, Protestants and Catholics. In its restaurants, top chefs use local and seasonal ingredients to create stunning dishes, while quality cheap eats are found around town at places like St. George's Market. In its museums, stories are reflected on with guts, like the newly revamped Titanic Belfast, set on the very spot where the ill-fated ship was built. This a city that's as inspiring as it is full of a hefty dose of fun—spend one night in the vibrant Cathedral Quarter, with its trendy bars, clubs, and arts centers, and you'll feel the full force of what this city is capable of.

Good to know: Book a Black Cab Tour for insight into the city's recent history from those who lived through it.

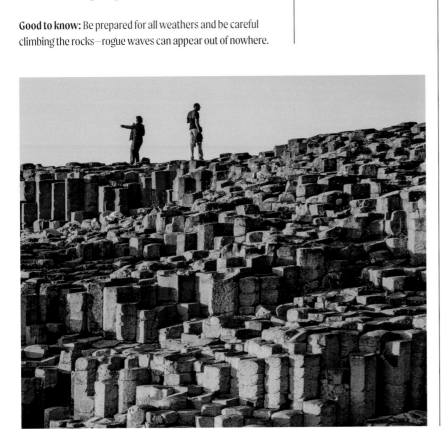

165

SCOTLAND

Drive the epic North Coast 500

Rugged coastlines, expansive bays, cloud-scraping mountain passes: it's not hard to see why this road trip is trending. The North Coast 500 takes drivers through Scotland's most dramatic and desolate landscapes for a glorious 516 miles (830 km). Setting off from Inverness, the beginning and end of the journey, the road north hugs the coast, revealing the history of the land at every turn. Through your rain-flecked windshield you'll spot imperious castles, Pictish ruins, and charming seaboard villages. In Sutherland, hailed as Britain's last great wilderness, Norse fortresses and Iron Age brochs pepper the hillsides, while eerie ruins serve as reminders of the Highland Clearances. To make the most of your time on the road, make sure to get off it too. Wander down to bone-white beaches, peer over heart-quickening clifftops, and enjoy a warm Highland welcome (and perhaps a traditional folk tune) at the local pub. Some describe this road trip as Scotland's answer to Route 66, but that's all wrong. The North Coast 500 is uniquely Scottish, through and through.

Good to know: This road trip is popular, so visit slightly off-season in late spring or early fall, and leave no trace behind.

166

SCOTLAND

See the Highlands aboard the Jacobite Steam Train

The Jacobite Steam Train is perhaps now better known as the Hogwarts Express for its role in the *Harry Potter* movies, but you don't need to be a Potterhead to be dazzled by this journey. On leaving Fort William, the Jacobite chugs its way through Scotland's most jaw-dropping landscapes, while inside, the carriage's vintage charm and mahogany interiors bring a touch of old-world magic. Gazing out across the shores of Loch Eil—which, on a still day, mirrors its surrounding, looming peaks—you'll feel the anticipation build as you approach Glenfinnan Viaduct. This concrete colossus with 21 enormous arches sweeps its way across Glen Shiel in a feat of Victorian engineering. Your journey concludes, not at Hogwarts of course, but in the coastal town of Mallaig, a fishing port where ferries cross crystal clear waters to Skye and the Outer Hebrides. All in all, this journey will leave you spellbound.

Good to know: Trains run April to October. Consider opting for a first-class compartment for added comfort.

167

SCOTLAND

Celebrate Burns Night

For the uninitiated, the rituals of a traditional Burns supper on January 22 may appear a little strange at first. A sheep's stomach, stuffed with minced offal and served on a silver platter, is heralded into the room to the rousing drone of bagpipes, and lovingly addressed in Scots verse before being pierced open and served to all for supper. Why, you ask? Well, it's to mark the birthday of Scotland's much-loved national bard, Robert Burns (affectionately known as Rabbie Burns to his fellow countrymen), and is celebrated with enough pomp and ceremony to blow away even the most stubborn cases of January blues. Celebrations, including whisky tastings, exquisite haggis suppers, and boisterous ceilidhs of which the party-loving poet would surely approve, take place all across the country. At each event, attendees take turns performing misty-eyed readings of the poet's best-loved verse well into the night, with recitals becoming increasingly theatrical as more whisky is consumed. The Scots certainly know how to have a good time, and Burns Night is no exception.

Good to know: Non-meat-eaters, fear not: some say veggie and vegan haggis tastes even better than the real thing.

168

SCOTLAND

Drive the Malt Whisky Trail®

Fiery and heart-warming, whisky is the pure essence of Scotland. The area of Speyside alone is home to more than half of the country's malt whisky distilleries, and in many ways, its whiskies are not unlike the landscape from which they hail—soft, gentle, and full of warmth and depth. It's said that the perfect balance of climate, terrain, and water from Highland springs is what makes the whisky here so good, and you can try it for yourself on the Malt Whisky Trail®, a signposted route through bucolic countryside. This peaty pilgrimage is made up of nine unmissable sights, including the historic Dallas Dhu distillery, where you'll gain a glimpse into the alchemy of spirit-making, and the Speyside Cooperage, where you'll discover the ancient art of barrel production. For many, though, it's about sampling the good stuff at the seven working distilleries, like the "Rolls Royce of single malts" at Macallan or the Johnnie Walker whiskies at Cardhu, the first distillery to be officially run by a woman. Along the trail, local cafés and restaurants showcase all that the Speyside larder has to offer—perfect for the designated drivers in tow.

Good to know: Time your trip to coincide with the Spirit of Speyside Whisky Festival in May.

Have a laugh at the Edinburgh Festival Fringe

Elegant squares and sleepy courtyards transform into bustling hubs for mirth and mayhem. Street performers juggle, jest, and occasionally defy the laws of physics. Brash fliers cover every imaginable surface, each telling of yet another unmissable show. One of the greatest celebrations of arts and culture on the planet, the Edinburgh Festival Fringe in August is a playground of wit, satire, and uproarious performance that push the imaginations of even the most seasoned comedy fanatics. Step into an intimate venue and you're just as likely to come across emerging talents as you are renowned comedians from all over the world. And it's not just about one-liners: the Fringe is a celebration of the unexpected, about experiencing thought-provoking one-person shows, quirky musicals, and avant-garde absurdity. Embrace the festival spirit and you'll leave this city a little lighter than you arrived.

Good to know: Always make time for spontaneity. Some of the best shows are those you would never have expected.

> One of the greatest celebrations of arts and culture on the planet, the Edinburgh Fringe in August is a playground of wit, satire, and uproarious performance that push the imaginations of even the most seasoned comedy fanatics.

Tee off at the birthplace of golf

St. Andrews is so much more than just the place where Prince William and Kate Middleton fell in love. It was in this quaint coastal town that golf was born—more specifically, at the Old Course, where the 18-hole round was established. Its immaculate greens and windswept fairways have been the site of many a round since the 15th century, back when whacking pebbles over the dunes was the order of the day. The Old has grown alongside the game itself, and it's still as sharp as ever: just when you think you're on the verge of victory, the winds change and this braw course presents a whole new set of challenges. It's enough to keep anyone on their toes, so whether you're a scratch golfer or just trying to avoid a double bogey, grab your clubs, channel your inner Tiger Woods or Rory McIlroy, and savor the thrill of playing on the very same turf where this glorious game was born.

Good to know: The best way to secure a tee time is to enter the ballot before 2 p.m. two days before the desired day of play.

172

SCOTLAND

Attend a ceilidh

How did you end up in this situation? You're out of breath but full of adrenaline, and your face hurts from laughing. The last few minutes have been a blur of new faces and dancing partners aplenty. Then you spot your latest partner incoming: that whirling, bearded Scotsman who takes great joy in prancing at a pace faster than the speed of light. And he's holding out an arm for you. Everyone should attend a ceilidh at least once in their life, a lively Scottish gathering that brings together the spirited melodies of fiddles, bagpipes, and accordions with the clatter of dancing feet. Don't worry if you don't know the steps—perfection isn't the goal here. Plus, there's always a caller to guide newcomers through the choreography of each jig and reel, which soon become second nature. The climax of any ceilidh is a favorite, the Orcadian Strip the Willow, during which the dance floor becomes a blur of spinning couples, kilts twirling, and skirts swirling. Even the most rhythmically challenged will find themselves swept up in the contagious rhythms of Scotland's toe-tapping trad.

Good to know: Ceilidhs take place regularly across the country, especially on special occasions such as Burns Night.

171

SCOTLAND

Hike the Loch Ness 360

A monster swims within these depths—or so the legend goes. True or not, the majesty of Loch Ness is certainly no fiction. Cleaving its way through the heart of Scotland and cradled by the brooding heights of the Great Glen, this watery mass is one of the country's most beguiling places. Visitors come here in droves, many with hopes of spotting that elusive beast, others to enjoy its quieter beauty spots away from tourist shops touting monster paraphernalia. One of the best ways to take in the loveliness of the region is to walk the Loch Ness 360, a multi-day hike to and from Inverness that loops the circumference of the loch for 80 miles (129 km). Skirt fertile farmland, meander through young beech forests carpeted in moss, and marvel at the thunderous Falls of Foyers as they tumble into the gorge below, casting rainbows in their mist. At Dores Beach, you'll reach one of the most painterly views down the loch's length. On a dreich day, peering out across the water's vast surface, even skeptics would be forgiven for wondering: could there be something lurking beneath?

Good to know: Allow around six days to complete the entire loop, or complete one or two sections as a day walk.

Visit Pembrokeshire

With its windswept mountains and lush green valleys, Wales lucked out in the beauty department. Many would argue that the country's finest feature is Pembrokeshire, a ragged coastline comprising butter-soft beaches, wildlife-packed islands, and delightful towns and villages. It's so lovely, in fact, that the Pembrokeshire peninsula has been made Britain's only national park focused on a stretch of coast. Adventures are ten-a-penny here: for the energetic, coasteering will have you investigating sea caves and jumping off rocks into the waves; for those who like to take their time, the 186-mile (299-km) Pembrokeshire Coastal Path roller-coasters up steep limestone cliffs and down deep glacial valleys. Days pass easily ambling around seaside towns like Tenby; spotting local birdlife on Ramsey or Skomer islands; or exploring religious heritage in St. David's, the UK's smallest city. There's little doubt this part of Wales offers fun for all in spades, but sometimes the best thing to do is stop and stare a while. After all, perhaps what puts Pembrokeshire on the bucket list is simply those stunning good looks.

Good to know: Buses cover most of the coast seven days a week over summer, but are less frequent out of season.

173

WALES

Climb Mount Snowdon

Yr Wyddfa, or Mount Snowdon, isn't just the tallest mountain in Wales. Outside of the Scottish Highlands, it's the highest point in the entire British Isles, clocking in at an impressive 3,560 ft (1,085 m). That said, it's a surprisingly doable summit, tackled by everyone from veteran climbers to families on their summer vacations. While the 3½-mile (5.6-km) Pyg Track is the quickest route to the top, starting fairly high up and taking roughly two to three hours, it's steep and quite tricky in places. The Llanberis Path, though a mile longer, is better suited to beginners, being well marked and with no scrambles or scary drops. No matter the route you take, you'll be treated to some of the best views of Eryri (Snowdonia) National Park. The loveliest panorama, naturally, lies at the summit, looking out across the serene waters of Llyn Llydaw, over which King Arthur is said to have passed to his final resting place in the legendary Avalon.

Good to know: Between March and October, you can take the Snowdon Mountain Railway back down instead of walking.

ENGLAND

Tuck into fish and chips in Cornwall

When it comes to this nation's favorite dish, fish and chips is up there. You'll find a chippy in every English town, often with an excruciatingly punny name, but go figure that the country's best offerings lie in regions right by the sea. Stretching out into the choppy waters of the Atlantic, England's most southwesterly county of Cornwall is *the* place to tuck into a helping of fish and chips on the beach, looking out at dramatic stretches of coastline while seals frolic in the water and some of Britain's best surfers ride the waves. For the best offerings, you'll want the basics covered: perfectly flaky fish that's sourced from the region's very shores, batter that's crunchy but not greasy, proper thick-cut chips, homemade mushy peas, and tartar sauce. The Cornish are a friendly bunch, so ask around and you're sure to find a local spot that checks all the boxes. Just be on high alert for seagulls hoping to nab a chip or two—they'll be that good.

Good to know: Cod is the most popular choice, given its mild taste, but go for haddock—chefs argue it has more flavor.

ENGLAND

Pay homage to the Beatles in Liverpool

Beatlemania may have reached its peak in the 1960s, but yesterday is still today. For proof, all you need is Liverpool, where hundreds of thousands of people each year pour into the Beatles Story museum. Of course, the Beatles-related sights stretch far beyond this. Spare a thought for Eleanor Rigby at her gravestone by St. Peter's Church, snap a picture of Strawberry Fields, and keep an eye out for Penny Lane before heading to the Cavern Club, built on the site of the original venue where the group was founded. Perhaps the must-do moment of any tour, though, is heading to the boys' homes. While you can only see George and Ringo's childhood homes from the outside, you can visit John Lennon's teenage bedroom and the McCartneys' front room where the band practiced. Musical pilgrimages don't get much better than this.

Good to know: National Trust-run tours of John's and Paul's homes are limited to groups of 15, and fill up quickly.

WHERE ELSE TO PAY HOMAGE TO THE BEATLES

ABBEY ROAD, LONDON
Arguably the most iconic image of the Beatles is taken by the Abbey Road recording studio, showing the fab four crossing the road. Re-create the photo then walk by the studio where the magic happened.

LENNON WALL, PRAGUE
This large piece of rolling graffiti takes over the wall of the Grand Priory, and was created after John Lennon was murdered in 1980.

STRAWBERRY FIELDS, NEW YORK CITY
Located in Central Park, this small garden is Yoko Ono's tribute to her husband, John Lennon. Fans come to pay respect to the late musician on special anniversaries.

BRITISH LIBRARY, LONDON
View napkins with song lyrics on them alongside cards at this library's free memorabilia collection.

ENGLAND

Marvel at Stonehenge

As you walk across Salisbury Plain in the hazy morning light, the great sarsens of Stonehenge appear like specters out of the mist, until eventually the whole of the mysterious broken circle is visible. Gazing up at these stones, you'll understand why it's this—out of all of England's ancient sites—that has perplexed and entranced people for millennia. Of course, most don't get such a peaceful experience: Stonehenge is one of England's most popular tourist attractions, and thousands of people pour out of cars and buses daily to walk around and admire it from a strictly enforced distance. But there are still a few ways to take in the sight while experiencing a little more of their magic. Firstly, book well in advance, and pick an early slot to beat the tour buses. Secondly, though there's a frequent shuttle bus between the well-presented visitor center and the stones, opt instead for the half-hour walk. And thirdly, shell out on the Stone Circle Experience, if you can. For an hour before opening or after the sight closes, a few lucky people get to step inside the circle itself, which is an experience as powerful today as it must have been 4,500 years ago, when the sarsens were first raised—though how, we may never know.

Good to know: The Stone Circle Experience is only open to 30 people at a time, so be sure to book ahead.

ENGLAND

Hike in the Lake District

Up in the northwest of England, the Lake District National Park is famous for its stunning scenery: rugged fells, serene lakes, and green valleys that offer some of the most rewarding hiking routes in Britain. It's a terrain that famously once captivated the Romantic poets who waxed lyrical about its great peaks and bucolic hills, which did much to popularize fell walking—sauntering through the wild landscapes for the pleasure of it. Follow in their footsteps on the loop walk around Grasmere and Rydal Water, which passes Dove Cottage, where the poet William Wordsworth once lived. For some more challenging routes, hike the craggy horseshoe of peaks between gently sloping Eskdale valley and Wastwater, England's deepest lake, or take on the country's highest mountain, Scafell Pike. With sweeping views of stretches of still waters and swathes of daffodils come springtime, the Lake District still captures the imagination just as it did hundreds of years ago.

Good to know: If you come across cows and sheep on your hike, try to move quickly and quietly around the herd.

Rock out at Glastonbury Festival

For most of the year, Pilton is a sleepy village tucked in the rolling hills of Somerset. But, for a few days in June, it's transformed as revelers pour in from all over the world to visit Worthy Farm, the site of the legendary Glastonbury Festival. Its first iteration in 1970 was inspired by 1960s counterculture, drawing some 1,500 attendees. Since then, it's grown into a cultural behemoth: more than 200,000 festival-goers pack into the 900-acre (364-ha) site, while everyone else watches live streamed acts from home. Past headliners have included Sinéad O'Connor, Stormzy, Beyoncé, and David Bowie (twice), to name a few. Music is still the heart and soul of the festival, but it's far from the only thing to enjoy at Worthy Farm. From lectures to meditation, there's more to do than you could possibly fit into the festival's five days. Go with an open mind (and a pair of wellies), and you'll be all set for the festival experience of a lifetime.

Good to know: Tickets go on sale in November, often selling out within an hour. Preregister to stand a chance of getting one.

Stroll around Bath

Set among the rolling green hills of the Avon valley, the city of Bath is one of the most beautiful historic cities in England. The creamy stone of its buildings glows gold in the evening sun, and it's all too easy to imagine its fashionable 18th- and 19th-century inhabitants promenading along its Neo-Classical streets. Famously once the home of Georgian-era luminaries like author Jane Austen and dandy Beau Nash, its history stretches far beyond this period. The city was founded in the first century CE by the Romans, who chose the area for its natural hot springs—the only ones found in England. Today, you can still visit the Temple of Sulis Minerva and the bath complex, which date back to that period. Among the well-preserved remains are intricate mosaics, evocative stone carvings, and even parts of the hypocaust, an ingenious system of underfloor heating. After exploring the historic baths, head over to the neighboring Thermae Bath Spa. As you relax into the mineral-rich waters of this chic modern spa, you'll have no trouble understanding why the ancient Romans once chose to settle here.

Good to know: Visit Bath in September for both the Jane Austen Festival and the Bathscape Walking Festival.

ENGLAND

Sip a pint in one of England's oldest pubs

If Britain loves anything, it's a pub, the beating heart of social life. It's in these cozy drinking houses that celebrations, commiserations, or just a good old chinwag take place, always with a glass in hand. In a country of centuries-old establishments, loads of pubs claim to be the oldest, but Ye Olde Fighting Cocks in St. Albans makes a pretty good case. The thriving market town grew from a Celtic Catuvellauni settlement into a Roman town, and has survived the Peasants' Revolt and the Wars of the Roses—much like Ye Olde Fighting Cocks, which many date back to 793 BCE. The building's main structure was built in the 11th century, and only adopted its current name in the 1800s in reference to the cock fighting that's thought to have taken place in the bar area. The jury's out on whether it's the oldest or not, but it's safe to say it's everything a good pub should be: low ceilings, crackling fireplace, and plenty of nooks and crannies to enjoy a good ale in. Cheers to that.

Good to know: Draft bitter, drunk at cellar temperature, is the most traditional British beer to order.

ENGLAND

Enjoy a night out in Manchester

Manchester is deservedly one of Britain's great cities. The birthplace of the Industrial Revolution, it grew rapidly in the mid-18th century, primarily off the back of a flourishing cotton industry. But with every boom must come bust, and when the cotton trade left town, a network of canals and mills, old textile warehouses, and markets remained. Fast-forward a hundred years or so and these markers of Cottonopolis (as the city was once nicknamed) were the backdrop to another revolution, this time of the UK's music scene. Enter Madchester, a genre-bending blend of indie and acid house, pop and psychedelia. The movement launched the likes of the Stone Roses and Happy Mondays, and set Manchester up as the place for a night out. And what was good then is great now: Canal Street is a thriving LGBTQ+ hub; the Northern Quarter has an artsy, slightly grungy vibe (all converted warehouses and peeling paint); and the Oxford Road Corridor puts live music front and center. For a night to remember, Manchester remains top of the charts.

Good to know: Late August sees Canal Street abuzz for Manchester's Pride, which attracts more than 170,000 visitors.

ENGLAND

Tour literary Oxford

Mention Oxford and it's the scholarly heritage that comes to mind, for this is the rival to the university city that-shall-not-be-named. But the home of England's first university has not only produced great scholars, it's also inspired many literary luminaries, and every cobblestone lane, towering spire, and handsome college has a story to tell. More often than not, these stories are of the mystical kind; in the early 20th century, the likes of J. R. R. Tolkien and C. S. Lewis founded the literary group "the Inklings," and would gather in The Eagle and Child pub to discuss their work, *The Lord of the Rings* included. It's no Middle Earth, but this historic pub is a cozy spot to nurse a pint before moseying on over to St. Mary's Passage, where an ornate door is said to have inspired the portal into Narnia in *The Lion, the Witch, and the Wardrobe*. More into your daemons than your evil queens? Experience Lyra's Oxford on a walk through the compact center—you won't come across talking animals, but you will see the places that inspired Philip Pullman's epic *His Dark Materials*.

Good to know: To try your hand at punting, rent a boat from punt stations like Cherwell Boathouse.

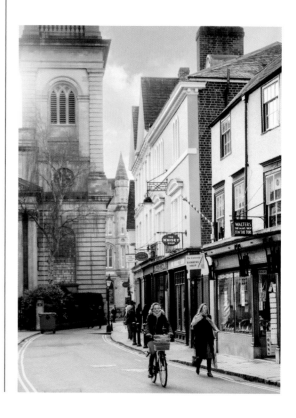

ENGLAND

Promenade through the grounds at Sissinghurst

"I saw what might be made of it. It was Sleeping Beauty's Garden," wrote Vita Sackville-West of the grounds at Sissinghurst. When the author and her husband, Harold Nicolson, moved into this tumbledown Tudor estate in 1930, she was instantly captivated by the possibilities of the 5-acre (2-ha) gardens, which she felt were "crying out for rescue." The couple worked tirelessly over the next three decades to achieve their vision of a poetic English country garden, blending Harold's perfectionism with Vita's horticultural vim. It was Vita's lush planting that brought the gardens to life, a profusion of color and scent that remains intoxicating decades later. Entering the space feels like taking a peek into a private Eden, a world where garden "rooms" are filled to the brim with delicate blooms and the air is fragranced with floral scents. England is certainly renowned for its gardens, in part thanks to Capability Brown's iconic creations like Blenheim Palace and Chatsworth, but this is truly one of the most brilliant.

Good to know: There are frequent events at Sissinghurst inspired by the life and works of Vita, Harold, and their circle.

> It was Vita's lush planting that brought the gardens to life, a profusion of color and scent that remains intoxicating decades later.

ENGLAND

See the choir perform at Canterbury Cathedral

The city of Canterbury is one of great religious import. It's been a major Christian pilgrimage site for the last 900 years, since the building of its cathedral in 1070 and the martyrdom of Thomas Becket a century later. The Trinity Chapel was built soon after as a shrine for his remains and famously inspired poet Geoffrey Chaucer's great 14th-century *The Canterbury Tales*, one of the most important literary works in the English language. Monarchs and archbishops come and go, but Canterbury Cathedral has been a constant across the rich tapestry of English history, and remains the oldest and most historic in the country. If that's not reason enough to visit, the famous choir that performs here is just as big a motivation. Hearing angelic voices soaring in the vast space, and witnessing the building's golden stone washed in warm candlelight or painted by the sun streaming through its stained glass, is an experience to remember.

Good to know: You can hear the choir at Evensong most days, as well as Sunday Sung Eucharist and special events.

LONDON

Samuel Johnson famously said that when one is "tired of London, he is tired of life"—often quoted it may be, but his observation remains true as ever. Always abuzz, London is ready to serve up something for everyone. Opulent landmarks? Check. Free museums and galleries? Check and check. It's hard to get bored here.

Join the crowds at a soccer match

There's so much about the experience of watching soccer live that can't be captured on a screen. The cheers, chants, and frustrated groans of the crowd; the sense of camaraderie, whether your team wins or loses; and the energy that buzzes through the stadium. Even if you're just a casual fan, you shouldn't miss out on the opportunity to watch the beautiful game in its home country. London has some 17 professional teams, seven of which are regulars in the Premier League: Arsenal, Chelsea, and Tottenham Hotspur among them. If you don't much mind who you see, you can't go wrong with a non-league match at the 90,000-seater national stadium, Wembley. But if you're a big fan of a particular team, then there's nothing quite like seeing them on home turf. Whatever you go for, you're in for a treat. Get the whole experience by dressing up in the team colors, forking out for food and drinks at the match, joining in on the chants (you'll learn as you go), and heading out for a few post-match pints to celebrate—or commiserate.

Good to know: Make sure you arrive well before the match starts, as it can take a long time to reach your seat.

187

Discover world histories at the British Museum

The oldest public museum in the world, the British Museum was established in 1753 to house the books, antiquities, and plant and animal specimens of the physician Sir Hans Sloane (1660–1753). The collection expanded rapidly, and during the 19th century the museum acquired a mass of antiquities from around the world—some by force or in other duplicitous ways, leading to intensifying calls in recent years that they be returned to their homelands. The objects now on show are drawn from a dizzying number of cultures and civilizations, from Stone Age Europe and ancient Egypt to modern Japan and contemporary North America. Here you'll see the famous Rosetta Stone, which was used to decipher Egyptian hieroglyphs; the hulking bust of pharaoh Ramses II, who reigned Egypt in the 13th century BCE; an old Roman floor mosaic purportedly showing one of the earliest-known images of Christ; and one of the biggest stashes of Anglo-Saxon treasure ever unearthed, the Sutton Hoo Ship burial finds. Little wonder this is London's most visited museum—there's something to interest everyone.

Good to know: The museum is free to enter, but you may need to pay to visit one of its temporary exhibitions.

MUST-SEE LONDON MUSEUMS AND GALLERIES

British Museum
Contains treasures from far and wide.

Natural History Museum
Life on Earth and the Earth itself are vividly explained here.

Victoria and Albert Museum
The V&A is a museum of art and design containing eclectic collections.

National Gallery
Houses one of the world's finest collections of European art.

Tate Modern
Covers modern international art of the 20th and 21st centuries.

Tate Britain
The oldest Tate gallery focuses on British art from 1500 to the present.

National Portrait Gallery
The world's most extensive collection of portraits, home to more than 220,000 paintings, drawings, and sculptures.

188

Catch a tennis match at Wimbledon

With the thwack of a tennis ball and the sweet scent of strawberries and cream in the air, British summer officially begins. The only Grand Slam tournament to be played on (perfectly manicured) grass, the Wimbledon Tennis Championship has been the sporting event to end all sporting events since the 1870s. All of the greats have played in this corner of southwest London, and history is made on the court year after year. It was here that Boris Becker became the youngest champion ever, at only 17; that Rafael Nadal beat Roger Federer after almost five grueling hours; and Serena Williams won her seventh Wimbledon title, making her the oldest champion ever, at 34. But scoring a sought-after ticket means more than just watching the greats battle it out. From your seat you can sip a refreshing Pimm's; keep an eye out for royalty in the Royal Box; and tuck into a portion of fresh strawberries, which have been synonymous with Wimbledon since 1877. So don something white (the crisper your outfit, the better), order some fizz, and watch history be made on the court.

Good to know: To buy tickets, you have to enter a ballot (usually open November–January).

189

Uncover royal London

Nowhere does pomp and ceremony quite like London. The royal capital of the UK for almost a thousand years, this city has been indelibly shaped by successive royal rulers (most of whom have lived here too). Start your tour at Buckingham Palace, the official London residence of the monarch since 1837—if the Royal Standard flag is flying, it means the King's at home. The Changing the Guard ceremony takes place behind the gates here, much to the delight of visitors peering in. More royal residences can be found around the city: Queen Victoria grew up in Kensington Palace, while Henry VIII lived large in Hampton Court Palace. Perhaps the most important royal landmark, however, is Westminster Abbey. Serving as the official royal coronation church since 1066, the medieval structure is also the final resting place of 30 British kings and queens. Passing through this hallowed space, you can't help but feel the weight of royal history.

Good to know: The Changing the Guard ceremony is free, but check the schedule on the Household Division website.

190

Let your hair down at Notting Hill Carnival

Notting Hill. All pastel-painted terraces, quaint market stalls, and foppish booksellers, right? Wrong. This multicultural neighborhood buzzes with international restaurants, reggae music bars, and community art centers. And at no point is the real Notting Hill more on display than during Carnival, a three-day extravaganza. Taking place over the August bank holiday weekend each year, the colorful celebration of the area's West Indian community and Caribbean culture draws crowds from far beyond the area. The event dates back to 1959, when the first carnival was organized by the area's Afro-Caribbean community, who moved in after the UK government opened up the country's borders to citizens of former British colonies. Fast forward to today and it's still as vital and vibrant as ever. Expect huge sound systems blasting out samba, calypso, and soca music; exuberant dancers in sparkling costumes; and crowds of people grooving in the streets. It's unashamedly loud and infectiously joyful—and it's impossible not to join in.

Good to know: Each day of carnival is different, but family-friendly Sunday is usually the best time to go for newbies.

191

See a world-class show in the West End

Battling Broadway for the title of "world's most famous theater district," the West End is a London institution. Or rather, it's full of them: the Adelphi, Apollo, Palladium, Theatre Royal—you'll find them all here. There's always a new production to enjoy, but some classics have been on for decades. *Mamma Mia* and *The Lion King* have been going strong since the 1990s, while the epic *Les Misérables* and *The Phantom of the Opera* have been rousing audiences since the 1980s. Agatha Christie's *The Mousetrap*, meanwhile, has been running since 1952. But that's nothing compared to the venues themselves. The Theatre Royal opened way back in 1663, marking the start of an influx of entertainment venues in the area. Since then, the West End has grown to represent the pinnacle of the country's theater scene: performers in West End shows are at the top of their game and celebrities are a common occurrence on the main stage. If you're looking to see a show in London, you might as well see the very best.

Good to know: Be spontaneous and swing by Leicester Square's TKTS booth for discounted same-day tickets.

192

Marvel at the architecture of St. Paul's Cathedral

For more than 350 years, the elegant dome of St. Paul's Cathedral has been one of the defining features of the London skyline, holding its own against a rising army of skyscrapers. It was completed in 1711 by Sir Christopher Wren, who was responsible for rebuilding more than 50 churches after the Great Fire of London; undoubtedly, it's Wren's masterpiece. Up close, St. Paul's is even more impressive, with its columns and porticoes carved out of pale Portland limestone. Its interior contrasts with the restrained exterior: the floors are paved in marble, while intricate carvings and paintings decorate the walls. Stand underneath the dome and gaze up at its trompe-l'oeil frescoes, which create the illusion that it extends even higher, before heading up. The Whispering Gallery displays the precision of Wren's design, its acoustics so finely tuned that you can hear something whispered against the wall from the other side. Yet perhaps the most magical moment in the cathedral is at Evensong. During this evening service, the choir's ethereal voices echo through the grand nave as candles flicker and the congregation falls silent in awe.

Good to know: Check St. Paul's website for times and tickets if you plan to stay for a concert or the choral Evensong service.

> During this evening service, the choir's ethereal voices echo through the grand nave as candles flicker and the congregation falls silent in awe.

LONDON

193

Walk through history along the Southbank

A stroll along the Southbank is to take a journey through the centuries. Running from Tower Bridge to the looming London Eye, this riverside area is packed with cultural venues. Catch a show in Shakespeare's Globe, an open-air reconstruction of the Elizabethan playhouse, or ride the Eye for stunning views of the historic Houses of Parliament (just across the river). Jumping forward a few centuries, there's the towering Tate Modern, which holds one of the world's premier collections of contemporary art; the Brutalist National Theatre, a world-class performance venue; and the no-longer-wobbly Millennium Bridge, a go-to for photographers. Icon after icon shares this riverside stretch, providing a whistle-stop tour of London's monuments. But that's not all the Southbank has to offer. Come any time, any day, and the area fizzes with energy. Skateboarders pass graffitied walls, couples browse secondhand book stalls, families feast at weekend food markets, friends catch up at alfresco bars, and locals enjoy a leisurely stroll past some of the greatest riverside views in the capital. Everything that makes London so special is right here.

Good to know: To view the Southbank from a different angle, hop on one of London's river boats.

195
PORTUGAL

Bite into a creamy *pastel de nata* in Lisbon

It's no surprise Lisbon is one of Europe's favorite destinations—365 days of sunshine, *azulejo*-lined streets, and picturesque views from countless viewpoints known as *miradouros* are some of its many charms. And if there's one thing you should do while here, it's tucking into a *pastel de nata*, the perfect pick-me-up after traipsing up and down Lisbon's famous hills. Invented by monks in a monastery near Lisbon, these tarts have three simple components: the hand-shaped crust, the custard filling, and the slightly burned top. One bite reveals the beautiful flakiness of the pastry and the creamy perfection of the lemon-and-cinnamon-flavored custard, with the caramelized top adding an unexpected smokiness that ties it all together. Enjoy yours fresh from the oven.

Good to know: Head to the Antiga Confeitaria de Belém bakery to sample the original recipe.

194
EUROPE

Interrail across Europe

Take stock for a moment. You've just bought a ticket that could transport you through a greater diversity of cultures and countries in a shorter space of time than is possible almost anywhere else in the world. With an Interrail ticket, you could, on one train journey with no changes, be in nations as contrasting as Spain and Germany or Austria and Türkiye. For this is the true beauty of traveling through Europe: not just that there is a mosaic of more than 40 countries in an area roughly equivalent in area to Canada, but that there is an efficient, environmentally friendly locomotive network linking up almost every major location within the European continent. And—from sunny Portugal to chilly Norway, and lively Poland to quiet Romania—Interrailing makes such rail adventures through 33 European countries accessible to all. Between the choice of a "One Country" or "Global" pass, you could find yourself trundling around one destination in-depth, alighting at local, little-visited stations along the way, or zooming across the continent on one epic multi-country expedition. What's it to be?

Good to know: There are discounted passes for under-27s and over-60s, so choose the best one for you when booking.

WHERE ELSE TO FIND FAIRYTALE CASTLES

BURG HOHENZOLLERN, GERMANY

Germany does fairytale castles well, and this hilltop example is no exception. The ancestral seat of the Hohenzollern family was remodeled in the mid-1850s, and tours lead through the revamped royal chambers.

196

PORTUGAL

Step into fairytale Sintra

Swoon-worthy palaces with vibrant towers; colorful castles complete with secret passages: Sintra could happily be home to a Disney princess. The town's stunning setting on the north slopes of the granite Serra de Sintra long made it a favorite summer retreat for Portuguese royalty, who built quirkily spectacular homes that still punctuate the hillside today. Most people picture the Palácio Nacional da Pena when they hear Sintra, a mishmash of pink and yellow towers and domes that has captured the world's imagination. But the fairytale landscape of Sintra really comes to life at the Quinta da Regaleira, where the palace grounds are littered with fantastical grottoes, secret tunnels, and a deep well complete with a spiral staircase. Once you've been swept up by the eccentric architecture, escape the crowds by heading to the trails of the untamed Serra de Sintra mountain range. Here, you're more than welcome to break into song, as any good Disney princess would.

Good to know: Overnight at Lawrence's, Sintra's oldest hotel and famously patronized by Lord Byron in the early 1800s.

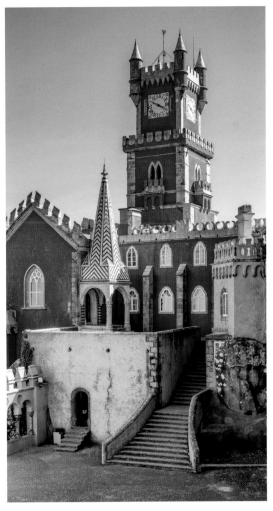

SCHLOSS SCHÖNBRUNN, AUSTRIA

Palace-hopping is a fine pursuit in Austria, and the lavish Schönbrunn Palace—the glittering heart of the imperial court—is a masterpiece of Baroque architecture. Even better, it's set amid exquisite landscaped grounds.

ALCÁZAR OF SEGOVIA, SPAIN

Rising sheer above crags with a multitude of gabled roofs, turrets, and crenellations, the Alcázar de Segovia appears like the archetypal storybook castle.

SPAIN

Walk the Camino de Santiago

According to legend, after St. James was martyred in 44 BCE, his disciples carried his remains to what is now Santiago de Compostela. When they were rediscovered in the 9th century, devotees flocked to pray at these remains, forging the famed route that's walked by hundreds of thousands of pilgrims each year. Except the Camino isn't one route, it's many, all following scallop-shell waymarks (the Christian symbol of St. James) from the south of France across northern Spain. The 500-mile (800-km) Camino Frances (French Way), from the Pyrenean town of St-Jean-Pied-de-Port in France to the Galician city of Santiago de Compostela, is the most commonly walked, which means you'll be far from alone en route. After a stiff crossing of the Pyrenees and over the border into Spain, you'll plow west through the rural province of Navarra, strike over La Rioja's heady hills, and enter the lush valleys of Galicia. Along the way are Roman ruins and medieval towns, not to mention welcoming tapas bars. And then there's the grand finale: the Santiago de Compostela Cathedral, where St. James's remains lie. But while the Camino has a very specific destination, it's really all about the journey—there are few better ways to reset than on a pilgrimage such as this.

Good to know: Get your *credencial* (pilgrim's passport) stamped en route to claim your *compostela* (completion certificate).

SPAIN

Visit the Real Alcázar

Not only is Seville's Real Alcázar one of the world's most beautiful buildings (so beautiful as to feature in *Game of Thrones* in 2014), it's also a portal to the age of al-Andalus, the Islamic kingdom of Spain. Created at the turn of the 10th century as a seat of Islamic power in the area, the Real Alcázar later became a royal residence when the kingdom was taken over by Christians in the mid-13th century. As a result of this change of hands, the complex showcases a fascinating blend of architectural styles. Walk through the glorious Salón de los Embajadores, craning your neck to admire its magnificent gilded dome, and pass the peaceful Patio de las Doncellas to see how the marriage of Christian and Islamic decorative styles has been incorporated over the centuries. Coupled with its lush plants, orange trees, and peacocks roaming the grounds, the Alcázar is an impressive testament to this side of Andalucían history.

Good to know: The building lacks signage, so hire a guide or rent an audiobook during your visit.

WHERE ELSE TO SEE MUDÉJAR FLOURISHES

LA SEO, ZARAGOZA
Zaragoza's cathedral displays a great mix of styles. Part of the exterior is faced with typical Mudéjar brick and ceramic decor.

PALACIO DE LEBRIJA, SPAIN
The home of the family of the Countess Lebrija since 1901, this mansion illustrates palatial life in Seville and has some beautiful Mudéjar features, including the arches around the main patio.

ARC DEL TRIOMF, BARCELONA
The gateway to the 1888 Universal Exhibition, which filled the Parc de la Ciutadella, is built of brick in Mudéjar style, with sculpted allegories of crafts and industry.

CATHEDRAL DE SANTA MARÍA DE MEDIAVILLA, TERUEL
This cathedral has colorful Mudéjar work, including a lantern dome of glazed tiles, and a fine tower.

199

SPAIN

Experience live flamenco in Andalucía

No art form is more closely associated with Andalucía than flamenco. More than just a dance, flamenco is a rousing artistic expression of the joys and sorrows of life, where yearning songs, expressive guitar playing, and exuberant hand claps beat the rhythm of southern Spain's soul. Flamenco has its origins with Andalucía's Romany community, and usually sees guitarists and singers accompanying one or more dancers, often decked out in eye-catching polka dot dresses. The city of Jerez de la Frontera is home to many *tablaos* (flamenco halls), but some of the most authentic places to catch a show are the *cuevas* (cave houses) of Sacromonte, a hill in Granada overlooking the mighty Alhambra fortress. These caves were the original homes of Granada's Romany community, where spontaneous outbursts of flamenco would take place. Feel the *duende*—the soul of flamenco—for yourself as you watch the *bailaora* skirt swirl.

Good to know: Visit Cuevas los Tarantos in Granada to take in a show while sipping on some local sherry.

200

SPAIN

Visit Córdoba's Great Mosque

Córdoba's Great Mosque was made to impress. Built between 784 and 786 CE, when the Caliphate ruled a number of Spanish kingdoms, the site has been extended and modified over the centuries. The biggest change came in the 16th century, when a cathedral was built in the heart of the reconsecrated mosque to complete the city's "Christianization." The result is a blend of many architectural forms that will have you reaching for your camera. Outside, neatly arranged orange trees preface the symmetry that lies within the building. Step inside and 856 columns support red-and-white horseshoe-shaped arches in the hypostyle hall, casting shadows across the marble floor. Passing through the space, there's a sense of peace that has remained despite the mosque's various changes over the years.

Good to know: The mosque is busiest on Mondays, so visit on any other day of the week for a more tranquil experience.

201

SPAIN

See the Alhambra

After a winding climb through the cobbled streets of medieval Granada, step into the grounds of one of the most famous palaces in the world. The Alhambra was constructed in the 13th century by the ruler of the Emirate of Granada. Intended to hold six palaces, two towers, bathhouses, and an irrigation system, it's almost a city in its own right. The palace astounds in its vastness, but its the tiniest intricacies that make it truly sing. All around you'll see bright geometric tiles and honeycomb-like vaulting. Look closer still, and you'll realize the poetry of the space isn't just visual—its walls are covered in verse, etched in Arabic calligraphy. The Hall of the Ambassadors is a highlight, but the exterior is monumental: with the Sierra Nevada mountains nearby, the red-hued Alhambra emerges perfectly from the dramatic landscape around it.

Good to know: You'll find little shade when exploring the grounds. Wear sun protection and bring water in the summer.

202

SPAIN

Tuck into a helping of paella

Gorgeously golden, satisfyingly hearty, and ideal for any social occasion: there's good reason paella is considered Spain's national dish. This rice dish is named after the large, shallow pan in which it's usually made, with saffron providing its rich color and flavor, and a traditional mix of chicken and rabbit—or sometimes seafood—its depth. Today, this once-humble Valencian meal can be enjoyed all over the country—pass a local restaurant, and you'll likely catch a whiff of this hearty dish being prepared. Paella is often served on Thursdays, perhaps because this was once the day that families usually ate out; a much more elaborate theory suggests 20th-century Spanish leader Francisco Franco was known to enjoy the dish on a Thursday, prompting restaurants to ensure it was on the menu that day. Either way, groups of families and friends will gather any day of the week to tuck into it together. For the true Spanish experience, keep in mind that it's a lunchtime affair; locals rarely eat paella for dinner.

Good to know: To enjoy the best paella, visit Valencia, where it originates from, and try a family-run establishment.

203

SPAIN

Contemplate Picasso's *Guernica* in Madrid

No modern painting is as bold a depiction of war as Pablo Picasso's 1937 masterpiece *Guernica*. Painted during the Spanish Civil War, it depicts the German bombing of the town of Guernica, located in Spain's Basque region. First displayed at the 1937 World Fair in Paris, it was shown around the world before it found its home as the crown jewel of Madrid's Reina Sofía Museum. *Guernica* is saturated in the symbolism and raw emotion that are the marks of a master, its lack of color in no way diminishing its power. From the moment you set eyes on it, it immerses you in the horrors of war. A distressed mother and a bull can be seen to the left, while the right shows a woman throwing up her hands to the sky as scenes of chaos, violence, and death entangle at the center. At more than 20 ft (7 m) long and 10 ft (3 m) high, the painting doesn't just command space—it demands viewers confront the grim realities of war.

Good to know: The painting is on permanent display in Madrid at the Museo Nacional Centro de Arte Reina Sofía.

204

SPAIN

Launch tomatoes at the La Tomatina Festival

This is the food fight to end all food fights. On the last Wednesday of August, the Valencian town of Buñol engages in a 20,000-strong battle with just one weapon of choice: the tomato. It all started in 1945, when a tomato stall fell over during a procession; revelers picked up the fruits and threw them at each other, and a glorious, very messy tradition was born. Proceedings begin somewhat bizarrely with festival-goers trying to climb a tall greased pole, on top of which sits a joint of ham; once it's dislodged and drops to the ground, chaos officially erupts. For an hour, it's every person for themselves. Ripe, juicy tomatoes are hurled with reckless abandon and pulp paints the town red. There's no deeper meaning to La Tomatina—it's just fun for fun's sake—and there's nothing quite like hurling a tomato at a total stranger.

Good to know: The event is now ticketed, so book online in advance and stay in nearby Valencia, since Buñol is small.

205

SPAIN

Celebrate Fallas Festival

> For an hour, it's every person for themselves. Ripe, juicy tomatoes are hurled with reckless abandon and pulp paints the town red.

Heralding the arrival of spring like little else, Valencia's Fallas Festival is an almost anarchic celebration in honor of St. Joseph, the patron saint of carpenters. Tradition has it that the festival began when Valencia's carpenters would burn their leftover wood to mark the new season; since then, it's evolved into a boisterous burst of colorful costumes, fireworks, and spectacular pyrotechnics. Each March, more than 300 elaborate papier-mâché sculptures—the *fallas*—are set up in the city to be inspected and judged on their artistic merit; all but two will eventually be set ablaze. On the final night, the sculptures are packed with fireworks. As the flames consume each work of art, ecstatic onlookers pull back to avoid the heat, while firefighters nonchalantly hose down nearby buildings, occasionally flicking plumes of water over the spectators. Within minutes, each sculpture, which has typically taken six months to create, has been burned to the ground in a spectacular fiery climax of wanton destruction.

Good to know: The La Plantà event, during which you can see the huge figures being built, takes place on March 15.

206

SPAIN

Go on a *pintxos* crawl in San Sebastián

Pintxos are par for the course throughout northern Spain, but in San Sebastián, they're something special. These slices of baguette, covered with anything from *tortilla* (potato omelet) to foie gras, are the Basque answer to tapas, and often arrive artfully arranged on a small plate, like a gift from chef to diner. The bar counters of San Sebastián are heaped high with the snacks, and the beauty of their small size means you can spend your whole trip hopping from restaurant to restaurant and trying as many *pintxos* as you can. And, since *pintxos* come in all different forms—savory, sweet, and everything in between—you'll never get bored. The Gilda, a skewered olive, anchovy, and pickled pepper, is the most famous, but be sure to also try *boquerones* (marinated anchovies), *piparra* (a type of chile pepper), and *rabas* (fried strips of squid). It's a full experience for the taste buds.

Good to know: For the lowdown on where to eat, download the Pintxos app, where chefs share their favorite *pintxos* spots.

207

SPAIN

Party in Ibiza

The Balearic Islands have long been known for their heady mix of sun, sea, and raucous partying, and Ibiza is the nightlife spot par excellence. One of the world's most infamous electronic music destinations, the island is a love letter to pounding beats, epic drops, and collective revelry lasting all night. Think of beach bars drumming out laid-back versions of club classics as the sun sets, or languorous summer mornings soundtracked by trendsetting DJs. Sure, there are plenty of rowdy clubs, but Ibiza is also known for its gentler, Balearic-beat-infused dance music scene. Ibiza's nightlife can be broken down into four main areas, each catering to a different taste: Ibiza Town is where you'll find sophisticated lounges and chic nightclubs; Playa d'en Bossa is home to huge superclubs hosting world-renowned DJs; San Antonio has chill bars as well as nightclubs; and Santa Eulalia is best for a laid-back beach bar. It's not all after-hours fun, of course: quiet coves, nature spots, and woodland walks abound on this beautiful island—perfect for some downtime before heading back out into the party come nighttime.

Good to know: The weather is best between April and October, but visiting out of season can be more affordable.

208

SPAIN

Step inside the Sagrada Família in Barcelona

The architect Antoni Gaudí transformed many of Barcelona's streets with his unrivaled vision. But his greatest legacy is one of the towering achievements of global architecture: the Sagrada Família. Under construction since 1882, it's the world's largest unfinished Roman Catholic church and will be the tallest religious structure in Europe once completed. Since Gaudí's tragic death, some of the brightest minds in European architecture have been drafted in to see it to completion. Outside, the Sagrada Família's three facades are infused with religious symbolism—from the colorful fruit towers to the animal-adorned porticoes—but it's the interiors that steal the show. Step inside and you'll be drenched in a kaleidoscope of color as light passes through the huge stained-glass windows. Fusing grand tradition with a modern sensibility, the church is a unique gem in Spain's peerless architectural crown.

Good to know: It's worth renting an audio guide to hear about the church's complex symbolism as you tour the building.

FRANCE

Step into history in the Loire Valley's châteaux

More than 300 châteaux pepper France's Loire Valley, with their towers and turrets emerging along the riverbanks; hidden among vast, forested estates; or—in the case of the Château de Chenonceau—even straddling the river. Until the French King Francis I transferred the monarchy back to Paris in 1528, the Loire was where the royals lived, constructing châteaux that became ever more opulent. The creamy yellow color of these buildings is an iconic feature of the region: tuffeau stone, a porous local limestone, was mined in quarries throughout the Loire Valley. The best way to explore multiple châteaux is to rent a bike and castle-hop on two wheels (thankfully, the region is largely flat). Even better? Take to the skies with a hot-air balloon ride over the region at sunrise. There's no better way to soak up the charming valley views; look out as you glide over the riverside town of Saumur, where the château dates back to the 10th century.

Good to know: To fully immerse yourself, stay in one of the châteaux—many rent rooms at surprisingly affordable prices.

FRANCE

Go wine tasting in Bordeaux

Fine wines and the region of Bordeaux have long been synonymous. The perfect combination of rich soil, warm climate, and generations of wine-making expertise have made the region the home of sophisticated drinking. With velvety, crimson hues and notes that are bold, fruity, and elegant, it's little wonder the world cherishes its vintages—the region is France's biggest exporter, after all. For a perfect introduction, visit Saint-Émilion. Nestled at the heart of the region, the town sports a spindly little church spire that rises up among the vines. Many of the *domaines* (wineries) are spread out around a château where tastings take place. Tours involve an introduction to the winery's *cru* (the name for a vineyard considered of superior quality) and a closer look at the cellars and vines. If you love excellent vino, nothing beats contemplating a glass of the good stuff at sunset, watching the golden leaves shimmer away in the warm evening breeze.

Good to know: During the Marathon du Médoc in September, the original boozy marathon, you can sip Bordeaux as you run.

WHERE ELSE TO GO WINE TASTING IN FRANCE

LOIRE VALLEY
The third-largest wine-producing area in France, the Loire Valley is dotted with fields of vines along its famed river. The white Sancerres have an excellent reputation, as do the rosé wines of Anjou.

CHAMPAGNE
A glass of bubbly is essential when visiting the Champagne region, and Reims is the epicenter of champagne houses, home to world-famous producers such as Taittinger.

PROVENCE
The hinterland of Cotes de Provence and the sandy coasts of Camargue produce complex red wines, luscious *vins doux*, and flinty rosé—the signature wine of the Provencal summer.

RHÔNE
The 14 wine routes of France's second-largest wine-growing region showcase the likes of Hermitage and Côte-Rôtie.

Fall in love with *fromage* in France

Cheese is a source of fierce national pride in France, and deservedly so: it's estimated that there are well over 1,000 varieties, 46 of which have an AOP (protected designation of origin) stamp. Here, cheese belongs to the people and is bound up with regional identity, longstanding traditions, and artisanal practices. You might have tried a good Camembert in your time, but there are so many other classics that can't be missed. Take, for example, gloriously mottled Roquefort, so brilliantly blue and tangy it rattles the roof of your mouth. Or creamy Reblochon melted into an unctuous tartiflette, best devoured after a day traipsing the Alps. For fans of the smelly stuff, the whiff of Morbier has an almost hallucinogenic buzz. Everyone has their favorite *fromage*, and a big part of the fun is debating the many merits of each.

Good to know: You can drive or cycle the Route des Fromages through Auvergne to try Cantal, Salers, and Bleu d'Auvergne.

211

FRANCE

See Monet's gardens at Giverny

It takes a truly special landscape to inspire some of the greatest paintings of all time, and Monet's gardens at Giverny are now seen in galleries the world over. It was here, in the countryside of the Seine valley, that Monet moved with his family in 1883, lured by the area's flower meadows, rolling fields, and pretty orchards. If you've always wanted to check *Bridge Over a Pond of Water Lilies* off your bucket list, just come straight to the source; in the shaded water garden, weeping willows drape across the water's edge, water lilies (the subject of some 250 of Monet's paintings) glide atop the surface, and that famous bridge reaches across the water. But this garden is more than a source of inspiration—it's an Impressionist painting in real time, bursting with the same vibrant hues that ended up on Monet's canvases. Sure, you can see Monet's work in galleries the world over, but immersing yourself in the real deal? That's priceless.

Good to know: Note that the gardens close for the winter, reopening in spring as the flowers begin to bloom.

FRANCE

PARIS

The City of Light tops many travel bucket lists, but it's more than just the sum of its famous sights and landmarks. In Paris, you can easily while away the day like a true *flâneur*—wandering along the Seine, taking in the long-inspiring views, and pausing at street-side cafés. There's no better place to embrace the joie de vivre.

213

Pick up a freshly baked croissant

Rumor has it some French boulangeries proudly waft the scent from their kitchen directly onto the street, which would explain the tantalizing whiffs of fresh bread you experience when walking past one. It's hard to resist the urge to walk in, and nor should you: sinking your teeth into a warm and buttery croissant is the only way to start the morning in Paris. The croissant might indeed be an Austrian creation, but it's become synonymous with the City of Light. While some believe Marie Antoinette first brought the pastry to the French capital, it was actually Vienna native August Zang who introduced it to Paris at his bakery, Boulangerie Viennoise. Patisseries and boulangeries now dot every corner of Paris's elegant streets, producing their own baked wonders. Whether you pick your buttery, moon-shaped croissant apart layer after layer, bite straight in, or—the most controversial method—dip it into your coffee, one thing's for sure: you'll never regret having opted for the delicacy that has made French breakfast famous.

Good to know: If there's a line at your chosen boulangerie or patisserie, chances are you've made the right choice.

Walk the Champs-Élysées to the Arc de Triomphe

Home to the president of France, luxury fashion houses, and high-end restaurants, the Champs-Élysées is Paris's most famous street. It hasn't always radiated wealth and power, though, being little more than an area of open fields until Marie de Médicis commissioned a tree-lined road in the 17th century. After landscape designer André Le Nôtre expanded on her plans, it became a fashionable location for the nobility to build townhouses. Today, the street bears witness to everything from national events to protests, and a walk along the 1-mile (2-km) avenue from Place de la Concorde to Place Charles de Gaulle always throws up something interesting to take in. Something that never changes, however, is what greets you at Place Charles de Gaulle: the Arc de Triomphe, which has sheltered a tribute to those who died during World War I for the past century. Ending at one of Europe's most recognizable sights, this is certainly a walk to remember.

Good to know: The viewing platform at the top of the Arc de Triomphe affords one of the best views in Paris.

MUST-SEE HISTORIC BUILDINGS IN PARIS

Versailles
The royal residence for more than a century lies in Greater Paris.

Palais-Royal
This former royal palace was the childhood home of Louis XIV, and now houses state offices.

Palais du Luxembourg
Marie de Médicis had this palace modeled after her childhood home, the Pitti Palace in Florence.

La Sorbonne
France's first printing house was established here in 1469, before it became the University of Paris.

Palais de Justice
Dating back to the Roman times, this enormous building houses the French law courts today.

Hôtel de la Marine
A splendid colonnaded 18th-century building, which used to be the royal storehouse then the ministry of naval affairs, is a public monument today.

Overindulge at Versailles

Versailles was built to impress, but still, nothing prepares you for the overwhelming scale and opulence of this royal residence. The epitome of royal grandeur, everything about this vast château complex and its seemingly endless gardens is perfectly extravagant. It's there in the rich marble decor of the sumptuous main apartments on the first floor. It's apparent in the oversize statues, grandiose fountains, and razor-sharp topiary dazzling in the formal gardens. And it's visible in the glorious Hall of Mirrors, where 357 mirrors face 17 looming arched windows. This fine creation is the brainchild of Louis XIV, the Sun King, who turned his father's royal hunting ground into a palace and made it the seat of the French court; his grandson Louis XVI lived here with his wife, Marie Antoinette. The pair might have been toppled during the French Revolution, but Versailles makes it feel like royalty never left, as all good palaces should.

Good to know: A frequent train service runs daily from Paris to the Palace of Versailles.

See the stained glass of the Sainte-Chapelle

The most precious Christian relics demand a home of the utmost splendor, and few sights are as splendid as Sainte-Chapelle. Constructed in the 13th century to house the Crown of Thorns and other relics of the Passion, the chapel is a radiant example of the Gothic style. It's tucked away in the small cobbled streets of Île de la Cité—you'll stumble upon it almost unexpectedly and be greeted by an imposing Gothic facade formed of intricate stone carvings, a mere hint of what lies within. The huge stained-glass windows—there are more than 1,000 in the chapel—seem to climb into the sky in an astounding interplay of light and color. Under the vaulted ceilings, biblical scenes are depicted and sculpted religious figures abound. Even the most jaded observer will feel a sense of reverence when confronted with the chapel's beauty.

Good to know: The chapel is best enjoyed on a sunny day, when the sunlight ripples through the stained glass.

Scale Montmartre and its Basilique du Sacré-Coeur

As you venture up countless steps on your way to hilly Montmartre, rest assured: this hip village within the City of Light is well worth the climb. Montmartre's winding cobbled streets and cozy cafés were the epicenter of Parisian cool in the 19th and 20th centuries. Today, the creative legacy of the area's visionary locals remains alive, and the cabarets, galleries, and boutiques are redolent of Paris's legendary bohemian past (this was once the stomping ground of painters like Henri Matisse and Amedeo Modigliani). Standing in the middle of it all is the Basilique du Sacré-Coeur, a four-domed sentry keeping a steady eye on the bustling city below. From the basilica's top, the city's most beautiful panorama awaits, with all of Paris's prettiest monuments on show, from the Eiffel Tower to the Panthéon. This makes venturing to the city's high ground all the more worth it—stay a while and soak it all in.

Good to know: A funicular runs from the bottom of Montmartre hill to the top, providing access for those who can't take the stairs.

218

Watch the world go by from a café terrace

If you want to while away a morning French-style, there's no better place than a local café. Whether they're lining the canal, tucked inside a bookshop, or sitting pretty on a street corner, cafés are a Parisian institution, and all feature a simple but divine set-up: round bistro tables, wicker chairs, and umbrellas shading a large *terrasse*. Such a cozy spot is the perfect place to meet with friends to chew over the issues of the day or get lost in a book for hours. But perhaps the best thing to do at a Parisian café is absolutely nothing, simply watching the city saunter, sashay, and scurry by. After all, the café's lively *brouhaha*—the vaguely onomatopoeic word the French coined to describe the sound of many voices in a crowd—is an invitation to take things easy, so lounge on that *terrasse* for as long as you wish, enjoying the hubbub around you.

Good to know: An espresso might be the chic order, but a noisette is a lighter option: an espresso with a drop of milk.

> The café's lively *brouhaha*—the vaguely onomatopoeic word the French coined to describe the sound of many voices in a crowd—is an invitation to take things easy.

219

FRANCE

Lock eyes with the Louvre's masterpieces

One of the largest museums in the world, the Louvre is a repository of some of humanity's greatest cultural products. Sound overly grandiose? The roll call of names on display reads like a who's who of Western art's most renowned figures: Leonardo da Vinci, Caravaggio, Titian, Rembrandt—the list goes on and on. The unmistakable glass pyramid that signposts the museum is just the tip of the iceberg: dive in and you'll find a never-ending, all-encompassing labyrinth of rooms filled with artwork stretching back millennia. From the world-famous (*Mona Lisa*, anyone?) to the esoteric, the Louvre has you covered. Fancy seeing some Italian Renaissance paintings? You're in the right place. Passionate about ancient Greek fashion trends? Look no further. Interested in Byzantine coins? It's all here, and it's all unmissable.

Good to know: Download the app "My Visit to the Louvre" for a 3D map of the entire museum.

220

FRANCE

Explore the storied Notre-Dame

Few of Paris's monuments have ignited such fascination and spawned as many myths as Notre-Dame. The 12th-century Gothic cathedral is arguably Paris's *pièce de résistance* (though it's a crowded field, of course). Located on the edge of the Île de la Cité, in one of the city's oldest areas, the cathedral was severely damaged by fire in 2019, which led to the tragic loss of its spire. Herculean reconstruction efforts are ongoing, but it's still a wonder to behold. Inside, you'll see its high vaulted ceilings soaring upward, lit by large stained-glass windows surrounding candlelit artwork. If you can, it's worth climbing the 400-step spiral staircase to the top of the building to enjoy views of Paris, before descending into the enigmatic crypt. You'll leave with that distinctly spiritual appreciation that only comes from such an emblematic building.

Good to know: Entrance to the cathedral is free, but you'll have to pay a fee to climb up the towers or down into the crypt.

221

FRANCE

Marvel at the elegant Eiffel Tower

The Iron Lady: the most distinctive symbol of Paris and among the most recognizable buildings in the world. Emblazoned on tote bags and postcards, and seen in countless films, the Eiffel Tower's ubiquitous presence in no way lessens the excitement of seeing it. The tower may only be about a century old—a young building by the city's standards—but without it, the French capital would undoubtedly feel bare. This is somewhat ironic, given that the tower was never designed to be part of the cityscape; it was originally a temporary installation constructed for the 1889 World Fair. Needless to say, the structure stayed, quickly becoming a Parisian icon. Sitting firmly on its four legs right next to the Seine, the looming 1,000-ft (300-m) structure towers over the rest of Paris, attracting vast crowds who gaze skyward from its base. If you gave it a miss during the day, don't worry. It's at night that the Eiffel Tower is arguably at its best: every hour on the hour, it sparkles with golden and silver lights while its beacon shines over the whole city. It's a spectacle not to be missed.

Good to know: Gaze at the tower from a distance on a boat tour, cruising along the Seine.

222

FRANCE

Trek around Mont Blanc

You're standing in awe, looking up at Western Europe's tallest peak, and then reality sets in: how to reach the top? You could ride the cable-car up from Chamonix, but to do so would be to miss out on the epic 105-mile (180-km) Tour du Mont Blanc, deservedly one of the world's most popular long-distance hikes. This exhilarating circuit was pioneered over two and a half centuries ago by Swiss geologist Horace-Bénédict de Saussure, who found that walking around the Mont Blanc massif was actually pretty enjoyable, and it remains so today. On the world-famous Tour du Mont Blanc, you'll follow a path winding over high passes between France, Italy, and Switzerland, bedding down with fellow trekkers in homey *gîtes* (lodges) and remote *refuges* (mountain huts), refueling on decadent fondues, raclette, and pasta. This route reveals superb vistas of the massif; you'll pass glittering glaciers, aquamarine tarns, and rocky cols overlooked by chamois and big-horned ibex. Make no mistake, this hike is a demanding one. The rewards, however, are infinite.

Good to know: The highest parts of the mountain are generally snow-free mid-June to September.

223

FRANCE

Admire the Pont du Gard

Transport yourself back in time with a trip to the most visited ancient monument in France. The Pont du Gard is one of the best-preserved examples of Roman architecture in the world. Built in the 1st century CE to carry fresh water over the Gard River to the Roman colony of Nemausus (present-day Nîmes), the three-tier aqueduct is the only surviving structure of its kind. Walking across makes you wonder how this behemoth was built without the aid of modern tools. It's a conundrum made all the more perplexing when you learn that some of the bridge's stone blocks weighed up to 6 tons (5.4 metric tons). But the bridge is not simply a marvel of Roman engineering: it's a magnificent work of art in its own right, especially when it's reflected in the Gard, its arches forming perfect circles in the water below. Little wonder the Romans considered it the finest tribute to the greatness of their empire.

Good to know: The little beach at the bridge's base is the best spot to appreciate the aqueduct's impressive scale.

224

FRANCE

Smell the lavender fields of Provence

In midsummer, flower enthusiasts flock to the violet-hued lavender fields of sunny Provence, where entire hillsides burst into glorious shades of deep purple, plum, and blue-violet. Two types of lavender grow in this region in southern France: fine lavender, used to make perfumes and essential oils, and lavandin, used for creating dried bunches, all of which are sold at local farms and markets across the area. Part of the joy is letting the perfumed air guide you toward endless symmetrical rows of the aromatic plant. It grows across the plateau of the Gorges du Verdon, where precipitous cliffs plunge steeply down to meet a turquoise river, and all around the fortified hilltop town of Luberon. But the classic view—the one saturating countless social media feeds—is found in Valensole, France's most important lavender-growing area. The entire region is a bee-buzzing haze of heavenly blooms.

Good to know: Be responsible on your escapades—don't walk among fields if they're gated off, and watch where you step.

WHERE ELSE TO ADMIRE LAVENDER

HOKKAIDO, JAPAN
The world-famous Tomita Farm is a lavender holy grail, where the likes of Noushi Hayazaki and Youtei lavender bloom early to mid-July. The farm even sells lavender soft-serve ice cream at its café.

TASMANIA, AUSTRALIA
The French lavender on the Bridestowe Lavender Estate blooms from mid-December to late January, when the slopes roll with vivid purple waves.

HVAR, CROATIA
Lavender grows naturally on the hillsides of this Croatian island. See them in the areas of Zastražišće and Gdinj between June and July.

SURREY, ENGLAND
The Mayfield Lavender Farm has been growing rows of tidy flowers since the 17th century, turning the lavender into baked goods and essential oils.

225

EUROPE

Take the Orient Express

The world's most famous train journey remains as romantic as ever, so climb aboard to revel in the golden age of rail travel. No other train journey has captured the imagination quite like it, with scores of films and novels set on board (Agatha Christie's famous murder mystery foremost among them). Since 1883, the *Orient Express* has transported travelers across the countries and landscapes of Europe in its polished blue sleeping cars. The original route ran from Paris all the way to Istanbul, but today it has multiple lines leading through some of the continent's most exciting landscapes, linking cities like Brussels and Venice, Paris and Cannes, Budapest and Athens. On board, the suites are furnished with polished wood and bedecked with tapestries, harking back to bygone splendor. "Trip of a lifetime" may seem trite, but once you try a three-course meal with matching wines in the train's brocaded piano lounge, the phrase rings true.

Good to know: Advance booking is a must for this once-in-a-lifetime train journey through Europe.

226

FRANCE

Vacation in style along the Côte d'Azur

Who doesn't dream of spending their summers on the Côte d'Azur? With an average of 300 days of sunshine a year, sweeps of golden sandy beaches, and quaint seaside towns beside the ever-blue waters of the Mediterranean, Provence's coastline has an enduring appeal. This beach-hopping paradise is perhaps more popularly known as the French Riviera, and it's long been a celebrity playground. Elegant Cannes has become a household name thanks to the annual film festival in May, which sees stars in their hundreds flock to its red carpet premieres. Nearby, the Cap d'Antibes maintains a rugged beauty, full of rocky cliffs and outcrops (among which lies the so-called Bay of Billionaires, home to the super-rich). Nice, meanwhile, has a thriving arts scene, with the stunning Musée Matisse at its center. Wherever your trip takes you along this esteemed stretch of coast, it's bound to be luxurious.

Good to know: Finding space on the beaches of Cannes or Antibes in summer can be a challenge, so visit in late spring.

227

MONACO

Rev up for the Monaco Grand Prix

Ever since the Netflix show *Drive to Survive* zoomed into our living rooms, we've all been transfixed by the high-octane theatrics of Formula One. And the absolute pinnacle of that drama is the Monaco Grand Prix, the jewel in the championship's crown. For almost a century, the tiny principality has erupted with the roar of engines every spring. It's a curious alchemy; acrid oil fumes and burning rubber blend with high society and the smell of money, blending grit and grease with glamour. On the track, some of the world's fastest cars—and their adrenaline-addicted drivers—weave around hairpin bends and narrow roads that cling to Monte Carlo's cliffs. Friday practice sessions and Saturday qualifying precede Sunday's intensely contested race—78 laps of motorized mayhem. Sharp corners, fast climbs, and a notoriously dicey tunnel section make this one of the season's most demanding courses. But with Monaco's legendary casino, the Prince's Palace, and rows of superyachts moored in the harbor, it's undoubtedly the most picturesque. Don your glad rags and head to the stands to absorb the action.

Good to know: Official F1 seats are eye-wateringly expensive; entry to the Rocher standing area is a fraction of the price.

229

NETHERLANDS

Walk among blooming tulips in the Bollenstreek

Come spring, the flat bulb fields of the Bollenstreek (Flower Strip) erupt into dazzling color. Purple and orange crocuses are first to burst along this 30-mile (48-km) stretch of fertile farmland, followed by a kaleidoscopic riot of narcissi and daffodils, hyacinths and irises. But in this veritable Eden, it's the tulips that steal the show. The Netherlands has been synonymous with this delicate flower since the 17th century, when it was introduced from Türkiye. So-called "tulip mania" soon took hold of the region, with the immense popularity of these new bulbs tempting investors who saw their value soar. Luckily, all it takes to see these beautiful blooms today is good timing: visit in mid-April to behold row upon row of flowering tulips taking over most of the country. The town of Haarlem, the northern-most point of the Dutch flower empire, is the perfect place to begin a tour, walking or cycling south through rainbow fields nestled among ancient meadows, gorgeous dunes, and comely villages. The highlight along the way is the celebrated flower garden of Keukenhof, one of the world's largest. At this showpiece of Dutch floral wizardry, some 7 million bulbs have been nurtured to perfection.

Good to know: Check Bollenstreek's website to see when your favorite flowers will bloom.

228

BELGIUM

Dive into tradition in Bruges

Even if you haven't been to Bruges you can picture it. As if plucked from the pages of a medieval tale, this enchanting city is a jigsaw of chocolate-box houses, medieval churches, and colorful market squares, all surrounded by scenic canals. The Belgian city wears its history on its sleeve, and its traditions remain as strong as ever. Chocolate is still handmade, and deli-cate lacework has been created the same way since the 1500s—you can learn about it in Kantcentrum, a lace museum in a former convent. More history awaits in the city's 12th-century Basilica of the Holy Blood, believed to hold a relic containing a drop of Christ's blood, while the impressive Groeninge-museum whisks visitors through the illustrious history of Flemish art. End your day with one final tradition: a soothing glass of Belgian Trappist beer brewed within the walls of a monastery.

Good to know: See demonstrations of bobbin lace-making in the upstairs room of the Kantcentrum.

NETHERLANDS

Ponder the mysterious *Girl with a Pearl Earring*

Few artistic masterpieces have set the world's imaginations racing quite like Johannes Vermeer's 1665 magnum opus, *Girl with a Pearl Earring*. The painting, on display at Mauritshuis in The Hague, remains shrouded in mystery, despite centuries of academic sleuths and art historians poring over its method and conception. Who is the girl at the center of the work? And what is the story behind her elaborate dress? Unlike many of Vermeer's works, the girl in the painting is not engaged in a task like reading or playing an instrument. Rather, she coyly glances out, her enigmatic expression inviting speculation over her story. While many mysteries remain, one thing about the painting is certain: it was produced by a master at the top of his game. Vermeer would have been bewildered by the international acclaim generated by his work; he mainly made a living as an art dealer, dying in debt and obscurity. But Vermeer's intensely detailed workmanship would see him posthumously recognized as one of the greats of the Dutch Golden Age. This is your chance to see his original masterpiece, and let your imagination ponder: who *is* the girl?

Good to know: Make sure to book your tickets in advance from the Mauritshuis website to guarantee entry.

NETHERLANDS

Get on your bike in Amsterdam

Amsterdam was made for two-wheeled excursions. Home to around 880,000 *fiets* (bicycles) and 250 miles (400 km) of dedicated cycle paths leading just about everywhere, it's little wonder that more than a third of journeys in Amsterdam are made by bike. Meandering through the city's labyrinthine alleyways and past elegant 17th-century merchant houses is effortless in the saddle. So too is exploring Amsterdam's big-hitter highlights—hurtle through the vaulted passage underneath the Rijksmuseum before jumping off to see the Rembrandts and Van Goghs inside, or take a leisurely ride through the city's beloved Vondelpark, pausing by lovely lakes as you go. The best way to explore the city's wonderful cycling infrastructure is to forgo a map and get lost. You might find yourself coasting down somnolent backstreets, circling a quiet *hof* (courtyard) away from the canalside bustle, or venturing outside the city in search of vast nature reserves and tulip fields. And after a long day in the saddle, there's always a tempting café nearby in which to unwind.

Good to know: Ensure you're familiar with cycling etiquette, including signaling, parking restrictions, and use of bike lanes.

DENMARK

Cycle around Copenhagen

When it comes to crowning the world's most bicycle-friendly city, Copenhagen and Amsterdam are battling it out at the front of the peloton. The margins are thin, but the Danish capital might have its Dutch rival beat. It feels like the city's streets have been laid with bikes in mind: there are several bridges exclusively for cyclists, for one thing, and bikes get a head start over cars at all traffic lights (and the city has many). Most important of all is the sheer number of safe, paved cycle paths that snake through the city. A favorite is the waterside Havneringen (Harbor Circle), which perfectly encapsulates the city's bike-friendly philosophy. Coast along this 8-mile (13-km) loop slowly, pausing for a drink at a houseboat café in Sydhavnen or a refreshing dip in the harbor baths at Islands Brygge. As you cycle, you'll pass futuristic buildings like the Black Diamond Royal Library, before reaching the famous multicolored townhouses of Nyhavn. You're free to veer off course if you spot something fun too—Christiania's murals or the rides of the Tivoli Gardens amusement park are both within easy reach. And that's just what cycling around Copenhagen is like: easy. Whether it's better than Amsterdam is up to you to decide.

Good to know: Bike rental is abundant—rent one of Donkey Republic's ubiquitous orange cycles or find a local bike shop.

SWEDEN AND DENMARK

Cross the iconic Øresund Bridge

It's hard to put your finger on it, but there's something almost haunting about seeing the low, snaking form of the Øresund Bridge for the first time. Having gained notoriety as the star of the Swedish-Danish hit series *The Bridge*, this huge, arced feat of civil engineering has become a quintessential symbol of the Nordic noir genre. The 5-mile (8-km) bridge (Europe's second-longest) opened in 2000 after five years of construction and connects Sweden's third-largest city, Malmö, to the Danish capital, Copenhagen, via a combination of road and rail. As it spans the Øresund strait, the bridge joins the artificial island Peberholm before plunging into the subterranean, 2½-mile (4-km) Drogden Tunnel, finally emerging on the Danish island of Amager, home to Copenhagen. Whether you drive across or take a train, seeing the flat, blue expanse of the Sound strait spread out on both sides of the bridge is a remarkable experience. Noir-lovers might imagine themselves on their way to solve a gruesome crime; engineering enthusiasts will be overawed by the sheer length of the crossing; everyone else will be content to marvel at the spindly wind turbines dotting the tranquil horizon.

Good to know: Toll fares for cars mean it is generally cheaper to travel across by train.

234

SWITZERLAND

Take a boat ride on Lake Lucerne

Sprawling across the boundary between four Swiss cantons, its multiple arms twisting their way up fjord-like valleys, Lake Lucerne (known locally as Vierwaldstättersee) is one of the most beautiful lakes in Switzerland. It's surrounded by breath-taking scenery, with topaz glacial waters framed by snow-tipped mountain peaks, rolling green hills, and fairytale towns. Cruises around the lake (Switzerland's fourth-largest) typically offer the perfect combination of fine foods and epic views. The Lake Lucerne Navigation Company's fleet includes five vintage paddle steamers—among them the *Schiller*, built in 1906, and the *Uri*, launched in 1901 and officially the country's oldest operating steamer, its elegant first-class saloon featuring an intricately painted ceiling and ornamental wood decoration—as well as modern passenger boats. The picture-perfect lake isn't all Lucerne has to offer either. Don't miss the historic Chapel Bridge in the city itself, and if you're here early in the year, be sure to catch the Lucerne Carnival in February; this folk festival promises a six-day-long party.

Good to know: Steamers depart from the town of Lucerne and run to Flüelen and back.

> It's surrounded by breath-taking scenery, with topaz glacial waters framed by snow-tipped mountain peaks, rolling green hills, and fairy-tale towns.

235

SWITZERLAND

Marvel at the Matterhorn in Zermatt

Perhaps no other mountain on Earth is more iconic than the Matterhorn, a soaring, near-perfect pyramid straddling the Swiss-Italian border at Zermatt. Its four almost-sheer faces rise so steeply to the almost 15,000-ft- (4,500-m-) summit that they remain largely free from snow, each constituting some of the most perilous mountaineering routes in the whole of the Alps. Luckily for those untrained in Alpine climbing, the mountain's grandeur can be appreciated from the safety of the surrounding ground. The east face is the most familiar, if only because its slightly hooked peak was immortalized on the packaging of Toblerone chocolate. The mountain's prominence means there are many places from which to gain a jaw-dropping view—including the Kirchbrücke in Zermatt itself, but especially from one of the small Alpine lakes scattered around the foot of the mountain. For the ultimate vista of the east face, head up to Stellisee, a small lake near the Blauherd cable-car station. If there's not too much of a breeze, you'll find the peak reflected perfectly in the lake's still surface.

Good to know: The Five Lakes Trail is a moderate hiking route taking in several lakes, with views of the Matterhorn.

SWITZERLAND

Ski the Swiss Alps

There are many reasons why Switzerland is the destination of choice for Europe's most dedicated (and glamorous) powder hounds. It has nine of the ten tallest Alpine peaks, which reward skiers with reliable snow. It has the history: Alpine winter tourism was essentially invented in St. Moritz a century and a half ago. It has the chocolate-box looks: rolling meadows are studded with wooden chalets; waterfalls cascade down sky-scraping summits, including the Jungfrau, Eiger, and mighty Matterhorn; even the bell-toting cows are more picturesque here. Indeed, it has the chocolate and the cheese, not to mention a whole host of other culinary delights, to fuel long days out on the slopes (and the all-important après-ski revelry). There's also the famously extensive and reliable system of trains and cable-cars whisking skiers high into the mountains to tackle dizzying pistes. With a diverse menu of destinations ranging from glitzy resorts such as Verbier and Zermatt to cute traditional villages like Mürren and Saas-Fee, there's no finer place to clip on your skis and swoosh through the snow.

Good to know: Check that your travel insurance covers skiing at the altitude you plan to visit.

It might win an award for one of the world's slowest "express" services—the journey takes almost eight hours to complete—but why hurry when you're passing through some of Europe's most sublime mountain landscapes?

SWITZERLAND

Take the Glacier Express

Over the last few years, a full-blown rail renaissance has been underway in Europe, but it's still safe to say that nowhere does trains quite like Switzerland. From impeccably efficient intercity services to iconic bucket list routes to historic cog railroads, you could construct a whole itinerary around rail travel here and be hard-pushed to run out of things to do. One of the country's most famous rail routes, and justifiably so, is the Glacier Express, which runs between Zermatt at the foot of the Matterhorn and St. Moritz. It might win an award for one of the world's slowest "express" services—the journey takes almost eight hours to complete—but why hurry when you're passing through some of Europe's most sublime mountain landscapes? The train's enormous windows are perfect for taking in the views, while the lavish dining carriage offers a pre-bookable three-course menu, paired, of course, with delicious Swiss wines. If only all train journeys could be this magnificent.

Good to know: Winter is the most magical time of year to hop on the Glacier Express, when snow blankets the mountains.

VIENNA, AUSTRIA

Advent turns the city's market squares into Christmas wonderlands, with the best festive cheer found at the Belvedere's Christmas village or the Rathausplatz's Christkindlmarkt.

STRASBOURG, FRANCE

Hundreds of towns and villages have special markets around Christmas time, but the most outstanding is found in Strasbourg in Alsace to the east. Strasbourg's is thought to be one of Europe's oldest Christmas markets, having first taken place in the 16th century.

PRAGUE, CZECH REPUBLIC

Prague's most famous markets take place during Advent period. The Christmas markets are visually spectacular, especially the twinkling stalls on the Old Town Square.

238

GERMANY

Get festive at Nuremberg Christmas Market

Many of our favorite Christmas traditions originated in Germany, and the country sure knows how to mark the festivities. Come Yuletide, scores of *Weihnachtsmärkte* (Christmas markets) pop up in cities and towns nationwide. Nuremberg's Christkindlesmarkt is arguably the star atop the tree. Tracing its origins back to the early 17th century, it's one of the world's oldest festive markets. Nurembergers still take great pride in re-creating their ancient "city of wood and cloth," a maze of some 180 stalls huddled into the Bavarian city's medieval main square. Old German traditions are ripe for discovery here, from intricate toy-making to the spicy joys of freshly baked Spekulatius cookies. Yet it's the captivating quirks that make the market so unique: take the *Zwetschgenmännle*, a tradition of figurines crafted out of dried prunes. All that's left to do is grab a hot mug of aromatic *Glühwein* (mulled wine) and immerse yourself in the cheer: 'tis the season, after all.

Good to know: Combine your visit with a trip to the smaller (less crowded) Christmas market in the Gostenhof district.

239

GERMANY

Raise a glass at Oktoberfest

"O'zapft is!" And Oktoberfest begins. Locally known as Wiesn, the world's largest *Volksfest* (a traditional festival where the joy of the fair meets the debauchery of the bar) takes place in the city of Munich every fall. During the month-long celebrations, boozing happens in Herculean proportions—around 1½ million gallons of beer are poured throughout the festival's duration, with more than seven million global revelers descending on the Theresienwiese to take part. The festival might now be imitated worldwide, but there's nothing like the real thing. Dozens of beer tents and endless amusement rides are spread over 4 million sq ft (420,000 sq m). Inside the enormous tents, proud Bavarians strut around in traditional attire while jaunty oompah bands play over rapturous chatter from tables, many reserved months in advance. Outside, hundreds of food stalls offer Bavarian classics like *Käsespätzle* (Germany's answer to mac and cheese) or enormous *Schweinshaxen* (delicious pork knuckles). The vast beer gardens here are also prime suntraps, perfect for people-watching or befriending fellow drinkers over a *Maß* (one-liter mug). And after three or four of these staggering pints, you'll find making friends comes surprisingly easy.

Good to know: Bring enough euros, as many bars are cash only and lines at ATMs can get very long.

GERMANY

Hike through the Black Forest

Beneath its thick canopy of evergreen trees, Germany's Schwarzwald (Black Forest) holds mysteries as deep as the Brothers Grimm fairy tales it inspired. Exploring this dense woodland is like venturing into a parallel world half-remembered from childhood—while there are no gremlins, there is a feeling of the fantastical. Dark, pine-scented holloways lead down to calm, glacial lakes, and singing waterfalls echo through the surrounding hills. Take a detour and you'll end up deep in valleys so serene you can hear a pin drop. Yet the charms of this storybook region aren't just reserved to its wilderness. Take a break from hiking and find refuge in welcoming towns like Baden-Baden and Freiburg im Breisgau, with their vibrantly colored buildings. Follow your nose to rural restaurants offering hearty dishes cooked by wise Omas (grand-mas). Or, seek out the region's most famous dessert, Schwarzwälder Kirschtorte (Black Forest gâteau), reputedly named for the sweet cherry brandy crafted in the region—Hansel and Gretel would certainly be tempted to try it.

Good to know: Baden-Baden is a great place to base yourself for hikes around the forest, not least for its Roman-Irish baths.

GERMANY

BERLIN

Many cities are shaped by their past, but none more so than Berlin. A sense of defiant freedom—felt since the 1989 fall of the Berlin Wall, which divided the city for almost 30 years—lingers on. The result? A love of personal expression, as well as a penchant for all things edgy, which make this city such a hot spot today.

241

Hop around Museumsinsel

Where else in the world can you find an entire island dedicated to museums? Berlin means business when it comes to the arts, and in a city bursting at the seams with renowned collections, Museum Island (Museumsinsel) is a cultural haven in its own right. At the very heart of the central Mitte district, this long island nestles in the tributaries of the winding Spree River, providing a home for five epic museums that span 2,000 years of history. Before you even enter the museums themselves, the ensemble of buildings offers a striking showcase of public architecture. And once inside? Ascend a Greek altar in the Altes Museum, one of the world's most beautiful Neo-Classical structures, and home to stunning classical antiquities. Dive into an unparalleled collection of archaeological treasures at the Neues Museum, where Nefertiti's iconic bust stands proud. Lose yourself in swirling Impressionism and Gothic phantasmagoria at the Alte Nationalgalerie. Marvel at the Bode-Museum's medieval sculptures or take a trip to ancient Babylon at the Pergamonmuseum. Entire worlds await within the relatively small confines of this cultural epicenter. It would take weeks to see everything here, so it's time to decide: what period of history do you want to step into?

Good to know: Buy a Museumspass online and save if you plan to visit multiple museums (plus, avoid ticketing lines).

Climb the Reichstag's dome

A visit to Berlin's official parliamentary building might not sound like the stuff bucket list dreams were made of, but this isn't just any old parliament building. Much like Berlin itself, the Reichstag has survived a lot—fire, Nazi rule, wartime bombings, and a devastating division, all in little more than a century. Yet, in spite of it all, Germany's modern seat of parliament has emerged as one of Europe's greatest symbols of democracy—and the building it's housed in is to be just as admired. Built between 1884 and 1894 to symbolize the aspirations of the new German Empire, which was declared in 1871, the Reichstag was beautifully restored post-reunification into a modern emblem of unity. A tour through its interior is a great way to learn about modern German history, but the undisputed highlight is climbing the spiral walkway that winds around the building's glass dome, a symbol of transparency and openness in government.

Good to know: Send your online request for a guided tour no less than a month ahead.

MUST-SEE BERLIN BUILDINGS

Reichstag
The magnificent dome is the highlight of the seat of the German parliament building.

Hauptbahnhof
Europe's largest train station has an impressive glass and steel structure that doubles as a hospitality hub.

DZ Bank on Pariser Platz
This building combines Prussian and modern architecture, with a remarkable dome inside.

Center am Potsdamer Platz
The huge building complex has a glitzy steel-and-glass rooftop.

Hackesche Höfe
This complex of 19th-century buildings has eight interlinked courtyards.

Zeughaus
Berlin's first Baroque building, the former Royal Prussian Arsenal is now the Deutsches Historisches Museum.

Go clubbing in the world's techno capital

When Berlin's Wall fell in 1989, Berliners valued freedom like never before. Much of East Berlin was in tumbledown condition, and its empty warehouses and abandoned buildings quickly became places where rules were a no-go, setting the scene for nonstop raves. Techno music soundtracked this renewed taste for liberation, and this genre—coupled with that post-Wall spirit—lives on in Berlin today, where the world-renowned clubbing scene still prizes unity, self-expression, and tolerance above all else. Clubbing here is the ultimate hedonistic exploit, where night blurs into day. Berghain is the holy grail, known for its notoriously tricky door policy (wearing black and knowing the DJ lineup helps), but unrestrained clubs are everywhere you turn, from sex-positive KitKat Club where latex and leather rule to the no-frills 72-hour parties that take over ://aboutblank. Door policies might be strict, but it's all part of ensuring these are safe spaces where people can be whoever they want to be, and that's the beauty of Berlin.

Good to know: Increase your chances of getting past bouncers by carrying ID, knowing the lineup, and being polite.

Pass through the Brandenburg Gate

If the Brandenburger Tor could talk, this gate would tell of the military parades that have marched under its arches, or of John F. Kennedy delivering his iconic "I am a Berliner" speech here in 1963. Standing proudly in the middle of Pariser Platz, the Brandenburg Gate has borne witness to Berlin's turbulent history, but it's more than just a watchful eye over the city. It's the undisputed symbol of Berlin, a beautiful structure modeled on the temple porticoes of ancient Athens and built by Gontard and Unger in 1770 to celebrate Prussian victory in the Seven Years' War. Atop the graceful triumphal arch sits the crowning "Quadriga" sculpture, a four-horse chariot ridden by the goddess of victory, acting as a symbol of peace. Though, this being Berlin, the gate and its surroundings are anything but peaceful—in the best way. Everyone from diplomats heading into the surrounding embassies to climate activists protesting pass under it. Look up as you march through—it's a humbling experience.

Good to know: The 100, 200, and 300 buses carry passengers past major city sights such as Brandenburger Tor.

Visit the majestic Schloss Charlottenburg

Opulence might not be the first thing that springs to mind when picturing Berlin. But if you head west from the bustle of the center, you'll find an extravagant expression of the capital's rich, prewar past, a sight that gives Versailles a run for its money. Built toward the end of the 17th century, Schloss Charlottenburg was initially designed as a small pleasure palace for Sophie Charlotte, the wife of Elector Frederick III. His coronation as King of Prussia in 1701 saw the palace flourish into a magnificent Baroque masterpiece. A tour through its lavish private apartments and impressive festival halls reveals precious ceramic collections and artwork by esteemed 18th-century French masters. Highlights include the Oak Gallery, adorned with family portraits, and the breathtaking Porcelain Chamber housing Chinese and Japanese earthenware. A visit here isn't complete without wandering the palace's decorative gardens—its leafy paths, hidden mausoleum, and manicured flower beds seem a world away from Berlin's hubbub.

Good to know: Buy the Charlottenburg+ pass to visit all buildings in the palace complex for one price.

246

Walk alongside the East Side Gallery

In Berlin, no sight is more quintessential—nor says more about the city's past and present—than the East Side Gallery. The German capital might be a place of unmitigated freedom today, but for 28 years, it was divided by the Berlin Wall. When the Wall was finally dismantled, Berlin did what it does best: it reinvented tragedy with hope and wry humor, turning a stretch of it (now heritage-protected) into an anarchic collection of street art, graffiti, and social commentary. At the world's longest permanent open-air art gallery, global artists have perfectly captured the zeitgeist of the Cold War, blending political statements, psychedelic musings, and other diverse artistic visions. Some of the most iconic works include Dmitri Vrubel's disturbing depiction of Brezhnev and Honecker kissing in *Fraternal Kiss* (1990) and lurid cartoon faces painted by Thierry Noir. These long-preserved paintings are constantly joined by new, changing works, a moving embodiment of Germany's reckoning with its past and future.

Good to know: Sign up for a guided walking tour to learn more about the wall's history.

> In Berlin, no sight is more quintessential – nor says more about the city's past and present – than the East Side Gallery.

247

Tuck into currywurst

When *Imbiss* (food stand) owner Herta Heuwer spontaneously combined tomato paste, curry powder, and Worcestershire sauce, and slathered it on a bratwurst in 1949, little did she know the impact she'd have on Berlin's food scene. The capital's signature snack, Currywurst is exactly what its name suggests: a smoky, grilled, and sliced sausage, with a dollop of curry-spiked ketchup. And it's absolutely delicious. You can't move for Currywurst kiosks in the city, with cult favorites including Curry 36 on Mehringdamm, which has been slinging the iconic dish since 1981, and Konnopke's Imbiss, a fixture below the U-Bahn's tracks. Some have created their own secret sauces (Herta never disclosed her exact recipe, so a bit of originality is required), others serve theirs with mayo-dolloped French fries and a pilsner on the side, but they all have one thing in common: the ability to sustain ravenous Berliners day and night. Now the big question is, will you get your sausage with or without the skin?

Good to know: Visit Curry 36 post-partying at the adjacent nightclub, Zur Klappe.

GERMANY

Explore Schloss Neuschwanstein

Seen one castle, seen them all? Not quite. Schloss Neuschwanstein, the castle that famously inspired Disney's *Sleeping Beauty*, seems to inhabit a fairy-tale world, swaddled as it is by Alpine foothills. But the castle's fanciful turrets and arcades owe their ostentatious existence to a very real individual: King Ludwig II. The enigma around the Bavarian monarch is inseparable from the unfinished masterpiece he built—the castle ultimately plunged him into debt and might even have led to his mysterious death. Cross Neuschwanstein's drawbridge and you'll see the scale of Ludwig's vision. Once inside, marvel at Wagnerian frescoes, the gravity-defying chandeliers, and intricate mosaic ceilings, all of which provide some insight into Ludwig's vivid and complex imagination. The castle might stand as a cautionary tale against hubris, but it also represents one man's fanatical quest for beauty. In that, he certainly succeeded.

Good to know: Marienbrücke (Mary's Bridge), in Schwangau, is a good spot to take in a panorama of the castle.

GERMANY

Keep it cool in Hamburg

Gateway to the world? Hamburg's grandiose claim holds some truth: a founding member of the medieval trading alliance, the Hanseatic League, it's also Europe's third-biggest port after Rotterdam and Antwerp. Hamburg has a reputation for being effortlessly cool, having reinvented itself down the centuries to keep its finger firmly on the economic and cultural pulse. In the Altstadt (old town), you can admire bombastic buildings like the Neo-Renaissance Rathaus (city hall) and the Church of St. Nikolai, once the tallest structure on Earth. To really see Hamburg's soul, you'll need to head to the waterfront, the key to the city's wealth and ambition. Most flock to the UNESCO-listed Speicherstadt to check out its historic warehouses, but it's more relaxing to escape to the Elbstrand's sandy shores. Here you can while away a few hours on the beach, all while marveling at the mechanical workmanship of the functioning docklands, the city's powerful engines.

Good to know: Get up (or stay up) for a Sunday morning beer and fish sandwich at the famous fish market in the Altona area.

250

AUSTRIA

Hike in the Austrian Alps

Once you've tried hiking in the Austrian Alps, there's a very real danger of becoming addicted for life. Taking to the mountains here can mean many things: greeting the first rays of sunlight from the doorstep of your *Berghütte* (Alpine hut); spending a night in a tent beneath starry skies; or marveling at the reflection of craggy peaks on the surface of a pristine lake. Austria's alpine trails are, quite rightly, a matter of fierce national pride. The country boasts a developed infrastructure of chairlifts, gondolas, and cable-cars to facilitate easy access to its most scenic spots. The crown jewel of all Austrian mountain hikes is, of course, the long-distance 256-mile (413-km) Adlerweg in the region of Tyrol. The route is divided into 33 stages that can each be done separately—only a few daring souls would opt to do the whole route in one trip. The trail invites you to hike up to the top of the Krimml waterfalls, which are among the highest in Europe; gaze over the still grandeur of Kitzsteinhorn Glacier; and marvel at the frozen beauty of Eisriesenwelt, the largest ice cave in the world. That's not forgetting the plethora of well-stocked inns you'll pass by— perfect for a reinvigorating glass or two.

Good to know: The Adlerweg (Eagle Walk) runs between St. Johann in Tirol and St. Anton am Arlberg.

251

AUSTRIA

Indulge at a Viennese coffeehouse

The Viennese *Kaffeehaus* (coffeehouse) hasn't changed much in 100 years. Artists, politicians, intellectuals, writers, and socialites famously used these salons as their own personal living room, a place to see and be seen, to share ideas, make connections, and watch the world go by. Sure, nowadays you can pay with your phone and choose from a variety of lactose-free options, but the concept remains much the same. They are a cultural institution, embassies of *Gemütlichkeit*, that ephemeral and untranslatable Austrian concept of belonging, coziness, and friendliness all wrapped up into one. Having a coffee and a slice of cake at one of these historic cafés is a quintessential Viennese experience. Expect chic Jugendstil and Art Deco wood interiors, glittering chandeliers, and courteous tailcoat-wearing waiting staff. Even more enticing? Each *Kaffeehaus* has its own signature cake. You can't leave Vienna without trying the famous Sachertorte, an intensely rich chocolate and apricot layered cake—the epitome of indulgence and sophistication.

Good to know: Tables at some of Vienna's more renowned coffee houses can be reserved online before your visit.

WHERE ELSE TO SEE AN ORCHESTRAL SHOW

BERLIN PHILHARMONIE, GERMANY

Considered one of the best concert halls in the world, Germany's temple of classical music is the home of the Berlin Philharmonic Orchestra, who put on sold-out shows.

SALA SÃO PAULO, BRAZIL

Known for the finest acoustics in Latin America, this concert hall is São Paulo's premier classical music venue for symphonic and chamber music, and the home of Brazil's top orchestra, the Orquestra Sinfônica do Estado de São Paulo (OSESP).

PHILHARMONIE DE PARIS, FRANCE

Home to the Orchestre de Paris, this glittering futuristic concert hall caters mostly to symphonic concerts. Thanks to a clever design, you're never more than 105 ft (32 m) from the conductor, no matter where you're sitting.

252

AUSTRIA

See an orchestral performance in Vienna

If all the world's a stage, Vienna has to be the most opulent of concert halls. The Austrian capital's classical output is world famous, and its roll call of composers is second to none. Wolfgang Amadeus Mozart, Johann Strauss, Franz Schubert, Joseph Haydn, and Ludwig van Beethoven all called Vienna home and created many masterpieces here. Vienna even lent its name to a whole genre of music and dance, the vivacious Viennese Waltz, and the meandering melody of Strauss' *The Blue Danube*—named after the river that weaves its way through the heart of the city. Today, Vienna remains home to one of the most sophisticated classical scenes in the world, attracting thousands of discerning devotees. Whether you're a classical connoisseur or just curious, one thing's for sure, you can't visit this most musical of cities and not attend a concert. If you only have time for one, make it a Vienna Philharmonic performance at the ornate Ringstrasse-era Musikverein, easily one of the most beautiful concert halls in the world.

Good to know: Always book your tickets directly from the venue you're planning on visiting.

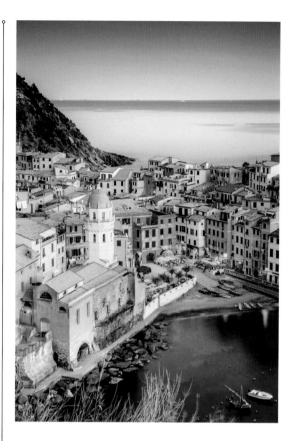

253

ITALY

Hike the pastel-hued Cinque Terre

Lying along the Ligurian coastline like a string of pearls, the Cinque Terre is archetypal Italian Riviera: a gorgeous collection of five pastel-hued villages that cling to the cliffsides in an unlikely defiance of gravity. Most of this area is effectively off-limits to cars, meaning the best way to explore is on foot; the Blue Path connects all five villages, through forests and along mountain trails and coastal mule tracks. The villages themselves make perfect stop-off points; colorful Riomaggiore, squeezed into a narrow bay, is famous for its winemaking, while Monterosso al Mare's convent is a treasure trove of Christian art. Vernazza, meanwhile, is rightly regarded as one of Italy's most beautiful villages—a harborside cluster of bright, elegant buildings that makes a particularly scenic spot to lunch on tasty local anchovies and sip on some limoncello.

Good to know: A Cinque Terre trekking card is required for entry to some of the trails.

ITALY

Admire Milan's beauty

Whether you want to look great, or look at the great, Milan is a must-visit. Italy's northern powerhouse oozes glamour and beauty, a product of notable artists, architects, and designers of the past and present. Stendhal syndrome might be synonymous with Florence, but it's a real possibility here too. Gaze up at the mighty Duomo di Milano, a Gothic masterpiece of a cathedral, and it's difficult to see beyond its staggering good looks. Admire Leonardo da Vinci's *Last Supper* in the modest Santa Maria delle Grazie and you would be forgiven for any rising emotions. For all its historic glories, though, Milan's creative streak isn't stuck in the past. This is the epicenter of European fashion, birthplace of couture houses like Prada and Armani, the influence of which can be seen among the city's well-heeled locals and in the windows of luxury designer stores. Milan is a feast for the eyes, then, but what sets it apart from other Italian cities is that it refuses to rest on its laurels. The next Leonardo or Miuccia Prada is surely just around the corner.

Good to know: Shoppers should head to the Galleria Vittorio Emanuele II, Europe's oldest shopping mall.

SHARJAH BIENNIAL, UAE

This large-scale biennial first took place in 1993, and has been presenting top art, music, and film on odd-numbered years since.

SÃO PAULO BIENNIAL, BRAZIL

The world's second oldest biennial, and now one of South America's most important art events, the São Paulo Biennial showcases art, architecture, and design from around the world, with no admission fee.

LIVERPOOL BIENNIAL, ENGLAND

Unusual and unexpected art in public places transforms the northern city of Liverpool at the UK's largest art showcase.

MALTA BIENNALE, MALTA

With the first event held in 2024, this biennial hosts top performances, enlightening lectures, and art films.

255

ITALY

See cutting-edge art at the Venice Biennale

Home to a slew of acclaimed galleries and museums, Venice brims with art all year round. Yet every two years, something special happens: the Art Biennale. Inaugurated in 1895 and usually running from April to October, the event sees artists from all corners of the world take over the city. Sculptures pop up on canalside rooftops, paintings line the walls of elegant palazzi, and installations draw visitors to lesser-known lagoon islands. Take a wrong turn down a narrow alleyway and you could happily end up in a secret gallery. Art is seemingly every-where—and much of it is free to see. Those keen to check off the main national pavilions, however, should head to the Venetian Arsenal. Originally built in the 12th century to create ships for the Venetian Republic, this collection of vaulted warehouses and colonnaded walkways makes for an impressive art space. Contemporary works are the main focus here, with eye-catching modern paintings and enormous installations filling the space. It's always worth paying for a ticket.

Good to know: Venice also hosts Biennales on architecture, dance, music, and theater, depending on the year.

256

ITALY

Hike the Dolomites

Jagged peaks, vertical drops, and sharp spires: the mountain range known as the Dolomites is truly one-of-a-kind. The dramatic peaks here rise to heights of more than 9,900 ft (3,000 m), with enough stunning highs and lows to warrant being described as one of the most captivating landscapes in Europe. And a striking setting such as this just begs to be hiked. Whether you're a novice or a seasoned climber, there's a route to be found for every ability, from straightforward strolls over undulating hills to the vertigo-inducing *via ferrate* (iron paths). For those with time to spare, the Alta Via 1—a 70-mile (115-km) hut-to-hut trek spread over 11 stages—is arguably the best introduction to the magic of trekking in this region. Reaching iconic peaks such as the Marmolada, Tre Cime di Lavaredo, or Cinque Torre, meanwhile, is the stuff of mountaineering folklore, and only reserved for the thrill-seeking climbers among us. However you explore this beautiful corner of Italy, make sure to pause to take it all in: you'll be hard-pressed to find such a jaw-dropping alpine landscape elsewhere in Europe.

Good to know: While accessible, some trails can be steep and exposed—ensure you're prepared and well-equipped.

Ride a Vespa through the hilltop towns of Tuscany

Ever since Audrey Hepburn and Gregory Peck explored Rome on a Vespa in the 1953 film *Roman Holiday*, this motorcycle has been a symbol of Italy. There's a magical novelty to hopping on a shiny Vespa here, as you explore winding cobblestone streets. While Hepburn and Peck ran amok in Rome, these little scooters are actually a Tuscan creation. An icon of Italian engineering, they've been produced in the Tuscan town of Pontedera since 1946, and have from the beginning been a unique combination of convenience, comfort, and, of course, Italian style. They're perfect for nipping around the narrow streets of Tuscany's historic towns, from medieval San Gimignano to the rolling hills of Siena. Perhaps the most wonderful stop of all, though, is going off-piste to San Donato in Poggio. Spying this hilltop walled village from the road is as enchanting as driving up to its little streets, where you can park up your Vespa and indulge in a true Tuscan holiday.

Good to know: Rent a Vespa in Piaggio from Multirent Toscana to start your Tuscan driving adventure.

Vineyards are spread across the golden Tuscan hills, with olive groves, oak forests, medieval fortresses, and old stone villages in their midst.

257

ITALY

Go wine tasting in Tuscany

There's no wine duel quite like that between France and Italy, two countries that have been battling it out for the title of "best wine producer in Europe" for centuries. France might have Bordeaux, but Italy has Tuscany, where the added bonus of ridiculously beautiful surroundings complement impeccable wines. Every bottle produced here is packed with flavor. There are the smoky reds produced in the Chianti region and the delicate floral notes of the crisp Vernaccia di San Gimignano whites. Then there are the Supertuscans, made using nontraditional grapes and methods, and often made in Bolgheri. Vineyards producing these world-class tipples are spread across the golden Tuscan hills between Siena and Florence, with olive groves, oak forests, medieval fortresses, and old stone villages in their midst. So, will Italy come out on top? Hit the Tuscan roads, stopping off at wineries and vineyards, and decide for yourself.

Good to know: Italy's oldest continuously operating producer, the Ricasoli 1141 winery, is found on the Castello di Brolio estate.

260
ITALY

Taste gelato in Florence

So you've seen Renaissance gems at the Uffizi Gallery, climbed the 15th-century Brunelleschi Dome at the cathedral, and crossed the shop-lined Ponte Vecchio. Think you've experienced Florence? Think again. This city is the birthplace of gelato, and an adventure here isn't over until you've got a cone in hand. The story goes that, tasked with organizing a banquet at the Medici court in 1559, the architect Bernardo Buontalenti invented a new dessert for the occasion. Flavored with citrus and chilled using his own ice storage system, it was a hit—and the rest is sweet history. Gelato isn't ordinary ice cream; it's made with more milk and less cream, churned slowly for a fuller flavor, and served at a warmer temperature. And not all gelato is created equal. To get the good stuff, avoid bright colors and favor those with lids on top, which keeps them fresh. If in doubt, go to Vavori, the city's oldest gelateria, or Gelateria Pasticceria Badiani, which once scooped up first prize in a Florence-wide competition to recreate the gelato most faithful to Buontalenti's original.

Good to know: Learn the secrets of gelato on a one-week gelato-making course at Florence Culinary School.

259
ITALY

Prop up the Leaning Tower of Pisa

Will you look silly doing it? Yes. Should that stop you? No. Taking photographs of you and your travel buddy propping up (or pushing over, if you're that way inclined) the famous, nay, infamous Leaning Tower of Pisa should be on everyone's bucket list, purely for the joy of it. One of Italy's signature sights, the tower has been amusing visitors for years, so much so that the Italian government has resisted repairing it beyond ensuring it won't actually fall over. The mystery behind its unique position, by the way, lies in its foundations, which were set in the Middle Ages. Construction of the tower stopped and started over hundreds of years, with engineers attempting to correct the lean. Today, after a significant project in 1990, it doesn't lean quite as dramatically as it appears in historical photos, but it still has its endearing tilt. After taking the obligatory snaps, be sure to explore Pisa itself; it's home to much more than the tower, after all.

Good to know: You don't need more than a day in Pisa to take in the tower and explore the historic center.

ROME

A city as impressive as this one definitely wasn't built in a day. And, like a living museum, Rome's rich past can be felt around every corner—among its splendid palaces and triumphal arches, iconic artworks and ancient ruins. True to its name, a walk through the Eternal City is like stepping back into another time.

Trawl through art history at the Vatican Museums

One of the oldest and largest collections in the Western world, the Vatican Museums are bound to impress even the most jaded visitor. The building itself is a maze of interconnected rooms, throughout which lie around 70,000 works of art by some of history's most acclaimed artists. There's the devastating *Laocoön*, a Hellenistic sculpture of the Trojan priest Laocoön and his sons struggling to escape from a sea serpent. There's Raphael's *The School of Athens*, a fresco depicting mathematicians, scientists, and philosophers from classical antiquity sharing their ideas under one roof. And there's the *Apollo Belvedere*, a sculpture by Giovanni Angelo Montorsoli considered a paragon of physical perfection by Renaissance artists. But the pinnacle of the museum—and often the very reason most people pass through these hallowed halls—is Michelangelo's masterful Renaissance frescoes, found on the ceiling of the world-famous Sistine Chapel. The artist's iconic depiction of the Christian creation story is one of the most famous paintings in art history, showing the hand of God reaching out to touch Adam's to bestow the gift of life. Glimpsing this masterpiece is as heavenly as it gets.

Good to know: The Sistine Chapel gets busy, but you can book an Extra Time Tour to visit after hours with just 20 others.

Experience ancient Rome at the Roman Forum

Even as the modern world rushes by, you can't help but time-travel into the past as you explore this 2,000-year-old city. Nowhere is that feeling more potent than among the remains of the Roman Forum. Now an archaeological park filled with ruined temples and basilicas, it was once the beating heart of the city, where citizens shopped, prayed, and socialized, and the columns left standing still echo with tales of the past. At the Basilica Aemilia, Roman coins are melted into the pavement, dating back to the 5th century BCE when the Visigoths invaded and set it on fire. At the Temple of Julius Caesar, an altar marks the site of the famed ruler's final resting place, where flowers are left for him. Every relic has a story, and with excavation still ongoing here, who knows what other chronicles are still to be told.

Good to know: The Forum is part of the Archaeological Park of the Colosseum, with free entry on the first Sunday of the month.

MUST-SEE ROME CHURCHES

The Pantheon
A Christian church dedicated to the Madonna and all martyrs,

Santa Maria Maggiore
One of the city's greatest basilicas dates from the 5th century, as do its earliest mosaics.

St. Peter's Basilica
This ornate church is the center of the Roman Catholic faith, and draws pilgrims from all over the world.

Tempietto
Rome's most quintessentially Renaissance building is a perfectly circular Doric temple built in 1501.

Santa Maria della Vittoria
Caked with gold and stucco, this is one of Rome's most lavishly decorated churches.

Santa Maria sopra Minerva
This church was built in 1280 on the ruins of a temple dedicated to Minerva, Roman goddess of wisdom.

Marvel at the Pantheon

Built around 113 CE as a temple "for all gods," the Pantheon is impressive indeed. But in a city of such heavenly buildings, what makes this one so special? Unlike many other Roman structures that fell into disrepair, the Pantheon became a church in the 7th century, its continual use making it one of the city's best-preserved ruins. Inside, the heavens shine down through the oculus, the world's largest unsupported cupola, providing the only light this structure sees. The unique feature also reveals the Pantheon's hidden genius: when rain falls, the water drains to the center of the structure. Add to that important shrines lining the inside walls, including that of the Renaissance artist Raphael, and you've got a truly remarkable building.

Good to know: It's free to enter the space; to experience it with smaller crowds, go early on a weekday morning.

265

Step into the Colosseum

As far as ancient sights go, the Colosseum might well be the most impressive. This is, after all, the largest amphitheater in the ancient world, and where the imperial passion for bloody spectacle reached its peak of excess. Commissioned by Emperor Vespasian in 72 CE and built by enslaved Jewish people, the arena opened in 80 CE with 100 days of celebratory games, some involving the massacre of 5,000 wild beasts. For centuries after, the arena was the site of wild animal fights and deadly gladiatorial combats, put on to entertain wealthy citizens, until they were banned in 404 and 523 CE respectively. Today, the main spectacle of this 2,000-year-old arena isn't bloody combat but the very building itself—a feat of great beauty, despite being damaged over the years by neglect and theft. Peer up at the arched entrances, walk its underground tunnels, stand on the arena floor—and try not to gasp at every turn.

Good to know: Book a spot on the Colosseum Underground tour for a fresh perspective on the ancient structure.

264

See the Villa Borghese

The stories of prominent families are woven into every brick of this city, and one such family was the Borghese—a powerful, wealthy, noble dynasty. The best way to get to know them? Poke around in their former home and backyard, of course. One of the largest parks in Rome, the Villa Borghese (yes, there's an irony to the green space being called the "villa") is an elegant expanse of landscaped gardens, artificial lakes, and soaring stone pine trees. This now public space was landscaped in the 1600s under instruction of the land's original owner, Cardinal Scipione Borghese. He also happened to be a keen art collector, and his rich collection of paintings and sculptures are housed in the park's Galleria Borghese, one of the world's greatest small museums. The dramatic marbles by the 17th-century sculptor Gian Lorenzo Bernini are the stars of the gallery, with his famous *Apollo and Daphne* sculpture, which depicts the moment of Daphne's metamorphosis into a tree, the ideal piece to see before strolling back out among tree-lined paths.

Good to know: Entry to the Villa Borghese park is free, but not to the Galleria Borghese, which is best booked ahead.

Uncover Palatine Hill

Rome was famously built over seven hills, and as well as being the centermost of them all, Palatine is also the most famous. The importance of this hill, which towers over the Roman Forum and the Circus Maximus chariot-racing stadium, was established well before Augustus's time. According to the founding mythology of the city, the twins Romulus and Remus were once nursed in a cave on Palatine Hill by the wolf Lupa and, as the city's first king, Romulus built his home here. By the 1st century BCE, Palatine was Rome's most desirable address, with Augustus being the first Roman emperor to move in here. His successors followed suit by building grand palaces until the fall of Rome, and the ruins of these palaces still dot the hills, the remains of elaborate fountains and colorful marble floors visible among the wreckage. This is the place to soak up the faded grandeur of ancient Rome—and watch a magical sunset over the city below.

Good to know: You can walk through parts of the hill for free, but you'll need a ticket to see the ruins of the imperial palaces.

Admire St. Peter's Square and Basilica

No basilica and its piazza are quite as famous as this pair. Based in the independent Vatican City (located within Rome), this is where the Pope holds liturgies and worshippers arrive en masse. The square, often packed when the Pope is due to appear, is an architectural marvel of symmetry, while the basilica is the largest church in the world. St. Peter's Basilica sits on top of the site where the saint was martyred and buried in 61 CE. Replacing a small 4th-century basilica, it was built throughout the 16th century, taking more than 100 years to complete, and filled with ornate gold ceilings, sculptural masterpieces, and sacred relics. Scale the heights of its dome, designed by Michelangelo and the tallest in the world, by climbing the stairway up to the dome's exterior. From here, an epic panoramic view of the ancient city can be enjoyed.

Good to know: Entry to the church is free, but expect to find a long (but quick-moving) security line at peak times.

Throw a coin into Trevi Fountain

Emerging in the Piazza de Trevi, you'll find crowds gathered in front of this famous Baroque fountain. And with every click of the camera, you'll hear a coin splash in the water carrying a wish to return to Rome. Designed by Nicola Salvi in the 18th century, Trevi fountain has served as a symbol of Rome's magic and potential for romance, appearing in films like the 1960s classic *La Dolce Vita* (just don't step into the fountain, as seen on screen). It may feel relatively modern compared with the city's much older ruins, but the site of the fountain in fact sits on the terminus of an ancient aqueduct. Rising above the fountain, Salvi's looming sculptural design depicts the Greek god Oceanus, flanked by the goddesses of abundance and health. Its details are a love letter to water, the life-sustaining element that, through the impressive engineering of their aqueducts, Romans commanded to grow their empire.

Good to know: One of the most popular places in Rome, the fountain draws fewer crowds in the earlier part of the day.

Trevi fountain has served as a symbol of Rome's magic and potential for romance, appearing in films like the 1960s classic *La Dolce Vita.*

Ascend the Spanish Steps

A flight of 135 stone steps leading up to the church of Trinità dei Monti, the Spanish Steps are not only one of the most iconic sights in Rome—they're also the longest and widest steps in Europe. Since the 18th century, this stairway has connected the church to the Piazza di Spagna below, its natural stone having been worn smooth by the countless numbers of people who climb it daily—a rite of passage when in Rome. It's not just the impressive scale that draws so many visitors, though; they've also captured the imagination of film lovers globally, featuring in pictures like the romantic *Roman Holiday* and compelling *The Talented Mr. Ripley.* Sitting on the steps is forbidden, but stairs were made for climbing: take your time as you walk up to the top, admiring the beautiful symmetry of the travertine terraces flanking the steps on either side.

Good to know: Eating on the steps is banned too, so take your picnic to the nearby Villa Borghese instead.

270

ITALY

Indulge in the art of the *aperitivo*

When the sky is starting to dim and it's too early to start thinking about dinner, you know it's time for a reviving *aperitivo*. This Italian tradition is the golden hour (or two) when locals drink, snack, and wind down after the working day before beginning their night plans. Head to a table set in a scenic city piazza, on a terrace overlooking the trim rows of a vineyard, or with views of the sunset across the sea and luxuriate—there's no rush when it comes to indulging in this tradition of a drink paired with complimentary nibbles in the early evening. In most of Italy, the drink order is usually simple and can be anything from the classic and vibrant Aperol Spritz to a delicious glass of local wine, but it's almost always accompanied by a plate of savory snacks, brought to the table without needing to order them. Whether you plan to indulge in the traditional drink in the company of friends, or want to enjoy a moment of solitude as the sun sets, an *aperitivo* is when you can pause and enjoy the *dolce vita* of it all before carrying on with your night.

Good to know: *Aperitivo* usually takes place between 6 and 8 p.m., with characteristically late dinners following from 8 p.m.

271

ITALY

Taste Italy's finest pizza in Naples

The story of Neapolitan pizza began back in the 19th century, when Italy's old suspicion of tomatoes began to fade as locals saw how sailors would eat them smeared over flatbread. Legend then tells how, in 1889, tavern owner Raffaele Esposito made a dough topped in fresh tomatoes, mozzarella, and basil (replicating the colors of the Italian flag) for the visit of Queen Margherita of Savoy, who gave her blessing, and name, to the beloved margherita pizza. Fast-forward to today, and Neapolitan pizza is now celebrated globally with a protected status. Its base needs careful hand-shaping before being adorned with San Marzano tomatoes and buffalo mozzarella. Simple but special, it's a dish that's hard to beat. And there's no finer way to appreciate the knack of the Neapolitan than a pizza-making class. A *pizzaiolo* (pizza chef) will teach you the arts of pizza-making, from the best ingredients to methods, before you get to dig in and enjoy your doughy masterpiece.

Good to know: There are pizza-making classes lasting anything from a few hours to a day, like those with Eat and Drink Italy.

ITALY

Drive the Amalfi Coast

Winding coastal roads, the smell of lemon trees on the breeze, and the Tyrrhenian Sea glittering blue beneath the rugged cliffs—the Amalfi Coast sets the scene for a truly unforgettable road trip. Stretching along Campania's Sorrentine Peninsula for around 30 miles (45 km), this has long been a region famed for its glamour and sea views, as shown by the many grand villas standing proud along the way. The most famous of these is the achingly luxurious hotel Villa Cimbrone, which offers the quintessential Amalfi panorama from its grand terrace, the Belvedere of Infinity. For all the beautiful views from up high, don't forget to descend to the coastline itself— there's a gorgeous beach, hemmed in by dramatic cliffs, at Praiano, while the town of Amalfi itself is home to many cozy tavernas where you can feast on the catch of the day as colorful fishing boats bob in the harbor. While it's far too tempting to linger at each pit stop, don't forget to keep driving. You never know what's waiting around the corner (another sweeping Mediterranean view, most likely).

Good to know: The Amalfi Coast has narrow, winding roads, so it should only be driven—slowly and carefully—by confident drivers.

272

ITALY

Step back in time in Pompeii

Along with the meteor that once wiped out the dinosaurs, the eruption of Mount Vesuvius back in 79 CE is one of the most famous natural disasters of all time. A huge cloud of ash, gas, and molten rock was thrown more than 20 miles (30 km) into the air, smothering the city of Pompeii and the neighboring town of Herculaneum under layer upon layer of ash and lava, preserving them for posterity. Both remained unknown for over a millennium until Pompeii was discovered in the 16th century, and Herculaneum a century after that. Arrive in Pompeii today and you can walk through Roman streets, amphitheaters, and private villas. Thanks to conservation work, colorful paintings and mosaics, which have since had a huge impact on Western art, can also be seen. But the most moving aspect of this ancient city is the devastating impact of the eruption, which can be seen at the Pompeii Antiquarium. Here, preserved remains in their final moments are displayed—horses and dogs lying on the floor, people huddled together in a last embrace. It's a humbling reminder of the sheer power of nature.

Good to know: The best way to get to the ruins of Pompeii is by train from the nearby city of Naples.

ITALY

Get to know Sicily

Rising out of shimmering cyan seas, sun-kissed Sicily and its satellite islands are some of the most beautiful in the Mediterranean. The endless coastline encircles a landscape of rolling farmland, windswept peaks and amber-and-green hued vineyards. Aside from its undeniable beauty, there's more to Sicily. Sitting to the west of Italy's boot, it's untethered not only by landmass but state of mind too. This isn't really Italy, it's just Sicily, a place that's carved out its own distinct identity, one shaped by a patchwork of cultures and civilizations, unrelenting invaders, and uninvited rulers. An abundance of archaeological sites and architectural landmarks attest to the island's tumultuous history, while generous locals insist on sharing stories and sweet treats—*cannoli* is a fierce source of pride here. Quite simply, Sicily has something special. Come and see for yourself.

Good to know: The easiest way to explore is by car, although you can also see some key sights using public transportation.

MALTA

Admire the golden hues of the silent city of Mdina

When you visit Malta, one of the first things you'll notice is the stone that makes up much of the cities. It seems like every other building you pass, whether a tumbledown farmhouse or an ornate Baroque church, is made from the island's trademark, pale gold-hued Globigerina limestone. It's been used as a building material here for more than 6,000 years, hewn into vast rough blocks for Megalithic temples and weathered into honeycomb patterns where it faces the sea. Probably the best place on the island to appreciate this stone is Mdina, the old capital. With its hulking walls, the fortified city looks intimidating on the approach. But once you've passed through its huge 18th-century Mdina Gate, you may be surprised by how peaceful it feels. Its streets seem to follow no set pattern, with narrow alleys opening into stunning vine-garlanded squares, or leading unexpectedly to viewpoints along the city walls that look out to the sea. There are plenty of churches, museums, and palaces to visit, but Mdina's real charm lies in getting lost in those meandering, golden streets. Stay overnight if you can; the "silent city" lives up to its nickname after the day-trippers have left.

Good to know: Regular buses run from Malta's capital city Valletta to Mdina—the one-way trip takes about 45 minutes.

> There are plenty of churches, museums, and palaces to visit, but Mdina's real charm lies in getting lost in those meandering, golden streets.

SLOVENIA

Peer into the Škocjan Caves

Slovenia has green credentials, and it looks after its natural landscapes. This is a country of snow-dusted Alpine peaks, lush forests, and startlingly clear lakes. Yet Slovenia's real natural treasures are the cathedral-like caves that lie beneath the earth. The best known is Postojna Cave, but the Škocjan Caves, one of the largest cave complexes in the world, are the real show-stoppers. Located just outside of the town of Divača, this cave complex was formed thousands of years ago by the underground course of the Reka River. At its heart lies one of the largest underground river canyons in Europe, the scale of which is unbelievable: more than 460 ft (140 m) high in places, it's spanned by bridges with the river churning far, far below. The main tour of the caves is led by a guide, but then you'll have a choice of three routes back to the entrance by yourself—the longer routes, leading through two collapsed dolines, more caves, and a natural rock bridge, are the most rewarding.

Good to know: There's a footpath to the caves from the train station at Divača, which is an easy 2-mile (3-km) walk.

278

CROATIA

Chase waterfalls in Plitvice National Park

Croatia's biggest draws may well be found along its coastline, but there are treasures to be discovered inland too. Set in the heart of the country, the Plitvice Lakes National Park is Croatia's most dramatic lakeland landscape, full of tranquil azure pools, flourishing foliage, and thundering waterfalls. This remarkable landscape has been shaped over several millennia by the confluence of rivers, underground waterways, and the deposition of minerals, creating 16 labyrinthine lakes that snake for 5 miles (8 km). With paths intertwining the lakes, it's easy to get up close to the famous waterfalls that dot the upper and lower lakes. At the lower lakes, you'll feel the cooling spray of the likes of the Veliki Slap Waterfall, the highest in the park at 256 ft (78 m), and the gorgeous Sastavci Waterfalls. Head to the upper lakes and the pretty Galovački Buk might greet you, the sun's rays breaking through the surrounding trees. Simply head onto one of four designated hiking trails or the seven marked tourist walking routes and let the water be your guide.

Good to know: Not up for hiking around? Several shuttle boats ferry visitors around the lakes.

> Set in the heart of the country, the Plitvice Lakes National Park is Croatia's most dramatic lakeland landscape, full of tranquil azure pools, flourishing foliage, and thundering waterfalls.

277

SLOVENIA

Gaze out across Lake Bled

To see one of Slovenia's most iconic views, head to Lake Bled. Surrounded on three sides by forested green hills, this enchanting body of water is famous for the little Bled Island at its center. No more than 358 acres (145 ha) big, the island is home to the small Church of the Assumption, which has long been a focus of Catholic pilgrimage. The best way to soak up the view of this fairytale church is by walking along the asphalt path that leads right around the lake; at the western end, you'll be treated to a view of the spire set against the stupendous backdrop of the snow-capped Karavanke Alps. Along the walk, you'll also come across the old Bled Castle perched above the water, where a terrace commands even more spectacular views of the shimmering lake below. All view'd out? Take a little boat to the center of Bled Island to visit the church itself, where it's said that those who ring the Wishing Bell above the nave will have their wishes granted.

Good to know: The lake waters are warmest from June to August, reaching a pleasant 77°F (25°C) during these months.

280

CROATIA

Immerse yourself in the Blue Cave

Croatia has many sea caves along its coast, including one where Odysseus is thought to have met the water nymph Calypso, but Biševo's Blue Cave is the most mesmerizing. Located on the east coast of Biševo island and only accessible by water, this cave is named after the ethereal turquoise light that appears in the cave at certain times of day. It's the result of a cave opening that allows light to filter through, the sun's rays making the water's surface glow a luminous blue. To visit the cave, you'll need to take an organized tour or public boat. As your chosen vessel approaches the cave opening, the island's limestone cliffs form gatelike rocks that provide a natural entrance. Inside, the darkness is short-lived before the cave's beauty reveals itself and the light kicks in. Your journey is over in the blink of an eye, so if you didn't spot a nymph this time around, you'll just have to pass through again.

Good to know: The light is at its strongest between 11 a.m. and 12 p.m. in the summer months—the busiest time to visit.

279

CROATIA

Sail around the islands of the Dalmatian coast

Warm, calm seas; craggy coves; and hundreds of islands to cruise around: welcome to the yachtie heaven that is Croatia's Dalmatian coast. Stringing this shoreline and its nearby islands together in a succession of scenic sea voyages is an essential experience in Croatia, where chartering a private boat will let you have full autonomy over where to drop anchor. The city of Split is the perfect place to set off from, where after a day exploring the cultural hub, you'll set sail for the tiny island of Hvar. Ancient fortresses, lavender fields, and hip beach bars keep you busy until your next stop: the sleepy isle of Vis, where a jagged coastline of beaches awaits. Strolling along Vis Town's seafront to the suburb of Kut is one of the most gorgeous shoreline walks in all of Croatia. From here, you can set sail to the medieval streets of Korčula, visit the 44 islands and islets of the Lastovo archipelago, and coast over to the forested isle and shimmering lagoons of Mljet. If you can tear yourself away from the seas, finish up at the ancient city of Dubrovnik; if not, simply let the wind be your guide.

Good to know: It's possible to explore by ferry too. Most are run by the Jadrolinija company, and timetables are available online.

281

CROATIA

Explore Diocletian's Palace in Split

There are palaces and then there's Diocletian's Palace. Commissioned as a vast city-palace, sea fortress, and imperial residence for the Roman emperor Diocletian between 295 and 305 CE, it's one of the largest and best-preserved examples of Roman palatial architecture in the world. But don't expect a stuffy museum or crumbling ruins. This sprawling marvel of architectural ingenuity, half Greek, half Byzantine, is very much the cornerstone of the city (in the literal sense) and about half of the Old Town exists within its walls. Labyrinthine streets echo with the hum of cafés, bars, and busy restaurants. The Peristyle, once an imperial court, is now a stage for street performers, and the nearby alleyways house high-end boutiques and artisan shops. Looking down over it all is the Cathedral of St. Domnius, its bell tower dominating the southern side. Shipyards and a busy port might be the modern face of Split, but this vast palace is a firm and beautiful reminder of the city's ancient roots.

Good to know: Soak up the views from the cathedral's viewing platform, but aim to visit in the early morning to avoid lines.

282

CROATIA

Walk the city walls in Dubrovnik

Few places on Earth exude such timelessness as Dubrovnik. Once a mighty maritime town-republic, this ancient city is now among Croatia's most visited destinations (thanks in part to its role in the *Game of Thrones* TV series). If the weathered stones of these city walls could talk, they'd speak of great victories, tragic defeats, invasions, and occupations. The whole complex is a masterpiece of defensive engineering, with myriad towers, bastions, moats, fortresses, and drawbridges. Largely built between the 15th and 17th centuries, and reaching heights of 80 ft (25 m), the medieval city walls truly are the ultimate vantage point from which to grasp the scale of Dubrovnik's splendor. On one side, see the glistening Adriatic sea peppered with distant islands, and on the other, take in a view of the city's terra-cotta rooftops ascending the hillside. With its narrow, photogenic alleys overlooked by historic monuments, the walled city of Dubrovnik has few equals in Europe.

Good to know: For the most dramatic views, plan to walk the walls just before sunset.

WHERE ELSE TO WALK OLD CITY WALLS

WALLS OF STON, CROATIA
Known colloquially as "Europe's Great Wall," these walls are the second-longest defense barrier in the world, after China's—a looped walk takes three hours. Most of the original 14th-century wall survives, along with around half the towers.

CARCASSONNE, FRANCE
The huge and impressive citadel of Carcassonne is a perfectly restored medieval town, and is protected by UNESCO. It crowns a steep bank above the Aude River, a fairy-tale sight of turrets and ramparts overlooking the lower town below.

YORK, ENGLAND
York's medieval walls were first built as part of a Roman military camp but took much of their shape in the 12th and 14th centuries. They are studded with imposing city gates.

HUNGARY

Dip into a thermal bath in Budapest

Nowhere does thermal baths quite like Budapest. This "City of Spas" has been famed for its hot springs since Roman times, and more than a dozen still exist across the city, drawing their healing powers from a network of springs simmering below ground. And soaking in the hot waters above is a beloved local pastime. Groups may gather for a semi-submerged game of chess in the outdoor pools at Széchenyi, while a younger crowd are drawn to its late night "sparty" events featuring DJs and a lively bar. Széchenyi is the largest spa complex in Europe, practically palatial and instantly recognizable by the bright yellow Neo-Renaissance facade that overlooks its sprawling outdoor pools. See it at its best during the winter months—what could possibly trump a warm outdoor dip surrounded by a light dusting of snowfall? For a more refined experience, there's no beating Gellért, an Art Nouveau gem of a bathing house with turquoise tiles and elegant interiors, while atmosphere awaits over at Rudas, a dimly lit hammam built during the time of Ottoman rule. Choose your bath wisely, sit back, and soak.

Good to know: Head to the baths early in the morning to avoid crowds; on weekdays, there is often a reduced entry fee.

SERBIA

See the Belgrade Fortress in Kalemegdan Park

Belgrade's fortress looms over the confluence of the great Sava and Danube rivers, commanding what is unquestionably the best view in Serbia's capital. No wonder, then, that this hilltop spot has had fortifications for some 2,000 years—the strategically placed fortress was built and rebuilt over the centuries by Byzantine, Ottoman, and Austrian rulers, to name a few. Today, its grounds make up the Kalemegdan Park, which is the best place in town for a stroll, dotted with modern sculptures among its centuries-old walls. The centerpiece of these is the 45-ft- (14-m-) tall *Pobednik* monument at the main viewpoint, which commemorates Serbia's victory over the Ottoman and Austro-Hungarian empires and is a beloved symbol of the city. On Kalemegdan's lower slopes down to the Danube, you'll find the ivy-covered Ružica Church and the only remaining medieval tower of the fortress, Kula Nebojša. On the other side, the grounds meet Belgrade's buzzing center, where the influences of its historic empires continue all along its narrow, cobbled streets.

Good to know: Belgrade Fortress is free to explore, with tourist information available on the key sites within its walls.

SLOVAKIA

Stroll through the streets of Bratislava

When it comes to Europe's great capitals, Bratislava still somewhat flies under the radar—surprising, given how utterly enchanting this city is. Bratislava's Old Town is a warren of numerous ornate facades and pedestrianized cobbled streets where fin-de-siècle palaces jut up against Baroque houses and spiraling Gothic cathedrals. Here, you'll find remnants of an old-world elegance inherited from a century of Austro-Hungarian rule, the enduring imprint of postwar brutalist architecture, and the dynamic energy of a new capital at the very heart of central Europe. Everywhere you look, the city embraces an unhurried joie de vivre. It's the place to while away the hours at pavement cafés, sip *burčiak* (new wine) at cavernous wine bars, and tuck into local delicacies at cozy traditional restaurants. Whatever you do, you can't leave without trying a hearty portion of *bryndzové halušky* (traditional dumplings with soft sheep cheese) or *makovník* (poppy seed pie), the perfect sustenance after a day of exploring the city sights.

Good to know: Most restaurants and pubs offer a great-value *obedové* (lunch) menu from Monday to Friday.

286

CZECH REPUBLIC

Explore historic Prague

Winding cobbled streets, reaching church spires, manicured gardens, and an enchanting atmosphere—there's just something about Prague. And, despite becoming the bachelor party capital of Europe, it's managed to retain its appeal. All those who visit are bewitched by the spires, cobbles, and tiny lanes, best appreciated from the medieval Old Town Square. Here, the Old Town Hall's Astronomical Clock still chimes the hour, trams trundle past the world's biggest castle complex, and the Gothic Charles Bridge continues to dazzle. Beyond the rounded cobbles of the Old Square are many exciting neighborhoods to explore, each with their own identifiable character. Head to Vyšehrad for its fortress and greenery, or Karlín for its post-industrial revitalization and burgeoning foodie scene. The area of Vinohrady, meanwhile—so-named for its former role as the city's royal vineyards—is the place to go for elegant architecture, leafy parks, and great nightlife. And when you've had your fill of this cultural mosaic, don't forget to take time out to enjoy Prague's unsurpassed beer. Little wonder Prague is one of Europe's top vacation spots.

Good to know: Prague's public transit system is affordable and efficient, making getting around the city a breeze.

POLAND

Walk through Kraków

Standing in the middle of Rynek Główny, Kraków's grand Main Square, you may wonder which century you're in. Medieval architecture abounds, while the vibrant hues of Baroque and Renaissance facades compete in color. Its streets are home to a wealth of historical buildings, in part owing to the fact that it was less damaged during World War II than other cities in the region. Walk around to take in the towering St. Mary's Basilica, before following the Royal Road straight to the most grandiose of all Polish historic buildings. The mighty Wawel Royal Castle is a popular sight, which looms high above the Vistula River on its vantage point on Wawel Hill. Kraków's story is also a tale of two cities: the Christian and the Jewish. Its Kazimierz neighborhood, once among the most important centers of Jewish life in Central Europe, was brought to a tragic halt as a result of Jewish persecution during World War II. Today, its centuries-old synagogues and cemeteries remain part of the city's historic fabric, telling the story of its past alongside the restored buildings of the city center.

Good to know: Kraków is well connected by inter-city bus and train services, and it also has its own airport.

> **Medieval architecture abounds, while the vibrant hues of Baroque and Renaissance facades compete in color.**

POLAND

Get to know Warsaw

Resurrected from the devastation of World War II to become one of the most vibrant cities in Europe, Warsaw is built on resilience and determination. And what better place to begin your exploration of the dynamic Polish capital than at its very heart? The beautiful Old Town is a feat of reconstruction work, meticulously rebuilt after the war using archival footage. Stroll through scenic Rynek Starego Miasta, the city's old market square; flanked on all sides with pretty pastel-hued buildings, it belies the city's painful past. History here is never that hard to find, and the POLIN Museum of the History of Polish Jews and the Warsaw Uprising Museum are great spots to learn about the turbulent events that shaped Warsaw. But the city also surprises with a modern vibrancy—skyscrapers surround the iconic Palace of Culture and Science, a buzzing art scene thrives, and cutting-edge restaurants serve up Polish dishes as well as international cuisine. All that's to say, visiting this UNESCO World Heritage Site is a must.

Good to know: Metro and trams cover all the major attractions, and a 24- or 72-hour ticket will help you save on travel.

EUROPE

Cruise along the scenic Danube River

Winding from the Black Forest to the Black Sea, the Danube is a continental best-of, a celebration of Western, Central, and Eastern Europe. The river counts Bavaria; Linz; and capital cities Vienna, Bratislava, Budapest, and Belgrade along its banks before it empties through Europe's second-largest river delta into the Black Sea, along the edges of Romania and Ukraine. Checking off these famous destinations while gently sailing down the river is a treat, but no cruise covers the entire course, so you may have to make decisions. Will it be the ornate Baroque architecture and artistic splendor of Vienna? Or northern Hungary's Danube Bend, which opens up to one of the river's most dazzling panoramas? Or perhaps the spectacular Iron Gates, where precipitous gorges separate Serbia from Romania? In between such storied stops, your vessel of choice will keep you entertained with an array of fine-dining restaurants, cozy cinemas and top-tier wellness centers. Yet, with so many scene-stealing views along the way, you may find you spend most of your time on the upper deck, weather-beaten but well-rewarded.

Good to know: Plenty of companies offer cruises down the Danube, including Viking and Uniworld.

ALBANIA

Discover the Albanian Riviera

Albania's long, sun-soaked coastline stretches some 100 miles (170 km) alongside the jewellike Adriatic and Ionian seas. It's studded with a succession of genuinely gorgeous beaches and historical sites, to which you can add plenty of delicious food and the incredible warmth of the local people—and yet, compared to neighboring Corfu or indeed most of the Mediterranean, until fairly recently the Albanian coast remained pretty much terra incognita to most travelers. However, that might be about to change. Head to the south for the Albanian Riviera, a place of turquoise waters, rocky cliffs, and crescents of golden sand. Here, the village of Ksamil, home to both beautiful beaches and intriguing archaeological sites, is a go-to for travelers. For a more secluded experience, venture to the canyon-backed bay of Gjipe or the 4 miles (7 km) of fine sand that can be found at the village of Borsh. While not quite the undiscovered coastline it was a few years ago, few destinations along the Mediterranean have maintained more genuine charm than the Albanian Riviera.

Good to know: Looking to party in paradise? Head to Kala Festival, a music event that takes place here in June.

BULGARIA

Explore the sweet-smelling Rose Valley

Imagine a valley where the Damask rose (*Rosa damascena*) is grown in such profusion that its cultivation defines the whole region. And, imagine that when they come into bloom in the spring, their pink and white petals cover the landscape like a huge, sweet-scented tapestry of fuchsia tones. That's the Rose Valley of Bulgaria for you, which lies between the Stara Planina and Sredna Gora mountain ranges in the center of the country. The importance of roses to Bulgaria cannot be overstated—it's the world's largest producer of rose oil. To celebrate the flowers' importance to the region, an annual Rose Festival is held each June, with rose-picking ceremonies and rituals taking place in and around many local villages. The festivities are a perfect way to witness traditional folk costumes and dancing, while also rolling up your sleeves and joining in with the rose harvest. Find a place to stay that's nestled into the valley, and each day you'll really be waking up and smelling the roses.

Good to know: Visit between mid-May and mid-June, when the roses are in full bloom.

ROMANIA

Get spooked at Bran Castle

For better or worse, Transylvania is associated with the blood-sucker that is Count Dracula, a character made famous by 19th-century author Bram Stoker. In Stoker's novel, the namesake vampire lives out his days in a Romanian castle perched high above a valley, eerily similar to Bran Castle in Brașov. This 14th-century fortress, which perches on a crag high above hillsides in a flurry of towers and terra-cotta-tiled turrets, has become known as "Dracula's Castle." But, unlike other places in Romania, this spot has no documented connection either to Stoker or Vlad Tepes, the ruthless medieval Romanian ruler on whom the Dracula legend is based. That does little to diminish its Gothic credentials, though, with its dingy passageways, weaponry-hung walls, and views out over thickly tree-clad slopes evoking the far-removed moody mountain atmosphere we have come to associate with any Dracula tale.

Good to know: Base yourself in Brașov to visit the castle easily; you can take a bus or taxi from the village.

294

GREECE

Catch a sunset across the blue domes of Santorini

The Greek island of Santorini is home to some of the world's most famous sunsets, and, as you stand on the island's western coast watching hues of pink and gold dip beyond the Aegean Sea, it's easy to see why. There are a multitude of places from which to watch the spectacle, from terrace bars where drinkers clink cocktails as the day fades away, to the popular hilltop panorama beside the Oia windmill, but the most famous spot might just be near the old castle, where the sun sinks into the horizon over the sky-blue domes of whitewashed churches. Just don't expect to have the view to yourself, mind. A "world famous" tag comes at a cost: crowds. Big ones. To escape them, make for the former donkey tracks that hug the hillside in the village of Fira, a much more peaceful option. A 3-mile (5-km) drive or slow hillside hike from the village of Pyrgos, meanwhile, takes you up to the highest point on Santorini, the Prophet Elias Monastery, from which you can watch the sundown surrounded by gorgeous Byzantine architecture and with nothing but the rustling olive and almond trees for company.

Good to know: Santorini is rarely cloudy or rainy between April and October, ensuring stunning sunsets on a daily basis.

293

GREECE

See the Parthenon atop the Acropolis in Athens

A timeless symbol of the birth of democracy and Western civilization, the Parthenon is one of the world's most captivating ancient ruins, built almost 2,500 years ago and still standing strong. Remarkably well-preserved, it continues to command views over Athens thanks to its position atop the Acropolis, a hilltop citadel on a rugged outcrop overlooking the modern Greek capital. The Parthenon was first built as a temple to Athena, the ancient Greek goddess of wisdom and warcraft, and even for modern visitors the hike to reach it—an uphill walk of around half an hour—has the feel of a pilgrimage. It's easy to imagine yourself walking in the sandals of Socrates, the great Greek philosopher who helped build the Acropolis during his days as a stonemason, and sense the history that radiates from its limestone columns. Once you get to the top of the hill, explore the remains of crumbling ancient stone amphitheaters surrounding it. Then, delve inside the ruins of the Parthenon itself, where the majestic sight of the monumental golden statue of Athena once proudly stood.

Good to know: Between November and March, entry to the Acropolis complex is free on the first Sunday of every month.

296

GREECE

Island-hop around Greece

Greece is home to more than 6,000 islands, each with its own charm and character, so knowing where to visit can feel overwhelming. Fortunately, you don't have to choose just one island—take your pick and embark on a Greek island-hopping tour. Start your adventure on the glam island of Mykonos, where you can enjoy seafood in pastel-hued harbor-front tavernas and indulge in some of Greece's liveliest nightlife. From here, set out on a ferry tour around the islands of the Cyclades. Step back in time in Naxos, where the doorway of the unfinished Temple of Apollo frames the blue sky like a portal to the past, and linger on one of its quiet beaches. Enjoy the island's slower pace of life, indulging in leisurely lunches washed down with Naxos's signature citrus liqueur, *kitron*. Splendid Byzantine churches and monasteries wait to be explored on Paros, while Ios is the perfect place to end your trip; feel the sand between your toes as you watch the sunset over the blue Aegean Sea.

Good to know: Midsummer is extremely busy, and midwinter sees reduced ferry routes, so visit in spring or fall.

295

GREECE

Explore the ruins of Crete's Palace of Knossos

Once the capital of the ancient Minoan civilization, the remains of Crete's most important ruins ooze grandeur. As you approach the Palace of Knossos, you're greeted by a fresco of a bull charging across an exterior wall, its rich hues of blue, red, and gold just as vivid as they would have been in the 16th century BCE. The modern (albeit controversial) restoration of its paintwork makes you feel like you're right there, walking through the past of Europe's first advanced civilization. It's also known as the home of the Minotaur, the legendary half man, half bull trapped in a mighty labyrinth. Hard evidence of this mythical maze is yet to be found, but, tantalizingly, plenty of bull-related art and objects have been. In addition to the exterior fresco, you'll find an indoor gallery depicting the ancient sport of bull-leaping alongside paintings of dolphins and griffins. Beyond the beauty of their art, the Minoans' ingenuity will surely impress you with their intricate waterways and vast wine cellars—after all, this was the largest and most sophisticated of the palaces on the island.

Good to know: A combined ticket allows entry to both the Palace of Knossos and the Heraklion Archaeological Museum.

CYPRUS

Visit Paphos

Located on the southwest coast of Cyprus, Paphos has a timeless charm. The town is really two towns in one—Kato ("lower") and Ktima ("upper") Paphos—with a history dating back to the Neolithic period. Evidence of its storied past can be found almost everywhere you look. It's said to be the mythical birthplace of Aphrodite; legend has it, the goddess emerged from the sea-foam on nearby Aphrodite's Rock. And the distant-past is ever-present here, with excavations turning much of Paphos into an archaeological site. It's home to the Tombs of the Kings and the Paphos Archaeological Site, which offers a fascinating journey through the remnants of Greco-Roman civilization. Along the waterfront, though, modern living thrives. Vacationers flock to the many resorts and hotels spread along the coast, while the center is packed with vibrant bars and convivial tavernas. After a day of beach relaxation, head here to enjoy the national dish, *fasolada* (a hearty bean and vegetable soup) along with local white wine, and indulge in island life.

Good to know: The best way to explore more of the island beyond Paphos is by renting a car.

> Standing beneath its arches, you can sense the whispered prayers of pilgrims that have soaked into the stones over centuries.

TÜRKIYE

Marvel at the Hagia Sophia Grand Mosque

Istanbul's skyline is punctuated by two landmarks unchanged since the heyday of the medieval Silk Road: the candle-like minaret of Galata Tower and the almighty dome of Hagia Sophia. Around 1,500 years old, the Hagia Sophia was first built as the Church of God's Holy Wisdom under Byzantine emperor Justinian I. Although it was once a church, today it's a mosque and a museum, with signs of these varied uses visible across the interiors. Pace across smooth slabs of stone and look for the many glittering remnants of gold-tiled mosaics embedded into the walls, including a glittering 9th-century mosaic of the Virgin Mary and baby Jesus. Standing beneath its arches, you can sense the whispered prayers of pilgrims that have soaked into the stones over centuries. The Hagia stands as a testament to the many changes and visitors it has witnessed over the last millennia.

Good to know: To visit as a tourist, there is a ticketed separate entrance to the second floor; the ground floor is for prayer only.

299

TÜRKIYE

Travel back in time in Ephesus

Time-travel back around 3,000 years while walking the streets of Ephesus. Now in ruins, this ancient city was once the main commercial hub of the Mediterranean and a prized location to both the Greeks and Romans. Sense the history of the place among the remains of ancient baths, squares, and innumerable temples. One of the most famous of these is the Temple of Artemis, one of the Seven Ancient Wonders of the World. Where 127 columns more than 40 ft (13 m) high once stood supporting a great roof, now only a single lonely column remains. Far more evocative, though, is the site's crown jewel: the so-called Terrace Houses. Only uncovered in 1962, they belonged to rich merchants who flaunted their wealth by adorning their homes with marvelously preserved mosaic-covered floors and hand-painted murals. Packed with monuments, Ephesus is a site where every stone is imbued with history—meaning you can't leave any (metaphorically) unturned.

Good to know: To beat the crowds, arrive for the 8 a.m. opening or buy the Museum Pass Aegean to skip the ticket lines.

300

TÜRKIYE

See Cappadocia aboard a hot air balloon

A hot-air balloon ride is a flying experience like no other. And, sure, there are plenty of places where you can take to the skies, but what about a land that was recorded as early as the 6th century BCE? The region of Cappadocia in central Turkey is hewn with stories. Millions of years ago, volcanic eruptions produced tuff rock, which the natural elements slowly sculpted into rock formations known as "fairy chimneys." The Silk Road once ran through this otherworldly land, and many empires laid claim to it; when the Romans invaded, Christians fled to the region's main town of Göreme. Here, they dug many tunnels, homes, and churches in the chimneys. To see this landscape from above, looking down over the many 130-ft- (40-m-) high cone-shaped formations, is to see it in all its glory. Little wonder this is one of the world's most famous places to peacefully float across the sky.

Good to know: Inevitably for a sunrise hot-air balloon ride an early start is a must, usually around 4 a.m.

WHERE ELSE TO RIDE A HOT-AIR BALLOON

VANG VIENG, LAOS
The beautiful Laos countryside is home to majestic karsts, cool limestone caves, and ethereal landscapes that feel out of this world. Many people see it from the water, but taking to the skies is just as special, drifting over dramatic karst cliffs above the Nathong valley.

BAGAN, MYANMAR
Hot-air balloons have become synonymous with Bagan, and offer the chance to look down upon Bagan's iconic skyline of more than 2,000 temples and pagodas poking through the clouds.

LUXOR, EGYPT
Ancient Thebes, the temple complex of Karnak, the Valley of the Kings: Luxor is often touted as the world's greatest open-air museum. Floating over these incredible ancient temples and ruins on the banks of the Nile is certainly a pinch-me moment.

301

TÜRKIYE

Bathe at Pamukkale Hot Springs

If a dip in a natural hot spring is on your bucket list, then you might as well go to the best. Pamukkale, or "Cotton Castle," is a snow-white staircase of travertine rock, upon which pool a series of thermal springs. At a first glance, this surreal landscape might look artificial, but it has in fact existed since antiquity. Famous figures such as Cleopatra came here to bathe in the warm natural waters; back then, the springs were overlooked by a temple to Apollo and, higher still, the Greco-Roman city of Hierapolis. Although these sights have long since become ruins, they add to the classic feel of the springs—some ornate columns can even be seen beneath the water. While Pamukkale may now be one of Türkiye's top—and busiest—tourist sites, soaking in these pools still delivers a dose of muscle-easing mineral therapy in a unique setting.

Good to know: To experience a more forgiving heat, visit between April and June.

302

GEORGIA

Visit the land where East meets West

Few countries better typify the collision between European, Asian, and Middle Eastern cultures than transcontinental Georgia. Such a mix infuses the country with rich tradition, best explored in the capital of Tbilisi, where eclectic architecture reflects the city's location on the historic Silk Road and the many invaders who left a mark. Here, grand Art Nouveau mansions share space with domed Persian-style bathhouses and medieval forts, and Islamic and Neo-Gothic mosques jostle for attention alongside petite churches and red-brick synagogues. At every turn, you feel as if you're entering both a different era *and* country. Brasseries recall scenes from Paris, spice markets are reminiscent of Middle Eastern bazaars, and ornate courtyards feel plucked from Italy. But Tbilisi is still constantly evolving and trying on new faces, with its growing urban touches giving it the moniker of "new Berlin"—think cool street art and wine bars housed in former Soviet-era warehouses. A Georgian proverb claims that "every guest is a gift from God," and it often seems as though its many unique sights might just be too.

Good to know: Explore beyond Tbilisi to find some of Europe's most unspoiled mountain hiking and beautiful scenery.

304

FINLAND

Bed down in an igloo

When you're living in freezing Arctic conditions (long before the days of indoor heating), you have to get creative with your shelter. That's exactly what the Inuit peoples did centuries ago, using blocks of compacted snow around them to construct an *iglu*, the Inuit word for "home." There's hardly a better way to test your mettle than bedding down in a room made completely of snow and ice, made possible at Finnish Lapland's Arctic SnowHotel. This is one of the world's biggest snow hotels, where the igloos are sustainably built afresh yearly and are open to those with a taste for the polar from mid-December to March. Inside, ice-carved furnishings (including a bed that's a block of ice) average just above 32°F (0°C); even with a hotel-provided extra-warm sleeping bag, you'll feel comfortably close to the Arctic weather. If you can't bear to face the cold, a glass igloo is the next best thing, and these lodgings are scattered all around Finland. And, unlike bona fide igloos that are entirely hemmed in by snow, these glass roofs offer the perfect chance to view the Northern Lights. Bucket list stays rarely get much cooler.

Good to know: Find out more about a stay in the snowy Finnish Arctic—and how to prepare for it—via the Arctic SnowHotel.

303

ESTONIA

Wander through Tallinn

Given its geographical position at a crossroads between Eastern and Western Europe, Estonia has had a tumultuous history. Over the centuries, the country was considered a prize strategic asset by neighboring ruling powers, but since regaining independence in 1991, it's been a model example of how to rapidly modernize while preserving national heritage. And its capital, Tallinn, is the poster child for such a feat. At the city's heart lies the UNESCO-listed Old Town, which has managed to entirely preserve its medieval and Hanseatic structure, its cobbled streets full of hidden courtyards, spired Gothic buildings, and massive defensive walls complete with towers. As if in a blink of the eye, once you step out of the Old Town's perimeter, you're hit with the "Manhattan of Tallinn," where the old, industrial Rotermann Quarter has been transformed into a buzzing area of skyscrapers, shopping centers, and fancy restaurants. So, will you step full throttle into a medieval storybook, or see what the city's modern face has to say?

Good to know: Visit Tallinn in July, when Medieval Days transform the Old Town into a medieval city for four days.

306

FINLAND

Spot a bear in Kainuu

The Finnish language has more than 200 words for "bear," a testament to just how important the country's national animal is. The ancient Finns feared and respected the sacred brown bear so much that they didn't dare utter its name out loud, instead using euphemisms like "honeypalm" or "king of the forest" to speak of the animal. Europe's largest predator is still woodland royalty across the country today, and nowhere more so than in Kainuu, a pocket of eastern Finland that's become the epicenter of bear-watching. When the snow begins to melt here in April, some 2,000 bears awake from their hibernation and begin to stalk the landscape until around August. The best way to catch a glimpse of the creature is on a specialized tour, sticking to designated bear-spotting facilities for safety. Or see them prowl from the comfort of a luxury cabin, where huge windows offer a grand (and secure) look out from which to watch the "kings of the forests" guard their kingdom.

Good to know: The best time of year to spot bears is from April to August; choose afternoon tours as the days begin to shorten.

WHERE ELSE TO GO BEAR-WATCHING

CANADA
In national parks and remote areas across Canada, such as the Rockies, you may see grizzlies, black, and brown bears. The Great Bear Rainforest on the Pacific Coast is the best place to catch a glimpse of the unique spirit bears—black bears with a recessive gene that makes them white.

ALASKA
With the exception of the Aleutian Islands, Alaska is prime bear habitat and home to three species of bears: black, brown, and polar. They're mostly active in the summer, retreating to dens in the winter.

BORNEO
The Bornean Sun Bear Conservation Center is dedicated to help protect the sun bear, the world's smallest bear. It's possible to see around 30 to 40 rescued bears roaming the forest enclosures here, which provide the bears with a home.

305

FINLAND

Say hello to Santa in Lapland

Here comes Santa Claus! The official hometown of the white-bearded face of Christmas, Lapland has been synonymous with Santa since 1927, when a Finnish radio host declared the region to be the home of his workshop. You may no longer believe in the big man, but it's impossible to be a Scrooge at Lapland's capital city, Rovaniemi, where every day is Christmas at the Santa Claus Village. This amusement park brings out the inner child in everyone who visits: say hello to Santa at his office, write letters with the elves at his post office, meet the famed reindeer in his backyard, and even hear stories from the legendary Mrs. Claus herself. As if it couldn't get any more magical, the Arctic Circle cuts right through the village, so you can cross the northernmost circle of latitude and step into Christmas at the same time.

Good to know: To experience Lapland's stunning snowscapes while you're here, aim to go between November and April.

307

FINLAND

Visit Helsinki

To understand why Finland is always voted the happiest country in the world, start at its capital. After all, why would you feel anything *but* joy when your days can be spent unwinding at a sauna, people-watching from waterfront cafés, and perusing contemporary art museums, all in a location that's spread along the scenic shores of the Gulf of Finland? Helsinki has been Finland's buzzy capital since 1812, when it was designed in line with architectural ideals of antiquity. It continued to enhance its skyline in the 20th century, erecting everything from the Functionalist Olympic Stadium to the Romantic National Museum of Finland. Fast forward to today, and it's this eye-catching architecture—both old and new—that first strikes you as you stroll through the center, where the likes of the copper, glass, and rock Temppeliaukio Church and the futuristic Kiasma center bring a little bit of "wow" into the everyday. And if you still don't feel like the happiest person on Earth before these epic constructions, well, there'll be a sauna waiting.

Good to know: The city center is walkable, but it's also very bike-friendly—rent one of the yellow bikes around the city.

308

SWEDEN

Celebrate Midsummer

The enchanting backdrop of Sweden's serene lakes, verdant forests, and gently rolling farmland set the stage for celebrations.

The longest day of the year is a special time to be in Sweden. On a Friday between June 19 and 25, Midsummer festivities celebrate the summer solstice, when Swedes don flower crowns, adorn maypoles with fresh blooms, and eat traditional delicacies like pickled herring. Dating back to agrarian times, Midsummer originated as a way to welcome in the summer season and ensure a good harvest. Rituals included collecting flowers, lighting bonfires, and casting love spells, all reflecting the belief that this was a magical time of good luck and fertility. Traditions have evolved over the centuries, and today, Midsummer is both a celebration of summer and Swedish customs. The enchanting backdrop of Sweden's serene lakes, verdant forests, and gently rolling farmland set the stage for celebrations, which start with a seemingly endless lunch from midday and continue into the early hours, often with the help of sing-songs and bracing drinks. You'll be wishing the day was even longer by the end.

Good to know: Book a ticket to celebrate at the Skansen Open Air Museum, which is at the heart of Stockholm's festivities.

SWEDEN

Set sail around the Stockholm archipelago

With some 30,000 islands, skerries, and rocks, the Stockholm archipelago is made for leisurely exploration. From the froth-lapped prow of a boat, beach-fringed atolls, ancient villages, and dynamic neighborhoods dotted with copper-colored summer houses unfurl in front of you. Idyllic scenery aside, what sets this archipelago apart from many others is its accessibility, a mere paddle away from Stockholm. The capital city itself is in fact built across 14 islands, making it part of the larger Stockholm archipelago. Sailing here is easy, with light winds to carry you forth and few tides to disrupt your flow—the only hurdle is deciding where to set sail for next. You could opt for the islands of Vaxholm and Svartsö, brightened up by their painted wooden houses, or moor up at Nynäshamn, adored for its craft beer scene. Or maybe you'll head to Grinda, the city's wild-swimming capital. So difficult is your choice, you'll want to extend your trip to see it all. And so you should: in Sweden, the freedom to venture into nature—*allemansrätten*—is a human right.

Good to know: Opt for a regular boat trip from Stockholm's city center if you'd rather not steer your own vessel.

NORWAY

Experience the midnight sun in Lofoten

It's midnight on the craggy archipelago of Lofoten, but it's not dark—far from it. In the "land of the midnight sun," the sun stays above the horizon permanently in summer, casting a red glow over the landscape as sunset merges into sunrise. This natural phenomenon is caused by the tilt of the Earth's axis and its rotation around the sun during the northern hemisphere's summer; the farther north of the Arctic Circle you venture, the more endless, rose-gold sunshine you get. Northern Lofoten is one of the top places to experience it, especially if you head to one of the beaches or set out on a hike up a mountain. The route to Reinebringen in Moskenes is the most popular, overlooking the surrounding mountains and the village of Reine below. For something even more memorable, hit the water and kayak under the glow of this nighttime sunshine. It's mind-boggling to be able to see the sun at a time you'd expect it to be dark.

Good to know: The midnight sun usually shines across Lofoten from the end of May to mid-July each year.

Drive the Atlantic Road

Among the most memorable drives in the world, the Norwegian National Scenic Route, or "Atlantic Road," seems to roll into the Norwegian Sea. Set on a truly exquisite location on the West Norway coastline and winding for more than 22 miles (35 km), the road has been taking the brunt of the Atlantic waves since 1989, when it was first opened. This marvel of engineering took six years to complete due to the unforgiving weather conditions, and today unfurls along tiny islets from the mainland all the way to the island of Averøy and across eight scenic bridges. The journey here is incredible in itself; it's worth taking time to see the striking architectural installations which punctuate the route. There are snaking boardwalks and wide viewing platforms thoughtfully distributed to allow visitors space to stretch their legs and savor the scenery's impact. Slow down as you drive: picture-perfect landscapes unfold at every turn, while at times the Atlantic Road surrenders to the waves that crash defiantly over its path. In some ways, the Atlantic Road is more than a scenic drive—it's a journey through the heart of Norway's untamed coastal splendor.

Good to know: In September and October, strong winds occasionally cause the waves to crash over the bridges.

ALASKA
Chasing the Northern Lights around the city of Fairbanks is easy: the light season is long (from late August to late April), the skies are dark and pollution is minimal.

ICELAND
Reykjavík is a popular base from which to chase the lights. Tours often head to Viðey, but the countryside offers clearer skies and a more dramatic backdrop of mountains or glacier lagoons.

FINLAND
The aurora borealis dance above the city of Rovaniemi, Lapland, around 150 nights a year, often between September and March.

GREENLAND
Way off the beaten track, Greenland is a great spot to see the lights without any crowds. Base yourself in the sparsely populated city of Ilulissat and prepare to be dazzled.

NORWAY

See the aurora borealis

You never forget the first time you see the Northern Lights, the green and red glow dancing between the stars. This natural phenomenon mystified the Vikings, who saw the lights as reflections of the Valkyries' armor, guiding warriors to the Norse god Odin in Valhalla. In reality, it's caused by the interaction of charged particles from the sun with the Earth's magnetic field. Seeing the Northern Lights is unsurprisingly high on every bucket list, and few places offer more opportunities to see them than Norway. Come between September and April, and head as far north of the Arctic Circle as possible—Bodø, Tromsø, and Svalbard are your best bets. Sightings are far from guaranteed, since the phenomenon relies on a perfect coalescing of conditions, but if you go as far as Svalbard, located halfway between Norway and the North Pole, you might even see the lights during the day.

Good to know: Give yourself a week to increase your chances of seeing the lights (they're usually visible from 6 p.m. to 1 a.m.).

NORWAY

Hike to Trolltunga

No hiker's bucket list is complete without the mighty Trolltunga, one of Norway's most spectacular scenic cliffs. Set among fjords and shaped by Ice Age glacial erosion, this bedrock hovers 2,300 ft (700 m) above Lake Ringedalsvatnet. And tackling the route up to it will really test your mettle. The challenging trek is a 17-mile (28-km) round trip, complete with an ascent of nearly 3,000 ft (900 m). Base yourself in Odda, on the edge of the sweeping Hardangervidda plateau in southwestern Norway, from which you can best set off to the trailhead in Skjeggedal. The hike itself can take anywhere from 8 to 12 hours, rewarding you with spectacular views over rocky valleys and clear-watered streams along the way. To really get in touch with the nature here, take advantage of Norway's famous *allemannsretten*, a rule dating from ancient times which allows you to roam, forage free on uncultivated land, and pitch a tent overnight (ensuring you leave no trace behind you when you leave). By the time you finally reach the Trolltunga cliff, you'll feel at one with the jaw-dropping views of the land below.

Good to know: Peak hiking season is from June to September, when buses and taxis shuttle between Odda and Skjeggedal.

NORWAY

Embark on a fjord cruise

Steep mountains, crashing waterfalls, and dark waters below: Norwegian fjords are packed full of dramatic sights. And a cruise through the fjords will take you right to the heart of these spectacular landscapes. There are enough scenic cruises to stump even the most decisive of travelers. Starting points include Stavanger, Flåm, and Geiranger, while the longest coastal route winds from Bergen to Kirkenes, in Finnmark. The route to the stunning Nærøyfjord is hugely popular, setting off from the village of Flåm and sailing through Aurlandsfjord before reaching the narrow Nærøyfjord. Opt for the route to Geirangerfjord, though, and you'll be taken down its 10 miles (16 km) of snaking, emerald waterways. The streams are bounded by tall cliffs that soar to 5,600 ft (1,700 m) and many waterfalls, including the Dei Sju Systrene (Seven Sisters) and the Brudesløret (Bridal Veil), which thunder down the mountainsides in an epic showcase of nature. Endless streams of visitors arrive in the summer to see this fjord, but a view of the bountiful, awe-inspiring landscapes make the crowds worth it.

Good to know: The peak season is between mid-April and September, with most cruises taking one to two weeks.

AFRICA AND THE MIDDLE EAST

MOROCCO

Hike the Atlas Mountains

Dawn in Morocco's High Atlas is almost a spiritual experience. The sun's early rays bring fingers of warmth to the steep slopes, and the only sounds are the wind and an occasional hawk wheeling through the thermals. The Atlas Mountains cut across much of North Africa, forming a rugged backbone to Morocco, Algeria, and Tunisia, but it is among the mud-brick mountain villages of Morocco that you will find some of the finest hiking in the region. Here, children shepherd their goats through isolated valleys, and Berber women, dressed in flowing headscarves, tend their crops of barley and corn on gravity-defying terraces. Follow old mule trails across gurgling streams or up to dizzying passes, stopping for lunch (usually a type of tagine) and a mint tea with villagers along the route to learn about the local way of life—many locals rely on tourism as their source of income. Most hikes depart from the trekking hub of Imlil, just two hours' drive from Marrakech—but a world away.

Good to know: You must be accompanied by a registered guide, who can also ensure you respect local customs.

MOROCCO AND MAURITANIA

Explore the Sahara Desert

The largest desert in the world, the sands of the Sahara stretch for more than 3,000 miles (4,800 km) across North Africa, covering large parts of 11 different countries and territories, from Western Sahara to Sudan. Head to southern Morocco for easy access and the classic Sahara image of ribbed dunes rolling away into the distance for as far as the eye can see. In places like Merzouga, at the edge of the Erg Chebbi sand sea, and M'Hamid, near the Erg Chigaga, you can organize tours that include camel riding, overnight stays in traditional Berber camps, and star gazing that is literally out of this world. The more adventurous can experience the Sahara in Mauritania, at the village of Atar, an oasis of lush vegetation and trickling streams that lies within easy reach of Chinguetti, a medieval trading center that is now a UNESCO World Heritage Site. For a different take on the Sahara, hop on the iron-ore train that departs from Choum, north of Atar, and trundles for more than 12 hours across the desert to the port town of Nouadhibou, a dusty, dirty, exhilarating ride through a sea of sand.

Good to know: Wrap up well at night, because temperatures in the desert can drop to 25°F (-4°C).

MOROCCO

MARRAKECH

For many people, Marrakech is the Moroccan city of their imaginations. In the tightly packed medina of twisting lanes and dead-end alleyways, stallholders in noisy souks sell intricately decorated metal lanterns, colorful patterned rugs, goatskin slippers, and everything else in between.

317

Visit the Jardin Majorelle

The frenetic sounds of the Marrakech souks slowly fade as you enter the garden sanctuary of the Jardin Majorelle, a small paradise in the heart of the city's Ville Nouvelle. Filled with exotic plants sourced from five different continents, this is the beautiful botanic creation of French artist Jacques Majorelle. Majorelle lived in the boldly colored cobalt-blue villa in the center of the gardens, where he painted and nurtured his many plants for almost 40 years. Following Majorelle's death in 1962, French fashion designer Yves Saint-Laurent purchased the striking property, and today the Jardin Majorelle forms one part of the Foundation Pierre Bergé—Yves Saint Laurent, a French nonprofit organization. Take your time to explore the luxuriant gardens, which are studded with yucca, bougainvillea, and hibiscus, and home to more than 400 varieties of palm tree and 1,800 species of cactus. Majorelle's Art Deco studio now houses a museum offering insight into the culture, clothes, and jewelery of the Berber peoples of North Africa. While the artist's iconic former home is off-limits to the general public, its magnificent exterior can be admired from the outside; guests at The Royal Mansour, however, can arrange a private viewing of the residence.

Good to know: The best time to photograph the gardens is during the golden hour around sunset.

318

Get lost in the souks

You might find a Berber cushion cover you never knew you wanted. You'll probably have to barter for a decent price on a finely woven rug from the High Atlas mountains. But one thing is for sure in the souks of Marrakech: you will definitely get lost. This seemingly endless maze of merchant's stalls and dead-end alleys dates back to the founding of the city, when Marrakech's earliest inhabitants made their living from trading goods such as gold, ivory, leather, and ceramics. Many of the individual souks are named after the products that were traditionally sold there, such as Souk el-Attarine, the Spice Market, and Souk des Teinturiers, the dyers' souk, where workers still rub dyes into hides from the nearby tanneries. The northern half of the medina is essentially one large market, covered in parts by wooden trellising, which throws slats of sunlight into the dark alleyways below. Dive right in and follow the flow of the buzzing stalls past leather pouffes, brightly colored slippers, metal lanterns, and pungent spices. Leave the map at home and follow your whims and the yell of vendors. And prepare to get lost.

Good to know: Always have a contact number from your riad (traditional house) or hotel, in case you do get truly lost.

MUST-BUY SOUVENIRS FROM THE SOUKS

Lanterns
Hundreds of mosaic table lamps and lanterns line the street shops, glistening in the afternoon sun.

Rugs
Carpets are typically woven in Rabat, Salé, and Casablanca and feature perfectly symmetrical patterns.

Tagine pots
Colorful, patterned tagine pots are ubiquitous in the souks.

Slippers
Embroidered slippers in vibrant colors have been sold in Morocco for centuries.

Spices
You'll smell the likes of cumin, paprika, and cinnamon before you see them, piled high at spice shops and stalls.

Teapots
For the perfect cup of mint tea, you'll want to purchase a silver teapot—it simply tastes better from these beautiful trinkets.

319

Enjoy the show at the Jemaa el-Fna

Nothing can prepare you for the vast array of humanity in the Jemaa el-Fna, the beating heart of Marrakech. All day long, this focal square is a throng of entertainers, tradesmen, and artisans, coloring a scene that has changed little in the last thousand years. Snake charmers coax cobras into a swaying dance, tooth-pullers advertise their services with ancient-looking pliers and battered trays of little white trophies, and men dressed in pompom-fringed hats serve water from hip pouches. As dusk descends, the square fills as crowds gather around the acrobats, musicians, dancers, and storytellers that have moved in. This is when the Jemaa is at its vibrant best. Come nightfall, dozens of food stalls set up shop in the center of the square, and you can tuck into a dinner of fried fish (or steaming snails or boiled sheep's head, if you dare) under canvas awnings and pungent clouds of cooking smoke.

Good to know: Café Clock, in the southern medina, holds traditional storytelling evenings on Mondays and Thursdays.

NIGERIA

Get swept up by the buzz of Lagos

Lagos is a city that's constantly on the go. You'll feel it as you weave through its notorious traffic on the back of an *okada* (motorbike taxi) or jostle for a serving of hot *suya* kebab, wrapped in a newspaper, from a street-food stand. There's a creative and cultural force at play here too. You'll sense it in the swanky cocktail bars of the affluent Ikoyi neighborhood and while browsing the shelves of *ankara* swimwear piled high in fashion boutiques on Victoria Island. Lagos is the dynamic heart of Nollywood, Nigeria's powerhouse film industry, which has developed into the second largest on the planet and whose stars gaze down at you from billboards across the city. Afrobeats was also born within these borders, championed by musicians like Burna Boy, Wizkid, and Davido. It's now a global phenomenon, but bouncing along to its drum-beat rhythms in a heaving Ikeja club seems to elevate the music to a different level. Unpeel the layers of Lagos: energizing and exhausting in equal measure, there's nowhere else quite like it.

Good to know: Detty December, the festive period at the end of the year, is a great time to visit.

GHANA

Haggle in Kejetia Market

The distinctive scent of ripe mangoes, dried fish, and sun-warmed cloth mingle as you weave through the crowds. The crowing of cockerels soars above the rumble of traffic, and vendors yell out their sales patter, their laughter ricocheting off the corrugated rooftops when they're offered a price they deem to be far too low. Every African market is a feast for the senses, but Kejetia, in Ghana's Ashanti city of Kumasi, packs a bigger punch than most. The largest single market in West Africa, it has more than 10,000 stalls, laden with chiles, bananas, cheap clothing, and plastic utensils in a blaze of color. If you're here to buy, don't expect matters to proceed too swiftly. As with all good markets, bargaining is expected, a cheerful verbal dance that takes patience and good humor to perfect. Haggling is hungry work, so you can refuel on street food such as *etor*, mashed yam or plantain with peanuts; avocado; and egg. Then it's time to shop once more.

Good to know: The market can feel quite hectic, so hire a local guide to steer you around the stalls.

SIERRA LEONE

Visit Freetown

History weighs heavy on Freetown, Sierra Leone's handsome capital on the shores of the Atlantic. Founded by abolitionists as a settlement for people freed from slavery, the city is dotted with reminders of its role in the transatlantic slave trade, none more evocative than the Gateway to the Old King's Yard, through which formerly enslaved people passed to freedom. Today's Freetown, though, encapsulates Sierra Leone's efforts to shake off the shackles of its past. Catch a *keke* (tuk-tuk) across the city and your driver will point out vibrant markets and hole-in-the-wall restaurants. While away the day by the beach before feasting on freshly grilled fish washed down with fermented *poyo* (palm wine). Come nightfall, dance your way into the early hours to the hard pulse of the *kelei* drum.

Good to know: Take a trip out to Banana Island, where palm-fringed beaches and diving are the name of the game.

THE GAMBIA

Cruise along the Gambia River

The Gambia is famous for the kind of beaches that winter sunseekers adore. But it's the Gambia River that defines this distinctively elongated West African nation, not its short, sandy coast. This freshwater lifeline snakes through the country from east to west, irrigating rice and groundnut fields as it goes. Hopping on a liveaboard motor boat and cruising upriver is a supremely peaceful way to explore the Gambia's rural heart, where villagers eke out a living from farming and fishing, and Mandinka cultural traditions such as harvest festivals, rites of passage, and musicianship remain intact. Tendaba, Bao Bolong Wetland Reserve, and the River Gambia National Park are particularly attractive areas to visit, lush with mangroves and palm trees and fluttering with kingfishers, darters, egrets, and bee-eaters. Eventually, the river spreads into the Atlantic via a yawning river mouth—and yes, those dreamy beaches too.

Good to know: Specialized tour operator The Gambia Experience offers cruises of the Gambia River.

TUNISIA

Embrace your inner *Star Wars* fan

Star Wars' otherworldly locations played as big a part in the saga's success as its storylines and stars. And while the films may have been set in a galaxy far, far away, four of the epics were actually shot, in part, in the vast deserts of southern Tunisia; Tatooine, the desolate home planet of Luke and Anakin Skywalker, is even named after the real-life Tunisian town of Tataouine. Just 12 miles (20 km) south of here, director George Lucas built a "spaceport" in the sands: the earthly setting for Mos Espa, which featured in *The Phantom Menace* (1999) and *Attack of the Clones* (2002). Although slowly succumbing to the desert, the domed buildings are still very much standing, as are the little pylons that every Star Wars fan worth their salt will recognize as "moisture vaporators." As you walk around the set, you can almost picture the film crew falling silent as Lucas shouts "Action!"

Good to know: Tataouine is around seven hours by road from the capital, Tunis; from there, hire a taxi for the day.

TUNISIA

Step back in time in Tunis's medina

Home to decorative palaces, great mosques, and scholarly madrasahs, Tunis was one of the greatest cities in the Arab world during the Middle Ages. Its medina (Arabic for "town") dates back to the 7th century CE, and is today a UNESCO World Heritage Site in its entirety. Duck into the medina through one of its monumental gates and while away an afternoon wandering its narrow, labyrinthine souks. Pass stalls where eager tailors display colorful kaftans, and follow your nose to sweet-smelling perfumes and homegrown herbs. You can seek refuge from the dusty streets at a shaded café off Souk Trok, in the shadow of the city's oldest mosque, and sip a refreshing mint tea as the muezzin climbs the minaret above you to sing the call to prayer across the medina.

Good to know: Most hotels and riads in Tunis can arrange private tours of the medina.

326

NAMIBIA

Explore the Skeleton Coast

Don't let the name put you off—barren and empty it may be, but there's nothing ghoulish about Namibia's far northwest coast. Sandwiched between the chilly Atlantic Ocean and a sea of tawny dunes backed by endless gravel plains, the Skeleton Coast is simply eerily pristine. The skeletal shreds of long-abandoned shipwrecks remain, rusting slowly, marooned. As do the bones of humpback whales, jutting out of the sand like dinosaur fossils, in a half-covered reminder of the bad old days when whaling was still legal. But take a closer look and this most unusual of places reveals its secrets. Surprisingly, perhaps, life clings on in this parched and unforgiving landscape. Beetles, lizards, and snakes survive on the moisture brought in by the sea mists that roll off the Atlantic each morning. Hyenas scavenge among the bleached bones that litter the beaches. And pale lions, adapted over generations to live within the desert, pad like ghosts along the shore.

Good to know: Skeleton Coast Safaris offers scenic flights, and there are a handful of high-end lodges on or near the coast.

WHERE ELSE TO SANDBOARD

HUACACHINA, PERU
The world's tallest sand dune, Cerro Blanco, lies near Nazca at a huge 3,860 ft (1,176 m). Sandboarding down it takes a whopping four minutes.

GREAT SAND DUNES NATIONAL PARK, COLORADO
Sandboarding and sledding are permitted anywhere on the dunefield of North America's tallest sand dunes.

327

NAMIBIA

Climb the dunes of the world's oldest desert

The Namib-Naukluft National Park is a place of superlatives, home to the oldest desert in the world and one of the largest national parks in Africa. But it is the haunting beauty of this endlessly photogenic place that will stay with you. Stark, white salt pans stretch for miles in every direction, framed by orange sand dunes so gigantic that they tower up like pyramids from the desert plains. Visitors flock to Sossusvlei, in the center of the park, to make the dawn climb up Dune 45 or the aptly named Big Daddy, at 1,066 ft (325 m) by far the biggest of the dunes here. Reaching the top is an arduous task, but perfectly achievable if you follow in the footsteps of the people before you. You can't sandboard back down the slopes like you can at other dunes in Namibia, this being a national park and all, but the views from the top are ample reward: waves of sand rising and falling into the distance and, directly below, the white clay pan of Deadvlei, with its blackened forest of petrified trees.

Good to know: Even starting at dawn, the hike up Big Daddy is a hot one, so sunscreen, a hat, and plenty of water are a must.

CAPE TOWN

Nestled at the southern tip of Africa, cosmopolitan Cape Town exudes coastal cool. This is one of the world's most beautiful cities, where striking architecture meets rugged mountains and where a trip to the beach is as much about watching penguins as people.

Take the cable-car up Table Mountain

It's hard not to crush on Cape Town, a pretty city sandwiched between mountains, vineyards, and the sea. Its surroundings are truly spectacular, none more so than the flat-topped massif of Table Mountain. Wherever you are in the city, from the fashionable restaurants of the V&A Waterfront to the beach at Camp Bay, this iconic landmark is a constant companion. If the view of the mountain from the city bowl makes you weak at the knees, then the panorama from the top will simply knock you out. A hike up its well-marked trails can take three to four hours, leading from the botanical gardens at Kirstenbosch past rock hyraxes and indigenous green fynbos. You can makes things easier on yourself, though, and skip the tough trek up for something far more sedate. The Table Mountain Aerial Cableway will glide you up to the summit in just five minutes, and has huge wrap-around windows and a 360-degree rotating floor to ensure you don't miss out on any of the views. Atop the famous mesa, carved out by wind, rain, and ice over 450 million years, Cape Town is spread before you, some 3,560 ft (1,086 m) below.

Good to know: The cableway runs daily from 8 a.m. to 9:30 p.m., with cars leaving the lower station every 15 minutes or so.

329

Watch the penguins at Boulders Beach

In the southern hemisphere's summer, the blond strip of sand at Boulders Beach in Simon's Town, just outside of Cape Town, is dotted black and white. Milling around the seashore, waddling over granite boulders, and ducking and diving into the waves that lap the shoreline are innumerable little African penguins. Also known as jackass penguins, for the donkey-like braying sound they make, African penguins are an endangered species, so it comes as quite a surprise to see them gathered in such large numbers on this sheltered town beach. The first pair of penguins turned up at Boulders Beach in the 1980s, when food was abundant, and the colony was quickly populated. Today, the penguins face competition for breeding sites, while climate change has affected the number of fish available for them to eat; the beach's entrance fee goes toward protecting and preserving them. You can view the colony on boardwalks that run across the beaches—if you're lucky enough, you might even see a penguin couple holding wings.

Good to know: You can see penguins all year long, although there are fewer in September and October, when they are at sea.

MUST-VISIT WILDLIFE WATCHING SPOTS IN CAPE TOWN

Boulders Beach
The 2,000-strong penguin colony here was founded by two breeding pairs in 1982.

Duiker Island
This island supports a 5,000–6,000-strong colony of seals, three species of cormorant, and some penguins.

Inverdoorn Game Reserve
A few hours' drive from Cape Town you'll find lions, cheetahs, antelopes, and white rhinos.

Cape of Good Hope
The most southerly sector of Table Mountain National Park provides a home for bontebok, grysbok, and Cape mountain zebra.

Table Mountain
Cute, semi-tame dassies (rock hyraxes) sunbathe here.

Aquila Private Game Reserve
This reserve is inhabited by lions, elephants, and buffalo.

330

Tour the Zeitz Museum

Simply put, the Zeitz Museum of Contemporary Art Africa (Zeitz MOCAA) is the most influential museum on the continent. Located on Cape Town's buzzing V&A Waterfront, it is home to one of the largest collections of contemporary African art in the world, with paintings, sculptures, fashion, photography, and visual-media installations sprawled across 100 galleries over nine floors. The building itself, the tallest in sub-Saharan Africa, is an architectural marvel, a converted grain silo that was stripped away to make a towering atrium. Inside, its vaulted cutouts evoke the feeling of a mighty cathedral. Outside, its soaring geodesic windows reflect the waters of the Atlantic Ocean, soft light transforming them into a shimmering wall of burnt orange at dusk. Zeitz MOCAA features work by artists from Angola to Zimbabwe—take the museum's self-guided audio tour for an expert insight, with commentary from artists, curators, architects, and designers.

Good to know: The galleries wrap around the central atrium for several floors, making it easy to walk through in a circular flow.

331

SOUTH AFRICA

Track the Big Five in Kruger National Park

The rain falls in sheets, filling the air with the smell of wet earth. Seemingly indifferent to the weather, a leopard sprawls on a fat branch of the tree in front of you, a half-eaten kudu carcass hanging casually beside it. It's a sensational sight, typical of the safari experience in South Africa's Kruger National Park, but it might not even be the best thing you've seen this morning. There was also the lioness slinking through the tall grass toward a dangerously unaware zebra, and the old bull elephant at the salt lick, using his mighty tusks to gouge into the nutrient-rich soil. Kruger is Big Five country, its open plains and mopane woodlands home not just to leopards, lions, and elephants, but also buffalo and white rhinos. This is one of the best places on the continent to see them all—and to celebrate with a sundowner as the last beams of daylight dip below the horizon.

Good to know: You can spot the Big Five in Kruger on a game drive, a walking safari, and even at the waterhole of your lodge.

WHERE ELSE TO SEE THE BIG FIVE

WAZA NATIONAL PARK, CAMEROON In the northern-most part of West Africa, this remote national park is home to several savanna animals.

MAJETE WILDLIFE RESERVE, MALAWI The Big Five prowl this rugged reserve of granite hills and river valleys, while 4WDs and boat safari tours pass through.

332

MAURITIUS

Hit the beach in Mauritius

Endless stretches of powder-white sands. Warm turquoise seas. Swaying palms and dreamy resorts. Mauritius's beaches are the stuff of storybooks. There's a patch of paradise for everyone, whether you want to kick back and relax or spend your days snorkeling and windsurfing. Start with the sunrise, catching its early-morning glow on an east-coast beach such as Belle Mare, one of the longest on the island. The wilder south has a rockier coastline, full of hidden inlets that are perfect for a picnic: laze on St. Félix and watch the waves crashing against the cliffs at Gris Gris. On the west coast, the sea at Le Morne is so clear you can make out its famous "underwater waterfall" (actually sand falling off an ocean shelf). This is a great spot for kite-surfing, while the protected beach at Flic and Flac, farther along, is perfect for swimming. Round off your tour with some snorkeling at Trou aux Biches, in the island's northwest, where the reef almost reaches the beach. Or just relish the sweet languor of relaxing in a hammock while the sun dips into the azure sea.

Good to know: For a taste of local life, visit the beach on a Sunday, when locals meet up with family and friends.

333

BOTSWANA

Glide through the Okavango Delta

The Okavango is the only major river in the world that doesn't reach the ocean. It rises in the jagged mountains of Angola and, thanks to a quirk of geology, eventually disappears without trace into the sands of the Kalahari Desert. En route, the river creates a dry-season delta in the northwest corner of Botswana that is a latticework of water channels and lagoons, a lifeline for elephants, hippos, and crocodiles. Smaller creatures enjoy the Okavango Delta's bounty too: herons and cranes patrol the waterways, and jewel-bright malachite kingfishers glimmer among the reeds. Settle into the hollow of a mokoro—a traditional canoe, poled from the back like a punt—for a frog's-eye view of this glittering wilderness. Once crafted from sausage trees, mokoros are now fiberglass, but this doesn't dim the romance. Your boatman will skillfully glide you through the water, with only the grunt of hippos and the swish of reeds against the mokoro's hull disturbing the silence.

Good to know: Most Okavango Delta lodges and camps offer mokoro trips during the seasonal floods (Jul–Sept).

SÃO TOMÉ AND PRÍNCIPE

Hike the rainforest trails of São Tomé and Príncipe

Set in the Gulf of Guinea, the twin-island nation of São Tomé and Príncipe is volcanic in origin and lush in the extreme. Hiking trails on both islands lead through tropical rainforest full of gushing waterfalls, thick ferns, rare orchids, and brightly colored birds—the islands are so rich in endemic species, including the dwarf ibis and the São Tomé grosbeak, the world's largest canary, that they are often referred to as the African Galápagos. Obô Natural Park, on São Tomé, is dominated by the volcanic finger of Pico Cão Grande, which towers above the trees and is a magnet for climbers. Príncipe, a UNESCO Biosphere Reserve in its entirety, is the focus of a groundbreaking eco-tourism initiative, where old plantation houses, known as *roças*, have been given a new lease on life as eco-lodges. Locals work as nature guides, leading hikes up Pico do Papagaio, birdwatching tours into the interior or afternoon trips to the island's golden beaches to watch turtle hatchlings making their first frantic forays for the safety of the sea.

Good to know: Eco-tourism company HBD runs Roça Sundy, Sundy Praia and Bom Bom on Príncipe and Omali on São Tomé.

334

REPUBLIC OF CONGO

Watch wildlife in Odzala-Kokoua National Park

Relatively few tourists have seen western lowland gorillas in the wild. Critically endangered, they're threatened by bushmeat poaching, disease, and oil-palm plantations. There's something very special, therefore, about the moment you catch your first glimpse of one, deep in the forests of Odzala-Kokoua National Park. All the effort to get here, to travel by air, vehicle, and on foot to the northern reaches of the Republic of Congo, near the border with Cameroon and the Central African Republic, simply melts away. It's an immense privilege to be in the presence of such rare and powerful creatures, eye to eye, and to be treated with gentle tolerance. Your precious time with them vanishes in a flash, but there are plenty of other wildlife wonders roaming the park. Odzala-Kokoua is also famous for its *baïs*, swampy clearings in the forest where you can spot antelope species like spiral-horned bongos and sitatunga, as well as giant forest hogs and forest elephants. Relatively few tourists have seen these in the wild, either.

Good to know: Kamba Africa offers trips to Odzala-Kokoua, including a stay at its lodge overlooking Lango Baï.

337

ZAMBIA AND ZIMBABWE

See Victoria Falls

At the Victoria Falls on the border of Zambia and Zimbabwe, the Zambezi River is transformed from a languid flow of water into a ferocious torrent that blasts down dark basalt cliff into a series of dramatic gorges below. A mist hangs above the water, the reason the falls are called Mosi Oa-Tunya in the local language, or "the smoke that thunders." The views from the Zimbabwe side showcase the falls in their panoramic finest, a 1-mile- (1.7-km-) wide stretch of white noise. Cross the Zambezi Bridge to the Zambian side for spray-in-your-face close-ups of the falls' tumultuous power. At the aptly named Knife-Edge Bridge, the water pours in torrents and a thick fog blankets the Eastern Cataract, Main Falls, and Boiling Pot, which blurs into white obscurity in the distance. Among the din are locals washing in the water, which they believe to hold healing powers and good-luck properties.

Good to know: The falls are at their most impressive from February to May, when the Zambezi is swollen by summer rains.

The Zambezi River is transformed from a languid flow of water into a ferocious torrent.

336

ZAMBIA

Spot leopards in South Luangwa

The bark of a baboon is the first sign. Then the sharp, snorting "cough" of an impala. Alarm bells ring in the animal world: a leopard is on the prowl. Taking a leaf out of both their books, you stop scanning the treetops for a glimpse of a black-tipped ear or an elegant, roseate-patterned flank and start listening instead. Is that rustling just the sound of the wind or the crunch of padded paws? Welcome to Zambia's South Luangwa National Park, where there are so many of these beautiful big cats that the area has become known as the Valley of the Leopard. With abundant fresh water, plenty of grazing savanna for prey, and thick groves of trees, South Luangwa provides an ideal habitat for a cat that hunts stealthily and stashes its kills aloft. Game drives set off each dawn and dusk in search of this bucket-list predator, or you can explore on foot with a trained tracker—just keep an ear out for those animal alerts.

Good to know: Safari operators in South Luangwa include The Bushcamp Company, which runs six lodges in the park.

MALAWI

Snorkel in the Lake of Stars

It is said that Lake Malawi owes its evocative nickname, the Lake of Stars, to the Scottish explorer David Livingstone, who was the first European to document this remarkable body of fresh water for Western science when he arrived on its shores in 1866. Livingstone was particularly struck by the lamplight of the villagers' fishing boats, glowing like constellations on the water after dark. These days, the locals have honed their fishing technique, instead using LED lights to attract fish into their nets by night. In many ways, however, life beside Lake Malawi remains profoundly traditional, with just a smattering of low-key tourist businesses dotted around the coast. While the sandy banks invite you to relax, it's worth pulling on a snorkel and mask. With more species of fish than any other lake in the world, including more than 700 different types of jauntily colored cichlid, the lake's waters are an inland aquarium.

Good to know: Good snorkeling spots include Monkey Bay and Mangochi. There's a PADI dive center at Nkhata Bay.

UGANDA

Hike the Rwenzori Mountains

Home to six of the highest mountains in Africa, the mist-shrouded Rwenzori are better known by their mythical moniker, the Mountains of the Moon, a term coined by the Greek explorer Diogenes when he stumbled upon their snow-capped peaks while searching for the source of the Nile River. Today, you can explore the mountains yourself on a hike up through hardwood forest, past towering bamboo, and across Afro-alpine moorlands peppered with lobelias; glaciers and jagged peaks provide the dramatic backdrop. Rwenzori red duiker, found nowhere else on earth, dart among the gigantic foliage. L'Hoest's monkeys scramble through the trees and forest elephants crunch all before them. The trails here are still largely off the beaten path, giving the illusion that you too have just stumbled upon these majestic mountains.

Good to know: It takes seven to eight days to summit the Rwenzori. Local operators include Rwenzori Trekking Services.

340

RWANDA

Go gorilla trekking in Rwanda

There are times when you have to pinch yourself to make sure you're not dreaming. Sitting stock-still among the thick foliage of Rwanda's Volcanoes National Park is a mountain gorilla. Rolling around on the ground nearby are a pair of fluffy adolescents, play-fighting with each other while their mothers look on. Other gorillas are gorging on bamboo shoots, looking at you intently with eyes eerily like a human's. The encounter feels near-sacred, and since you only get an hour with them, you stay rooted to the spot, lest a twig snap beneath your boots, and speak only in whispers, afraid to break the spell and scare them off. Habituated over time, the gorillas can get so close that their thick fur brushes against your skin. There are only around 1,000 mountain gorillas left in the wild, so the rule is to stay at least 20 ft (6 m) away from them, to avoid spreading diseases—you don't need telling twice when the troop includes 400-lb (180-kg) silverbacks among their number. These males are so immense you'll pinch yourself again.

Good to know: Plan your trip in September to attend the Kwita Izina ceremony where newborn gorillas are named.

341

TANZANIA

Get spicy on Zanzibar

Is there anywhere in Africa that's more evocative than Zanzibar? The name conjures up a paradise of swaying palm trees, perfumed courtyards, and dhows with billowing sails. Even before you catch your first whiff of spices on the warm sea breeze, you'll be half-dizzy with the sheer seductiveness of it all. Zanzibar's tropical climate and rich soil provide the perfect conditions for cultivating spice plants, and the archipelago has been a focal part of the spice trade for more than 500 years. Today, some of the island's *shambas* (small plantations) offer tours, with a guide who will cajole you into stroking, smelling, and sampling specialties like cardamom pods, cinnamon bark, cumin seeds, ginger rhizomes, and the pods of the lipstick bush, which contain a scarlet dye. Zanzibar's signature spice, however, is the clove—dried myrtle bud— which has been prized for centuries. One sniff and you're transported to a traditional Christmas, and the scent of mulled wine and spiced oranges.

Good to know: Plantation visits last three to four hours and can be booked through any of Zanzibar's hotels.

TANZANIA

Climb Kilimanjaro

Rising above the coffee and tea plantations of equatorial Arusha, Kilimanjaro teases with glimpses of snowy peaks peeping through tangled clouds. Its name is a combination of words in the local Swahili and Chagga languages, which together mean Mountain of Whiteness, and its jagged summit calls adventurers like a shining beacon. Climbers who make it to the top, 19,300 ft (5,895 m) above sea level, are rewarded with the well-earned bragging rights of having conquered Africa's highest peak. Wildlife mills through the lush rainforest on the lower slopes, but most trekkers push through here quickly, their sights set higher. There's no need for complicated gear or mastering techniques, although getting to the top is no mean feat. You can climb for as little as five days, but allowing more time will help prevent altitude sickness—Kilimanjaro has subdued plenty of adventurers who tried to tame it.

Good to know: June is the clearest month for a climb, but is also wet, windy, and the coldest time of the year.

> Flamingos paint the shoreline of Lake Magadi in brushstrokes of blush pink and elephants graze among the acacia woodlands that dot the crater floor.

TANZANIA

See Ngorongoro Crater

Standing on the edge of the Ngorongoro Crater, its patchwork of habitats laid out before you thousands of yards below, feels like staring into a microcosm of East Africa. Everything that makes the region such a great safari destination is here. Flamingos paint the shoreline of Lake Magadi in brushstrokes of blush pink, hippos wallow around the scenic Ngoitoktok Springs, elephants graze among the acacia woodlands that dot the crater floor, and lions slink through its open grasslands on the hunt for impala and zebra. Venturing down into the caldera, you'll be struck by the sheer density of wildlife. The abundance of game is largely thanks to the wide availability of water, in swamps and permanent streams fed by run-off from the crater-rim forests. And to the fact that these animals are, for all intents and purposes, trapped within the crater's walls.

Good to know: You can easily combine Ngorongoro Crater with a trip to the Serengeti National Park for varied game viewing.

344

KENYA

Witness the Great Migration

Good things come to those who wait. Sitting in your jeep, parked up on the edge of the Mara River on the border between Kenya and Tanzania, you pass the time with your eyes glued to the opposite side of the river. Kicking up clouds of baked-earth dust, a mega herd of some 1,000 wildebeest have gathered, each one also waiting. Who will be the first to take the plunge, to lead the others to greener pastures, or to death? Between July and November each year, up to two million wildebeest migrate in a clockwise direction across the Serengeti-Mara ecosystem (in Tanzania and Kenya) to graze and calve. Watching them cross the Mara is the main draw, a loose column of half-swimming, half-jumping animals, hooves flailing as they run the gauntlet of crocodiles lurking in the muddy water. It's drama on an epic scale. Exhausted, the herd scrambles up the bank to continue their journey across the plains. Hidden in the tall grass ahead lie more predators, lions this time, watching, waiting.

Good to know: Wildebeest cross the Mara River around late July to August and again from late October to early November.

345

KENYA

Visit Nairobi National Park

Driving around the sequestered folds of Nairobi National Park, watching impalas drinking at a waterhole, you could be forgiven for thinking you were in the middle of the African bush. But then the Kenyan capital's office blocks loom up in the background and you remember you're just a few minutes' drive from downtown Nairobi. This is the only national park in the world within a city, where tales of lions straying outside the park and causing Monday morning traffic jams are not as uncommon as you might think. The park is home to four of the Big Five: as well as lions, you can also spot leopards, buffalo, and a dense population of black rhinos. Only elephants are missing. There are a few chic lodgings within the park, so you can fall asleep to the sound of hippos grunting outside your tent—and the low hum of distant traffic navigating the city's streets.

Good to know: Bring a packed lunch, because there are picnic sites and observation points where you can stretch your legs.

346

MADAGASCAR

Watch lemurs leap through the trees

Madagascar is an island of wonderful wildlife oddities, where miniature weevils have necks shaped like giraffes, chameleons come in all colors of the rainbow, and 99 percent of the 300 frog species are found nowhere else on earth. But above all, it's the lemurs, with their breathtaking agility and teddy-bear charm, that everyone wants to see. There are over 110 species of lemur, all endemic to the island and ranging in size, shape, and appearance, from the tiny Madame Berthe's mouse lemur, which can fit in the palm of your hand, to the honey-hued golden bamboo lemur, which was only discovered in 1986. Venture out after dark to look for nocturnal lemurs, directing your flashlight to avoid disturbing them too much, or scan the treetops during daylight. Almost every pocket of trees has its own specialties, from the balletic sifakas of the spiny forest to the indris, the largest lemurs of all, whose whooping, wailing calls ring out across the rainforest canopy.

Good to know: You'll spot more lemurs with a local naturalist guide, who can recognize, and mimic, their calls.

347

EGYPT

Cruise along the Nile

"To travel the Nile is to know the real Egypt," quips every local guide in Luxor, and they're right. Flowing down from Lake Victoria to the Mediterranean, the world's longest river is imbued with myth and legend. Cleopatra sailed it with Julius Caesar, aboard the pleasure barge *Thalamegos*; a young Florence Nightingale cruised its waters; and Agatha Christie turned her travels on the steamship *Sudan* in 1937 into the bestseller *Death on the Nile*. Book passage aboard a traditional hardwood *dahabiya* and drift the 143 miles (230 km) from Luxor to Aswan. The boat's barefoot crew handle the linen sails, so you're free to watch life unfold along the river banks and marvel at the molten sunsets. You'll stop at island villages farming alfalfa, explore the royal quarry of Gebel-el-Silsila—whose sandstone built the statues and sphinxes of Luxor and Karnak—and visit temples such as Kom-Ombo and Philae, where you can see the last hieroglyphs ever carved.

Good to know: Wild Frontiers offers a ten-day Slow Boat to Aswan tour. Historic sites are busy in December and January.

348

EGYPT

Climb Mount Sinai

Mount Sinai is perhaps the holy book's most famous mountain. And the views from the top at sunrise are truly biblical.

Believed to be the location where God delivered the Ten Commandments to Moses, Mount Sinai is perhaps the holy book's most famous mountain. And the views from the top at sunrise are truly biblical. Climbing up, you'll pass 6th-century St. Catherine's Monastery, where God appeared to Moses in the form of a burning bush. Beyond here, the trail splits in two. The Camel Path has a gentle gradient along a wide path; the Steps of Repentance follows a serpentine route up 3,750 steps carved by monks—it offers better views, but not all operators will let you use it. There are Bedouin tents en route for tea and a breather, and camels for those who'd prefer to save their puff for when the trails converge for the final 750 steps to the summit. At the top lie the ruins of a 16th-century church and a small mosque that's still in use, but all eyes—and cameras—will be trained on the panorama of russet red, as the glowing sun spills over the horizon.

Good to know: Hiring a Bedouin guide is mandatory. Carry your passport at all times—it's required for the trail checkpoints.

EGYPT

See the Pyramids of Giza

Few structures capture our collective imagination quite so much as the great Pyramids of Giza, the last remaining Ancient Wonder of the World. Like three wise men, the UNESCO-listed pyramids of Khufu, Khafre, and Menkaure—named after the kings for whom they were built—stand 8 miles (13 km) southwest of the chaotic capital of Cairo. To this day, they are still clinging on to their secrets. Quite how the two million bricks that it took to make each pyramid, each one of which weighed as much as an elephant, were arranged by the tens of thousands of paid workers (not enslaved people, as was originally thought) is still a mystery. And for what reason the pyramids were even built in the first place is also still widely debated. They're generally believed to be the burial sites for ancient Egypt's pharaohs, but alternative theories abound. Venture inside and decide for yourself.

Good to know: The pyramids are best visited during the Egyptian winter (Nov–Feb) when temperatures are milder.

351
EGYPT

Stroll around Alexandria

Although a far cry from the pyramids and temples that Egypt is famous for, Alexandria, the most populous city on the Mediterranean coast, is steeped in ancient history. It was founded by Alexander the Great in 331 BCE, and as you walk along the corniche, between sea and skyline, it's easy to picture sailing vessels of centuries past moored off Qaitbay Fort. The fort was built in 1480 on (and from) the ruins of the Lighthouse of Alexandria, one of the Seven Wonders of the Ancient World. A romantic stroll from here to the far side of the Eastern Harbor will take you to the soaring Biblioteca Alexandrina, Egypt's 21st-century answer to the long-lost Great Library of Alexandria. On the way, you'll pass mosques, elegant prewar hotels, century-old cafés, and the dignified, neo-Renaissance-style French consulate. Ramble inland to find St. Mark's Coptic Orthodox Cathedral and the Eliyahu Hanavi Synagogue, exquisite reminders of the city's multi-religious, multicultural, and very cosmopolitan past.

Good to know: Aside from walking, you can also get around Alexandria on the city's electric trams.

350
EGYPT

Camp in the White Desert

As you drive deeper and deeper into Egypt's vast Western Desert, the landscape makes a quite extraordinary transformation. Gone are the sun-bleached rocks and the palm-strung oases, and in their stead spreads the Sahara el Beyda—or White Desert National Park—a haunting lunar landscape of wind-whittled rocks. Submerged by sea some 60 million years ago, its leftover chalk and limestone rocks have been eroded over the millennia into inselbergs so zany in shape that they resemble an open-air modern-art gallery. Camping among such strange formations as Mushroom Rock and Crystal Mountain is an otherworldly experience and offers the chance to spot jackals, fennec foxes, and the endangered Rhim gazelle in the blissful serenity of sunset and sunrise.

Good to know: The Western Desert is best explored on a tour from al-Bawiti, 227 miles (365 km) southwest of Cairo.

353

EGYPT

Immerse yourself in ancient Egypt

The gem-encrusted treasures of King Tutankhamen cause an international stir every time a small part of the collection is allowed out of Egypt. And that's without the Boy King's iconic funerary mask, which is too fragile to travel. If you dream of peering into its quartz and obsidian eyes—and thus deep into the mysteries of Egypt's 18th pharaonic dynasty—you'll have to travel to Cairo. Here, behind a glass case in the capital's Egyptian Museum in Cairo, sits the gilded mask, created by master craftsmen some 33 centuries ago and displayed alongside King Tut's gleaming jewelry, furniture, and coffin. The world-famous museum, located just off downtown's Tahrir Square, is crammed with tens of thousands of other glories, ranging from granite royal statues to the preserved mummies of some of ancient Egypt's most powerful pharaohs. The mask will move, along with all 5,000 of Tutankhamen's treasures, to the Grand Egyptian Museum, which is scheduled to finally open near the Pyramids of Giza some time in 2024.

Good to know: The Grand Egyptian Museum's opening has been continuously delayed; check the website for the latest.

352

EGYPT

Learn to dive in Dahab

Few places on earth can match the Red Sea for its marine biodiversity, a spectacular array of underwater life that includes more than 200 species of coral and more than 1,200 species of fish. The gin-clear waters here allow for greater visibility than at many other dive destinations. The former Bedouin fishing village of Dahab offers easy access to a variety of well-preserved reef sites, from swim troughs and tunnels to colorful coral gardens and canyons. This is one of the best places in the Red Sea to learn to dive: PADI courses are affordable and the majority of dives start from the shoreline, so there's no need to master rolling backward off a boat. Dive locations include Eel Garden, Tiger Reef, Bannerfish Bay, and the Blue Hole, Egypt's most famous dive site, which is brimming with more underwater action than *The Little Mermaid*.

Good to know: PADI offers a range of open water and advanced open water training courses in Dahab.

> Few places on earth can match the Red Sea for its marine biodiversity, a spectacular array of underwater life that includes more than 200 species of coral and more than 1,200 species of fish.

354

JORDAN

Float in the Dead Sea

Super-saturated with minerals, the water feels thick and almost oily as you slowly wade into the Dead Sea. As the warm water rises up around your chest, your feet detach from the sandy floor and you find yourself floating in the syrupy slick. Lean back for the strange sensation of having your head, arms, and feet in the air all at the same time. You're being buoyed by incredibly high concentrations of salt— around ten times that of normal seawater—mixed with magnesium, potassium, chlorine, bromine, and so many other minerals that immersing yourself in the waters of the Dead Sea is a recognized medical treatment for skin diseases and joint disorders. Forming a natural border between Jordan, Israel, and the Palestinian Territories, the Dead Sea lies at 1,411 ft (430 m) below sea level, the lowest point on earth. The thick air here has the world's highest concentration of oxygen, its density helping protect against sunburn. Hotels along the shoreline offer bathing areas and saltwater spa treatments—and a heavy dose of blissful relaxation.

Good to know: Due to its high salt concentration, you should only spend around 20 minutes in the Dead Sea at any one time.

355

JORDAN

Stay overnight in the Wadi Rum desert

In the 1962 film *Lawrence of Arabia*, Lawrence (Peter O'Toole) is asked what attracts him to the desert. His response is brief, crisp, and memorable: "It's clean." Scoured by the sun and khamsin winds, the breathtaking desert panoramas that costar with O'Toole in that World War I epic were filmed in Wadi Rum. They are as magical and magnificent today as they have been for countless generations of Bedouin. In recent decades, those same desert nomads, renowned as much for their traditional Arab hospitality as for their intimate knowledge of the landscape, have moved into ecotourism, hosting visitors in everything from goat-hair tents to glamping domes. Your tour of the area's reddish bluffs, sand dunes, gorges, and rock carvings begins with traditional Arab coffee and a delicious Bedouin breakfast and ends with a BBQ over a roaring fire. After the sun goes down, gaze up at the heavens and you'll see the dazzling brushstrokes of the Milky Way twinkling across the desert sky.

Good to know: Hire a Bedouin guide with a jeep to tour the area or even camp out in the desert.

356

JORDAN

Visit Petra

You're walking through a narrowing gorge whose sandstone walls are so high they block out the sky. You follow yet another bend in the rock when suddenly, rising before you, stands a sight that will literally stop you in your tracks: a Hellenistic-style colonnaded facade emerging from the cliff face opposite. Known as Al-Khazneh (the Treasury)—though it's actually the mausoleum of a king—the columns, pediments, statues, and funerary urn of this etched work of art were carved nearly two millennia ago by the Nabataeans. The Treasury served as the spectacular introduction to their capital, the "rose-red city half as old as time" as the English writer John Burgon famously put it. A short walk through the main area of wadis and hills takes you to yet more structures carved into the landscape, including the so-called Monastery (another tomb), the 8,500-seat Theater, and the hilltop High Place of Sacrifice. At almost every turn, an astonishing panorama of desert bluffs unfolds, revealing more secrets hidden from the world for a thousand years.

Good to know: The adjacent town of Wadi Musa has a selection of excellent hotels and restaurants.

357

UAE

Go to the top of the Burj Khalifa

Big is definitely beautiful in Dubai. Towering some 2,717 ft (828 m) above the emirate, and with more than 160 floors, the Burj Khalifa is superlative in almost every sense—as well as holding the world record for the tallest building, and the most number of floors, it also holds records for, among others, the highest occupied floor and the elevator with the longest travel distance. It even holds the world record for holding the most world records. Designed to resemble a flower, the Burj Khalifa is home to a hotel, residences, and offices, though most visitors are here for the observation decks, on levels 124, 125, and 148, all of which allow guests to feel the thrill of being in, you guessed it, the world's fastest double-deck elevators.

Good to know: Why stop at level 148? The Lounge serves coffee and light bites on levels 152, 153, and 154.

WHERE ELSE TO FIND THE TALLEST BUILDINGS

MERDEKA 118, MALAYSIA

Kuala Lumpur is home to the world's second tallest tower, Merdeka 118, a 118-level building at 2,227 ft (697 m). On levels 115 and 116 you'll find Southeast Asia's highest observation deck.

SHANGHAI TOWER, CHINA

Shanghai's architectural symbol stands at a dizzying 128 stories, making it the tallest building in Asia. Most visitors head straight to the 118th floor to the Top of Shanghai Observatory, the world's second-highest deck after the Burj Khalifa.

LOTTE WORLD TOWER, SOUTH KOREA

Seoul's 1,821-ft (555-m) and 123-story building is the sixth-tallest tower in the world, and is home to a hotel, concert hall, shops, and a viewing platform, as well as apartments.

358

UAE

Explore historic Al Fahidi

Dubai might appear to be a thoroughly 21st-century city, but among the gleaming skyscrapers that spike the skyline there are vestiges of the original fishing village that existed here in the 1800s. Located in the heart of Old Dubai, on the banks of Dubai Creek, the winding alleyways of Al Fahidi Historical Neighborhood are home to some of the best-preserved buildings in the whole of the emirate. Most striking are the district's traditional sand-stone wind towers, or *barjeel*, which protrude from the houses like chimneys. They acted like early air-conditioning units, funneling cool air into the building and hot air out, lowering the interior temperature by around 50°F (10°C). One of the wind towers has been beautifully restored and now houses the Sheikh Mohammed bin Rashid Al Maktoum Center for Cultural Understanding (SMCCU), where you can enjoy a traditional Emirati meal while chatting with the center's host about life in the emirate. Other houses stage demonstrations by local craftspeople, their intricate work with palm fronds and embroidery a far cry from the glitz of downtown Dubai.

Good to know: You can book breakfast, lunch, dinner, or a Fuala (Emirati afternoon tea) at the SMCCU. Meals last 1½ hours.

UAE

Get cultural at the Louvre Abu Dhabi

A collaboration between France and the United Arab Emirates, the Louvre Abu Dhabi is the Arab world's first universal museum. Its permanent collection consists of pieces loaned from the original Louvre in Paris, the Musée d'Orsay, and other museums across France, a priceless ensemble of art that ranges from figurines from ancient Egypt to works of contemporary art. Alongside these, rotating exhibitions explore concepts such as the influence of Islamic art on 20th-century jewelery design. Set on the western tip of Saadiyat Island, the museum itself is a work of art. Designed by Pritzker Prize–winning architect Jean Nouvel, it takes inspiration from traditional Arabic architecture, the flattened dome acting as a protective parasol to the museum's medina-like white buildings, its layered steel reflecting the shimmering waters of the Arabian Gulf.

Good to know: You can get superb views of the Louvre Abu Dhabi by taking a guided kayak tour around the museum.

OMAN

Go on a desert safari

Located on the Arabian Peninsula, Oman's natural beauty ranges from hulking baobab trees to rugged, fjord-like inlets. But it's the vast sand seas covering much of the country that really capture the imagination. Easily reachable from the capital, Muscat, the Wahiba Sands (known as the Sahara of Arabia) is the desert of *One Thousand and One Nights*, a terra-cotta landscape of shifting dunes that stretches more than 3,850 sq miles (10,000 sq km). Thrilling desert safaris replace lions and leopards with camels and camping in Bedouin tents, and feature sunrise or sunset treks with a local guide—the region is named for the local Bani Wahiba tribe. Most Omani safaris feature a few days in the desert as part of a wider trip around the country, which also tends to include some time exploring the villages of Jebel Akhdar, swimming in jade-colored wadis, exploring the lively souks of Nizwa, and touring the ruins of the World Heritage–listed Lost City of Ubar in the Rub Al Khali, or Empty Quarter, an even greater expanse of desert than the Wahiba Sands.

Good to know: Multi-night Omani safaris are in a 4WD, departing from Muscat.

ASIA

UZBEKISTAN

See the incredible Registan Square

Not many places in the world conjure up such wanderlust as Samarkand, a city located along the route of the famous Silk Road. And in the epicenter of this ancient city is its stunning Registan Square, for which it's best known. Walk up the steps leading to the square and you'll be confronted by a trio of huge, sturdy *madrasahs*, colleges to study religion and other subjects. The facades of these structures line three edges of the square, each one tall and intricately decorated with colorful tiling typical of Islamic art. The oldest of the three is the 15th-century Ulugh Beg Madrasah, while the Sher-Dor Madrasah and the Tilya-Kori Madrasah in the middle both date back to the 17th century. It's easy to lose track of time as you peer closer at the ornate *muqarnas*, decorative niches above the entrances of the buildings, trying to take in all of the details. And, while the old city surrounds the square on every side, all that can be seen beyond the distinctive turquoise domes is an endless stretch of sky—an ideal setting for contemplation.

Good to know: The hottest days of the year are in July, so aim to visit at any other time.

UZBEKISTAN

Marvel at Samarkand's Shah-i-Zinda

In the north of the city of Samarkand lies a huge and intricate necropolis known as Shah-i-Zinda. A medley of turquoise domes and stunning blue tile-work facades, this site is made to impress. What once began as a Zoroastrian temple, part of ancient Persia, was subsequently turned into a mosque in the 7th century, before evolving from the 11th century into the memorial complex that stands here today. With such a changeable history, the mausoleums, mosques, and other structures that make up the complex are an embodiment of the Silk Road's very essence. There are Central Asian and Chinese motifs, turquoise and blue hues reminiscent of ancient Persia, and the ornate tile-work and geometric patterns of Islamic art traditions. The great significance of this site lies in its name: it means "the living king" in Persian, linking it to the legend of Kusam ibn Abbas whose final resting place is thought to be here. Walk around the tranquil space and take in the rich history it encompasses.

Good to know: The best time to visit Shah-i-Zinda is just after opening, in order to catch the site at its calmest.

363

PAKISTAN

Tuck into a plate of biryani

Fragrant steam fills your nose, pillowy piles of yellow rice hit your tongue, spiced meat awakens your taste buds … in Pakistan, biryani is not just a meal, it's a multisensory experience. This rice-based treat is India's most popular dish, but you haven't tried the best until you've eaten it in Pakistan. The edible art form was introduced during the Mughal Empire in the 16th century and has evolved into many regional varieties, including the popular Sindhi biryani and Karachi biryani. Rice is layered with meat tenderized to perfection by an intoxicating marinade of yogurts, spices, and herbs. A chef's unique stamp lies in the blend of spices they choose to infuse their dish with—sometimes cardamom, cloves, bay leaves; a touch of cumin, coriander, and turmeric; and often ginger, garlic, and a good shake of chili powder. For the full experience, forgo a fork or spoon and instead bunch the rice together with your fingers and scoop it into your mouth. Are your taste buds tingling yet?

Good to know: Madni Biryani is billed as the best biryani restaurant in Karachi (open daily, no reservations).

364

INDIA

Admire the Golden Temple

While the popular name for Harmandir Sahib, the Golden Temple, leaves little to the imagination, it still doesn't prepare visitors for what awaits them in Amritsar. This gurdwara is the spiritual heart of Sikhism and, as you approach from the causeway, known as the guru's bridge, verses from the sacred Guru Granth Sahib ring out across the water. Your first glimpse of the temple is its gilded heights reflected in the Pool of Nectar below it. Then, there it is. As you take it in, all the eye can see is gold: in fact, a reputed half-ton of gold leaf glitters across its central dome alone. First built some four and a half centuries ago, the site has suffered assaults by Afghan invaders and other destructive forces, yet retains a serenity ruffled only when free meals cooked up in the community kitchen are dished out to the 100,000 daily visitors of all nationalities, backgrounds, and faiths. Plan to visit in time for the afternoon golden hour and you'll really get to see the temple shine.

Good to know: Admission is free, but visitors must remove shoes and cover their heads before entering.

WHERE ELSE TO GO ON AN EPIC TRAIN JOURNEY

365

INDIA

Ride the Palace on Wheels

Short of a moat and a peacock, there's little to distinguish this luxury tourist train from the opulent monuments it visits on its tour of northwest India. Designed to evoke the golden age of the princely places through which it travels, the lavish decor of the *Palace on Wheels'* chambers, restaurants, and bars across its 14 cars is matched by the effortless service and gastronomy. But however glamorous it may all be, the real treasures are to be found at each carefully curated stop. On the eight-day odyssey through Rajasthan from India's capital, Delhi, you'll explore the exquisite palaces of lakeside Udaipur and the Pink City, Jaipur; gaze up at the imposing walls of fairytale forts in Chittorgarh, Jodhpur, and desert-encircled Jaisalmer; track tigers in Ranthambore National Park; and be dazzled by the birdlife of Keoladeo National Park. If you're going to have one lavish experience on your bucket list, this is it.

Good to know: Fares are lowest in September and April, the first and last months of the season.

CALIFORNIA ZEPHYR
Slicing through the landscapes of the American West, this train route links Chicago and San Francisco by way of the awe-inspiring Colorado Rockies and the snow-capped High Sierras. Opened in 1869, it was the first transcontinental railroad in the US.

QINGHAI-TIBET RAILWAY, CHINA
Crossing some of the most beautiful but unforgiving terrain on earth, the world's highest train route runs for 1,215 miles (1,956 km) from China's Qinghai province over the semi-frozen Tibetan Plateau and up into the soaring Himalayas.

SERRA VERDE EXPRESS, BRAZIL
Inaugurated in 1884, this route spans what was once inaccessible terrain. While chugging through tropical forest hillsides, you'll see parrots, clusters of bromeliad plants, and viewpoints by plunging gorges.

INDIA

Awe at Humayun's Tomb

It all began with a broken heart. When the Mughal Empress Bega Begum lost her husband, Emperor Humayun, in 1556, she dedicated her life to giving him an unmatched final resting place. And she succeeded. The grounds alone were made to impress, with 25 acres (10 ha) of waterways, pools, and many fountains set within a grand quadrilateral *charbagh* design, based on a description of paradise in the Qur'an. In the middle of it all stands the focal point on a raised platform: India's first garden tomb, a Mughal masterpiece made of red sandstone and marble, topped with a glorious dome. The interior showcases exquisite artistry, with stone latticework creating striking patterns of sunlight around the solitary sarcophagus placed at the center. As well as Humayun, the tomb is also the resting place of more than 150 relatives of the imperial family. A testament to their union, the empress's grief-driven architectural project led to one of the most impressive tombs in the region being built, paving the way for the royal mausoleums that followed.

Good to know: A guided tour will deepen your appreciation of the history and symbolism throughout the site.

366

INDIA

See the Lotus Temple

Upon seeing the Lotus Temple for the first time, you'd be forgiven for thinking it was sitting afloat the surrounding lawns and unfurling before your eyes. This huge, multi-award-winning Bahá'í temple—one of just seven around the world—is clad with 108,000 sq ft (10,000 sq m) of the same Greek marble as the Parthenon, took a decade to build, and receives 10,000 visitors a day, making it one of the most-visited religious sites on Earth. The lotus was constructed with three layers of nine petals, in keeping with the Bahá'í faith's reverence of the number nine, while nine pools surround the lotus to represent the flower's leaves and help keep the building cool. Unlike other places of worship, there are no icons, statues, or pictures inside, and the temple is open to all faiths. Like a true flower, the color of its petals is changing as the New Delhi air pollution takes effect, but its beauty still shines through.

Good to know: Followers of all faiths can attend daily 15-minute services (at 10 a.m., noon, 3 p.m., and 5 p.m.) in the auditorium.

369

INDIA

Take part in Diwali festivities

For five nights each fall, regions across India are transformed into twinkling constellations for Diwali. Homes and Hindu temples are decorated with candles, lanterns, and clay oil lamps called *diyas*, usually placed somewhere they can be seen from the outside. Now known as the festival of lights, Diwali was originally a Hindu celebration marking the end of the summer harvest and highlighting key events in epic myths, which vary by region. Today, Hindus, Jains, Sikhs, and Buddhists all take part. Watch where you step during this period: decorating pavements and doorways are gorgeous *rangoli*, rainbow-hued patterns and detailed designs that are lovingly created in colored powders, often surrounding candles and lamps. Each day of Diwali brings a different focus, but the events reach a crescendo on the third evening. On the night of the new moon, many devotees pray to the Hindu goddess Lakshmi for blessings, fueling up for further carousing and sharing traditional *mithai* (sweets). Let yourself get swept up in the jubilant atmosphere of it all, especially when a glorious night of fireworks lights up the night sky.

Good to know: Diwali falls on the full moon of Kartik, the eighth Hindu month, in October or November.

368

INDIA

Roam the Valley of Flowers

Orchids, marigolds, daisies, primulas, poppies, anemones—during the summer months, from July to September, all these blooms and countless more carpet the meadows of the Valley of Flowers National Park. Tucked away in the folds of the Himalayas in far northern India, this spectacular spot flanking the Pushpawati River in Uttarakhand province first became known to the outside world as recently as 1931. Having become lost during an expedition, British mountaineer Frank S. Smythe and his party stumbled upon the valley, and coined its evocative name. Now protected as a national park, the lush slopes of the Valley of Flowers harbor more than 600 floral species—many of them not seen anywhere else on Earth—plus rare animals including the gray langur, the Himalayan monal, and even the evasive snow leopard. Even more elusive are the mythical fairies who are said to protect the valley's enchanting beauty—who knows what you'll spot as you frolic through the flowers.

Good to know: The valley is accessible only by trekking from the road at Govindghat, via Ghangaria village.

The lush slopes of the Valley of Flowers harbor more than 600 floral species—many of them not seen anywhere else on Earth.

371

INDIA

Experience the colors of Holi

When choosing your outfit for India's most colorful festival, you could don your oldest clothes that you'd be happy to part with—they're going to be almost destroyed, anyway—or do as many locals do and dress all in white, creating a blank canvas for the millions of would-be Jackson Pollocks preparing to fling *gulal* (colored powders) and water at all and sundry. During Holi, the Festival of Colors, towns and villages across northern India erupt in a huge kaleidoscope of chaos, streets teeming with Hindu devotees celebrating the triumph of good over evil in the most flamboyant way possible. Each hue has meaning, of course: red dye symbolizes love and fertility; green represents new beginnings; and blue is the color of Lord Krishna, the deity whose eternal love for Radha is a focus of the festival. The revelry begins on the night of Holika Dahan, when blazing bonfires recall the demise of an evil demon, before mayhem ensues the next day. Munch on traditional Holi *gujiya*, fried parcels packed with spiced nuts and dried fruits, before getting sucked back into this rainbow riot.

Good to know: Holi is celebrated on the last full moon in the lunar month of Phalguna, usually in March.

370

INDIA

See the Taj Mahal

Unmissable, unmistakable, and undeniably beautiful, the great Taj Mahal is visited by millions each year. First and foremost a symbol of love, the mausoleum was built by the Mughal Emperor Shah Jahan for his favorite wife, Mumtaz Mahal. It took more than 20,000 laborers and craftspeople 17 years to build the sublime garden-tomb, which was completed in 1648. Even from afar, its curved domes and looming minarets are a marvel of Mughal architecture. The white marble absorbs and transforms in the light— a rosy pink in the dawn, white and pristine in the noon sun, and ethereal and ghostly in the moon's diffused beams. Then, when you see it up close, you really get to take in the artistry of it all: the swirling green floral patterns embedded into the stonework, made with jade, crystal, turquoise, and lapis; intricate marble latticework alongside Quranic verse; and delicate flowers carved into white marble. It's a structure you may think you know, but nothing compares to seeing the details of the Taj Mahal for yourself.

Good to know: Capturing that photograph of you, your loved one, and the temple is possible—just arrive at opening time, 6 a.m.

INDIA

Soak up the scenes along the Ganges

Emerging from the Himalayas and flowing across northern India into the Bay of Bengal, the Ganges is more than just a river. Many locals have made their homes along the banks of this mighty river, while others travel from farther afield to bathe in its waters. Seen as sacred, the river is of great importance for Hindus, who are attracted in their tens of millions each year to receive forgiveness for their sins and achieve salvation. In Varanasi, sets of steps leading down to the banks, called *ghats*, are busy with people washing clothes and performing religious rituals. The river is believed to have great healing properties for those who are sick (although it's known to be polluted) and is considered one of the most favorable places for Hindus to die and be cremated, with around 100,000 bodies cremated by the river every year. The best way to take in riverside activity while taking care not to disrupt ceremonies or the daily lives of local people is by booking a sunrise or sunset boat tour led by a local.

Good to know: The most popular city from which to see the Ganges is Varanasi.

> **The river is of great importance for Hindus, who are attracted in their tens of millions each year in order to receive forgiveness for their sins and achieve salvation.**

SRI LANKA

See the Temple of the Tooth

According to legend, Princess Hemamali wrapped the Buddha's left canine in her hair and smuggled it out of India to Sri Lanka. Safeguarding this sacred relic became the duty of the royal family and, ever since, it's been housed in the Temple of the Tooth, or Sri Dalada Maligawa. The temple shines white like a polished molar itself, at the center of Kandy's lakeside royal palace complex. Forever entombed in a series of seven jewel-encrusted golden caskets, the tooth is symbolically bathed every Wednesday during Nanumura Mangallaya. A replica casket is placed in front of a mirror, which is bathed with fragrant flowers and herbs while poems are recited. Make an offering of incense or a tealight in the courtyard outside as you leave, taking in the spiritual atmosphere of this temple.

Good to know: Aim to arrive in time for the 9:30 a.m. *puja*, when drummers in Kandyan attire perform.

374

SRI LANKA

Take a train through the Hill Country

There are few things that withstand a "world's most beautiful" moniker, but the train journey that runs through Sri Lanka's Hill Country pulls it off. This is a region of mist-shrouded mountains, rolling hillsides carpeted with lush green tea plantations, and rushing waterfalls—and there's no better way to see it than from the window of a train from Kandy to Ella. The most memorable section of this seven-hour route is at the highest point of the line, a four-hour stretch from Hatton to Ella. As the train grinds patiently upward, the epic "Ella Gap" panorama comes into view, framing the valleys between Ella's mist-shrouded mountains. But, really, every second offers up a new highlight, from the quaint stations complete with original hand-painted signs that punctuate the trip to the swathe of bright green tea bushes that creep up impossible gradients. Buy a snack from one of the roving hawkers visiting the cars and settle in for the journey of a lifetime.

Good to know: Reserve seats as far in advance as possible via the official website.

375

SRI LANKA

Ascend Adam's Peak

Adam's Peak, Sri Lanka's fourth-tallest mountain, has long attracted pilgrimages to its summit. It's here that you'll find Sri Pada, or Sacred Footprint. Buddhists believed this to be the footprint of Buddha, Hindus the imprint of Shiva, and Christians and Muslims the mark made when Adam first stepped out of Eden. To nonbelievers, the trek up to the summit is one of the best hikes in the region. No matter your beliefs, set off in the early hours of the morning from the town of Dalhousie, in the Central Province, to make your own way up. You may find yourself in the company of pilgrims, some dressed all in white, some walking barefoot. As you ascend, a string of delicate lights zig-zag their way up the mountainside like fireflies. From the summit, gaze on in awe as embers of light illuminate the often mist-shrouded valley below. Regardless of whose footprints you're walking in, the stunning views from the peak are enough to stir any soul.

Good to know: There are six routes to the top, and the most popular is the short-and-steep 3-mile (5-km) Hatton trail.

SRI LANKA

Explore the ancient rock fortress of Sigiriya

This is a sight that defies belief. Rising abruptly from the forest below, Sigiriya is a 5th-century palace, complete with gardens and reservoir, perched atop a nearly 660-ft- (200-m-) high column of volcanic rock. One of Asia's earliest royal cities, it served as the capital for King Kashyapa I, and was so ethereal that rumors of it being guarded by an army of wasp "soldiers" and a crocodile-infested moat were easily believed. It was dubbed the "Lion Rock," because to enter, visitors had to ascend a staircase that passed through the jaws of a stone-carved lion. Following the same staircase up the rock face, you'll reach the flat top, where crumbling terraces of brick foundations mark the last vestiges of this fortress in the sky, overlooking scenery worthy of Shangri-La: rice paddies and a pewter lake that melt into an amphitheater of silhouetted hills.

Good to know: Visit early to avoid the heaviest crowds and climb while the sun is less fierce.

 376

SRI LANKA

Head inside the Rangiri Dambulla cave temples

Slip off your sandals and feel the cool stones beneath your feet as you step inside Dambulla, Sri Lanka's best-preserved cave complex. The five cave shrines at Dambulla have been in use since the island's King Valagamba hid here in the 1st century BCE, after being overthrown by invading kings from southern India. When he later reclaimed power, he returned and filled the caverns with statues and a whole riot of frescoes, so beautiful they're considered the best in the whole of southeast Asia. Added to by the kings that followed, the caves are now home to 157 statues. Inside the first cave you'll discover a 47-ft- (14-m-) long Buddha reclining on his side, glittering with traces of gold and surrounded by offerings of fresh frangipani. Look for the underground spring that appears to flow up the roof of the cave before emerging back out into the daylight.

Good to know: To visit with ease, see the caves as part of a wider tour of the region; visiting without a tour is also possible.

378

MALDIVES

Luxuriate and explore in the Maldives

Ask anyone to describe a scene of island excellence and they are sure to describe the Maldives. Here, more than a thousand palm-fringed islands and sandbanks lie, ringed in by coral reefs filled with rainbow-hued fish and sea turtles. This paradise, where the skies are mirrored by a wide-blue ocean and romanticism is woven into the warm breeze, is inevitably popular among honeymooners, but there's more to the Maldives than white sand and five-star water villas. Local life thrives on a small portion—in fact, around 200—of the islands. Delve into this side of the Maldives by exploring on board a traditional *dhoni*. Hop off at your island of choice to shop at local fish markets, visit mosques, or tuck into Maldivian "short eats." Tasty bites like samosas make for a delicious snack, while heartier meals like *garudhiya* (a spicy fish broth) are perfect at the end of the day. Whether you decide to stick to one beach or explore all that the Maldives has to offer, here you'll get to experience true island living.

Good to know: The best way to get to the Maldives is by plane; boats and *dhoni* are the most efficient way to island-hop here.

379

BANGLADESH

Spot wildlife in the Sundarbans

Sprawling along the fringes of the Bay of Bengal, where the sluggish waters of the mighty Ganges, Brahmaputra, and Meghna rivers complete their long journey to the Indian Ocean, the Sundarbans are the world's largest expanse of mangrove forest, spanning some 3,860 sq miles (10,000 sq km) of land and water. Though part of this vast ecosystem lies in India, the lion's share is in Bangladesh. But forget lions, it's another big cat altogether that dominates here: this is a stronghold of the fierce Bengal tiger, whose numbers are, thankfully, rebounding following years of decline. An estimated 200-plus of the striped predators now stalk this landscape, alongside the various creatures on which they prey—wild boar, spotted deer, monkeys—as well as endangered Ganges river dolphins, pythons, estuarine crocodiles, and around 260 species of bird. The huge Sundarbans aren't only a wildlife-lover's paradise, but also a place where you can meet locals and producers. These groups continue to preserve traditional ways of living amid all the thriving mangroves and prowling tigers.

Good to know: The cooler, dryer months of October to March are best for exploring the Sundarbans.

WHERE ELSE TO SPOT BIG CATS

BANDHAVGARH NATIONAL PARK, INDIA
One of India's key tiger reserves, Bandhavgarh National Park sprawls across an area of 241 sq miles (625 sq km). Apart from some 50 tigers, the park's wildlife also includes leopards, Indian wild dogs, and 250 species of bird.

NORTHWEST SWEDISH LAPLAND
Arrive in March, find the most isolated spot in the mountains (you'll need a snowmobile to do so) and you might be lucky enough to see the elusive lynx prowling in the snow and ice.

LAIKIPIA WILDERNESS CAMP, KENYA
Try your luck at spotting the rare black leopard in northern Kenya. Its sleek coat looks black rather than golden due to melanism, a surplus of pigment.

380

NEPAL

Trek the Himalayas

The world's tallest mountain range holds varied meanings to those drawn to its slopes. For Nepali people living here, it's an "abode of snows"—the literal translation of Himalaya. For geologists, it's a vast crumple zone pushed up as the Indian tectonic plate plunges beneath the Eurasian plate. And for climbers, it's a playground of soaring peaks to be conquered—including the planet's tallest, Mount Everest, at 29,032 ft (8,849 m). Lace up your boots and head out onto one of the hiking trails yourself (with preparation and a guide, of course). Even the range's tallest summits can be seen from easy-to-reach spots: Pokhara provides views of Annapurna, while Everest can be seen from Dhulikhel and Nagarkot. Trekking along popular routes like the Annapurna Circuit, you'll be surrounded by sprawling mountain scenes, monasteries, and quaint villages—a whole high-altitude world of its own.

Good to know: The best times for trekking are the dry months flanking midwinter—October, November, and March.

381

NEPAL

Hike to Mount Everest Base Camp

For serious hikers, Mount Everest Base Camp is just the beginning of a life-changing adventure. The 12-day return hike to the foot of the world's tallest mountain is a transformative experience. After a nail-biting landing at one of the world's most dangerous airports, in the Himalayan town of Lukla, the famous trail will lead you up into a fairytale landscape of snow-capped peaks, Buddhist shrines, and remote Sherpa villages. Backed by the tinkle of yak bells and the fluttering of colorful prayer flags, it's a multisensory journey that almost carries you into another realm. As the air becomes thinner and the days cooler, the power of this white landscape is tangible at every stage of your journey. Reaching Base Camp is an exhilarating moment, but it's far from the only highlight. This is a journey that will see you forge friendships over teahouse suppers, discover what the human mind and body are capable of, and gain a new perspective. Up here, you're at the mercy of the mountains and you'll never feel more alive.

Good to know: Avoid the crowds by hiking to base camp in winter with a licensed guide.

382

NEPAL

Walk around the great Boudhanath Stupa

Spinning prayer-wheels rumble softly and incense spices the warm dusk air. The city of Kathmandu thrums beyond, while streaming bunting flutters in the breeze. This is Boudhanath Stupa, a shrine holding holy Buddhist relics and sacred texts within an immense domed structure that is sure to impress. For Tibetan devotees, a visit to the largest stupa in Nepal has added significance: it's one of the most important religious sites outside of their homeland. Entry into the main shrine at the center isn't allowed; instead, visitors circle the structure, turning some of the prayer wheels that line its walls as they pass by. Many ancient legends swirl around the origins of this stupa, but what is certain is that it has stood the test of time. Well over a millennium old, it has been restored after invaders' depredations and the impact of earthquakes over the years, including the shattering tremors of 2015. Despite such challenges, the mighty Boudhanath Stupa still stands true at the center of a thriving Tibetan community in Nepal.

Good to know: As at all Tibetan Buddhist monuments, circle the stupa in a clockwise direction.

MYANMAR (BURMA)

Get to know Myanmar (Burma)

It's no surprise that this beautiful region was long known as the "Golden Land." Gilded spires top countless Buddhist monuments, like the temples scattered across the hills around Mandalay. Some of these seem as though they're made of gold, from the glittering Shwezigon pagoda at Nyaung-U to the jaw-dropping Shwedagon Paya in former capital Yangon, described by awestruck writer Rudyard Kipling as "a beautiful winking wonder that blazed in the sun." In the Andaman Sea to the south, the soft sands fringing the castaway islands of the Myeik Archipelago gleam almost as brightly. But in truth, and despite the often violent political divisions that have wrought Myanmar (Burma) over the decades since the country's independence from British rule in 1948, its real treasure is its people. Whether you encounter a leg-rowing fisherman on the waters of Lake Inle, a red-robed monk walking among ancient temples on Bagan's plains, or the skipper on an Irrawaddy River cruise boat, you'll likely be met with a genuine and effusive warmth.

Good to know: The security situation in Myanmar (Burma) is changeable, so make sure to check the latest travel advice.

384

BHUTAN

Spend time in Bhutan

Unconquered, uncolonized, and famous for using the Gross National Happiness (GNH) index as the guiding principle of the government, Bhutan is recognized as a relatively peaceful place. Encircled by the toothy Himalayas, it's also a nature oasis: the law here dictates that 60 percent of the country must always be covered in forest to maintain ecological balance. With such admirable credentials, Bhutan, then, is somewhere to get to know, and the best way to do so is by immersing yourself in local life. Explore monasteries, where monks carve intricate butter sculptures in the courtyards; organize a homestay with a local family; tuck into steaming plates of the beloved national dish *ema datshi* (a spicy stew made with chiles and cheese); and head out into alpine hills to see the elusive takin. You'll likely leave with a burgeoning belief in the possibility of a more peaceful modern living.

Good to know: Only citizens of India, Bangladesh, and the Maldives can visit independently; all others must book a tour.

385

BHUTAN

Trek to Tiger's Nest Monastery

Clinging like a swallow's nest to the edge of a 10,200-ft- (3,120-m-) high sheer rock face, Paro Taktsang Buddhist monastery—better known as Tiger's Nest—seems so improbable that locals often say it was "built by men during the day and angels at night." Home to some 250 monks, it was first built in the year 1692 on the site where it's believed Guru Rinpoche (who brought Buddhism to Bhutan) landed onto the back of a pregnant tiger in his tantric, or aggressive, form while casting out local demons. Setting off along the 4-mile (6-km) round trip to the temple, you'll find spinning prayer wheels and brightly colored flags that wave in the breeze along the way. Once inside the temple, take a moment in one of the quiet rock-hewn rooms, which are dimly lit with traditional butter lamps. In these tranquil spaces, smoky wisps of incense swirl in the darkness and, always, the hum of prayers being chanted can be heard.

Good to know: There's a small cafeteria at the halfway point, where you can grab a drink and pause for great views.

386

THAILAND

Discover extraordinary northern Thailand

From misty mountaintops to sanctuaries shrouded in forest, Thailand's north is full of charms that set it apart from the beaches and islands of the south. Chiang Mai, the distinguished former seat of the Lanna Kingdom, matches historic allure with tranquility. Take a tuk-tuk around its Old City, where there are sites and shops to visit, before stopping off for authentic northern Thai cuisine. Dishes like *khao soi* (a restorative curry soup) and *sai ua* (a tasty spicy sausage dish) are hearty perfection—great for refueling after active days. Chiang Mai is also an excellent launchpad from which to explore the green rice fields, pristine rainforests, cascading waterfalls, and countryside villages of the surrounding region. This lush landscape is home to some of Thailand's most gorgeous *wát* (temples) and best ecotourism, from jungle trekking to zip lining to rock climbing. Between the stellar ancient city and abundant vistas beyond it, no two days need look the same as you explore this incredible part of Thailand.

Good to know: See Chiang Mai province from a covered boat on the Ping River, ending near the city's famed Night Bazaar.

BANGKOK

The capital of Thailand and one of Southeast Asia's great cities, Bangkok is full of sights, spiritual and cultural, which draw visitors in droves. It teems with life: customers seek out its famous street food, devotees visit temples, and markets buzz with hawkers. With such a ceaseless bustle, there's never a dull moment here.

Shop at the Damnoen Saduak Floating Market

There is no sight more quintessentially Thai than the region's century-old floating markets. Once big, vibrant hubs, these markets provided vital economic development and social connection to rural areas and communities. While many remain in the capital city today, none is as well-known and celebrated as the one found at Damnoen Saduak. Navigating the sleepy waters of the *khlongs* (canals), vendors in little wooden boats sell various goods to eager shoppers at this always popular and busy market. Sometimes dressed in *mo hom* (traditional bright blue farmers' shirts) coupled with wide-brimmed, conical straw hats, the traders paddle their wares out in the water in the early hours each morning, when it all kicks off. It's truly a riot of color and life: boat sterns overflow with fresh tropical fruits, traditional sweets, and endless knick-knacks as the haggling begins. The best way of getting around the floating market? By boat, of course. Trips can be taken along the labyrinth of narrow *khlongs*. The markets are able to endure in part as a result of interest in them. And, thankfully, they continue: beyond today's novelty, the tradition speaks volumes about Thai history and culture.

Good to know: Arrive at the market between the hours of 7 a.m. and 9 a.m., when it's really in full swing.

389

Tuck into Thai street food

Spicy, salty, sweet, savory, and bitter: Thai street food is renowned for hitting a full and intense range of flavor profiles with every bite. In Bangkok, the many street food markets make for a multisensory experience, where endless fiery woks, fragrant spices, and smoke-plumed grills build up anticipation for the dishes on offer. Snacks are fast, fresh, and made to order, with ingredients that often reflect Thailand's rich pantry: freshwater fish, pork, coconut milk, palm sugar, and seafood are expected. The most famous dishes like *pad krapao* (holy basil stir-fry) and *moo ping* (grilled pork skewers) are ubiquitous, while dishes from Muslim, Indian, and Chinese communities offer cultural insight. Relish the tasty, unique flavor combinations of your chosen dish before moving on to the next stall for a whole new taste experience.

Good to know: Carry cash and make sure to have small bills— vendors prefer not to break bigger notes.

Wat Arun
One of the symbols of Bangkok, this is an ancient temple with five iconic *prangs* (towers).

Wat Suwannaram
Home to some of Thailand's best temple murals, this *wat* is located on the Bangkok Noi canal.

Wat Suthat
One of the most important *wats* in Thailand and home to a 26-ft- (8-m-) tall bronze Buddha.

Wat Saket
The highlight here is the view of the Old City from the Golden Mount, a hill inside the temple.

Wat Pho
Bangkok's biggest and oldest temple, with a 150-ft- (46-m-) long Reclining Buddha.

Wat Phra Kaeo
The *chedis* of this temple are striking examples of Buddhist architecture.

Wat Traimit
Home to a Golden Buddha image made of gleaming solid gold.

388

Explore Wat Arun

Watching daybreak across Thailand's Wat Arun, or Temple of the Dawn, is an experience worth waking up early for. Named after the Hindu god of dawn, Aruna, the Khmer-style temple is one of Bangkok's most iconic sights. Legend has it that King Taksin, seeking a new capital for the kingdom after the fall of Ayutthaya, discovered a small shrine and decided to build a stunning temple instead. And Wat Arun really is impressive: the 230-ft- (70-m-) high spire is covered in shining Chinese porcelain shards, creating a dazzling, effervescent reflection onto the river at sunrise. Up close, marvel at the intricate floral mosaics adorning the temple before climbing the steep staircase to glimpse views of Bangkok's Old City—an invigorating sight, no matter the hour.

Good to know: For the best view, catch the sunrise from a rented long-tail boat or the (cheaper) express ferry.

Visit the Bangkok National Museum

Looking for an introduction to the arts, crafts, and history of Thailand? Then look no further. With one of the biggest collections in Southeast Asia, the Bangkok National Museum is Thailand's premier museum. Set around the Wang Na Palace, the building alone is worth a visit, particularly for the gold-adorned Buddhaisawan Chapel at the heart. This fine chapel is home to the Phra Buddha Sihing, one of the most venerated Buddha images in Thailand. Throughout the museum, remarkable artifacts, relics, and archaeological treasures span the kingdom's fascinating past, best seen at the Gallery of Thai History, which holds an informative and concise timeline of key events in the region. With all this and more to explore, the museum makes for a great base to acquire a deeper understanding of this region's long history.

Good to know: The museum is only open Wednesday to Sunday, so plan accordingly.

Get a front row seat at a Muay Thai match

It's a combat sport (and sometimes a bloody one), but Thais will tell you there is fierce beauty in the ancient tradition of Thai boxing. Known as "the art of eight limbs"—a nod to the Hindu god, Hanuman, who watches over fighters—it requires dexterity and skill. It's related to boxing and kickboxing but distinct from both, with fighters using their fists, feet, elbows, and knees. One-on-one fights in Bangkok's atmospheric Muay Thai stadiums are inevitably action-packed; the agile nature of the fighting style means there is never a dull moment. Plucky traditional Thai music soundtracks the experience, coupled with roaring crowds. Get there on time to see what's known as a *wai kru*—a ritual dance at the beginning to pay respect to the trainers and ask for Hanuman's blessing—before settling in for the match.

Good to know: Fights take place year-round; nab excellent seats by booking ahead at box offices or stadium websites.

Walk through imperial history at the Grand Palace

It may not have been home to a royal ruler since the 20th century, but Bangkok's Grand Palace still retains its regal air today. The 18th-century complex—found beside the country's holiest of temples, Wat Phra Kaeo—remains a highly sacred Buddhist site, eagerly visited by tourists and religious pilgrims alike. It's an essential stop to further understanding how Buddhism, which legitimizes monarchical rule through divine destiny, has historically defined Thai culture and society. The palace's buildings, ceremonial halls, pavilions, and gardens also showcase a unique fusion of Thai and Western aesthetics within their walls. The fusion of the old Ratanakosin style with foreign flourishes is most visible in the grand Chakri Maha Prasat (Grand Palace Hall), where Italian Renaissance and traditional Thai elements are blended together, and in the Borombhiman Hall, with its French-inspired design. It's practically a city within a city, and one of Southeast Asia's most unforgettable sights.

Good to know: Anyone inappropriately dressed is required to borrow clothes at the entrance gate on Na Phra Lan Road.

394

THAILAND

Unwind on the tranquil island of Phuket

Phuket, Thailand's largest island, is enjoying its glory days. Long hailed as one of Southeast Asia's most popular resorts, these southern shores have seen high numbers of Bangkokians, seeking out a calmer lifestyle, relocate here. The result? Phuket now has more top-tier bars and restaurants than ever before, while its nightlife can compete with the capital's scene. The surrounding Andaman Sea has long been home to some of the country's most breathtaking landscapes, which can be enjoyed while diving, rock climbing, or surfing. Phuket Town is not to be slept on, home to captivating museums, ornate Chinese shrines, and many historic Sino-Portuguese mansions. There's plenty of fiery southern Thai cuisine (among the country's spiciest) to indulge in too, while not one but two stunning national parks are within its reach. And to top it all off, there are countless pristine, white-sand shores that flank the island's shoreline; look hard enough and you'll likely find one to enjoy all to yourself.

Good to know: For the biggest choice of beaches to explore, head to the island's western Andaman Coast.

393

THAILAND

Dance at a Koh Pha Ngan full moon party

No other feature of Thai nightlife has achieved the same legendary status as Ko Pha Ngan's full moon parties. On this tiny southern island, thousands of revelers arrive monthly for the famous, neon-happy bash on Haad Rin Beach. What started out in the 1970s as a hippie ritual has exploded into a world-famous phenomenon, where dance music reigns supreme. Daily fire shows, thumping beats, and booze buckets come together to create a wild, free-spirited party atmosphere that has become a rite of passage for many a backpacker. Take on the intrepid, adventurous spirit of the party's founders and swap the main event on Haad Rin for some of the more elusive gatherings across the island. You'll find island locals, expats, and discerning travelers boogying to underground music until sunrise (and, often, beyond). And sure, these parties have a raucous reputation, but letting loose might be something everyone should do once.

Good to know: Arrive a few days before the main event for lively pre-parties across the island.

THAILAND

Celebrate Songkran, the Thai New Year

Come early spring, Thai revelers up and down the country eagerly anticipate the main celebration of the year: Songkran, the Thai New Year. Taking place in April each year, it's a time when families and friends gather, Buddhist worshippers bathe temple shrines, and water washes away the past year at water festivals. The northern city of Chiang Mai hosts some of the longest and liveliest festivities, where revelers splash around, sopping wet and wielding toy water shooters for days. Over in Pattaya, one of the largest water fights in the region erupts across the streets without fail. Among the watery scenes, pickup trucks with blaring boomboxes cruise around, turning it into a full-blown party. Whether you're throwing water with the locals or attending one of the calmer city parades, there's no escaping the jubilation of it all.

Good to know: This is one of the busiest times to visit Thailand, so make sure to book accommodation well in advance.

THAILAND

Uncover the past at Ayutthaya

Standing at the confluence of the Chao Phraya, Lop Buri, and Pasak rivers, Ayutthaya is Thailand's most epic temple town. Here, dozens of enigmatic ancient temples and ruins point to Ayutthaya's golden era. In its heyday, it was one of the most prosperous cosmopolitan centers in the world, home to more than 400 temples. Many have been restored, but some stand in various states of disrepair, revealing many exposed stupas, roofless chapels, and headless Buddhas. They nod to the kingdom's ultimate fate in 1767, when Burmese invaders ransacked it and took over the capital. Today, the town is a popular spot for Buddhist studies, with monks often seen in town. And the best way to discover it for yourself is by bike. Cycle over to the main ruins of Ayutthaya's Historical Park before continuing on to see more temples strung along the Chao Phraya River.

Good to know: Stay overnight to see stupa-peaked sundowns and night markets pop up among the temples.

THAILAND

Spot the world's largest flower in Khao Sok

The lush jungles of Khao Sok National Park, which are some of the oldest rainforests around, harbor myriad creatures and vegetation. Among them lies the ultra-rare and endangered plant *Rafflesia kerrii*. This red and white parasitic plant has no roots or leaves, but blooms out of its host plant into the world's largest flower, up to an impressive 30 inches (80 cm) in diameter. It has a pretty pungent odor too; likened to rotten meat and known as the "corpse flower," the smell works to attract pollinating insects but is foul to humans. That said, it can be a blessing in disguise when trying to seek out the flower. Since the *Rafflesia kerrii* requires specific growth conditions, its natural habitats are limited to certain regions of Southeast Asia, Khao Sok being one of them. Climate change means it's now even harder to see these power petals, so—for better or worse—follow your nose. No luck? Khao Sok offers up plenty of other delights, like the artificial Cheow Lan Lake and 188 species of bird to spot.

Good to know: Join a rafflesia hike with an expert guide to give you the best chance of seeking the flower out.

WHERE ELSE TO SEE BIG PLANTS

KEW GARDENS, ENGLAND
The *Victoria amazonica* is the world's biggest water lily. Growing to a diameter of 10 ft (3 m) along the Amazon River, it can also be seen in Kew Gardens.

SHARK BAY, AUSTRALIA
The world's largest plant, *Posidonia australis* (a fiber-ball weed), grows in a 110-mile (180-km) area and is said to be more than 4,000 years old.

THAILAND

Indulge in a Thai massage

It's thought that traditional Thai massage (*nuat paen boran*) dates back to the time of the Buddha, and the practice remains stronger than ever in Thailand today. Spas and parlors are found across most of the country—especially in bigger cities— and they're an ideal place to unwind after days of exploration and activity. The ancient practice isn't just about physical restoration, though. It's a therapeutic art deeply rooted in holistic practices. Using an effective combination of acupressure, rhythmic pressure, and gentle stretching, the body, mind, and spirit are harmonized along so-called "sen" energy lines to restore vitality and well-being. Settle in and feel every tension melt away as your body is expertly manipulated by skilled hands— you'll feel good as new after.

Good to know: Master the art of Thai massage yourself at Wat Pho's respected school in Bangkok.

MALAYSIA

Trek through the jungles of Borneo

Borneo: the name alone brings to mind dark rainforests, steaming rivers, and wild adventure, and there's no better way to experience it all than on a trek through its jungles. The third-largest island in the world, Borneo is split between the countries of Indonesia, Brunei, and Malaysia, and is home to the Dayak people. It's a veritable wildlife paradise, full of hornbills, long-nosed proboscis monkeys, giant flying squirrels, and so much more, all of which can be readily seen from hiking trails. By far the most famous species to call these lush, viridian expanses home, though, is the elusive orangutan. Trekking through the Danum Valley in Malaysia, it's possible to spot these fluffy, rusty-haired primates in the wild as they swing through the treetops and cling to branches, peering at you with curiosity as you gaze back at them. They are a critically endangered species, and Borneo is one of the only places in the world where orangutans can still be seen in nature, making such a sighting a truly unique experience—just ensure you don't disturb them or their habitat.

Good to know: Water-resistant hiking boots are a must on this trek, because it's soggy underfoot in the jungle.

399

THAILAND

Bask in the beauty of Ko Phi Phi

Bright turquoise waters, stretches of white sand, craggy green cliffs: Ko Phi Phi is *the* island to visit in Thailand. Located 25 miles (40 km) south of Krabi Town, it's in fact made up of two islands: Phi Phi Don and Phi Phi Leh. Both are famed for their spectacular landscapes, which include striking cliffs—tall walls of limestone rising to huge heights of 1,000 ft (300 m) on Phi Phi Don and 1,200 ft (370 m) on Phi Phi Leh—and seas teeming with marine life. Unsustainable tourism has taken a toll on some of the pristine shorelines, and in 2018, the popular Maya Bay beach was closed to the public. Following the break, its delicate ecosystem is recovering, with new coral growth and blacktip reef sharks returning. Strict restrictions on visitor numbers continue, meaning it's possible to travel responsibly and appreciate the stunning marine life.

Good to know: Check the opening hours—closures, sometimes for a few months, still take place on the islands for conservation.

> Borneo is one of the only places in the world where orangutans can still be seen in nature, making such a sighting a truly unique experience.

401

MALAYSIA

Scuba dive at Pulau Sipadan

The coasts of Malaysia are heralded as some of the world's best places for scuba diving, and the island of Pulau Sipadan—off the east coast of Borneo in the Celebes Sea—might just be the best of the bunch. Only 120 people are permitted to visit per day, meaning the technicolor scenes beneath the water can be explored uninterrupted. A world unto its own, here colorful clown fish relax in the floating tentacles of anemones and hawksbill turtles swim through limestone labyrinths. The flat-beaked face of a parrotfish may peer at you as you glide through reefs of vibrant coral. Look closely, and you may just be able to see tiny nudibranchs in all colors of the rainbow. Keep an eye out for bigger creatures, like the mighty hammerhead sharks and shoals of fearsome barracuda that also roam these waters. The most spectacular sight of all might just be the so-called Hanging Gardens, where cascading corals and sponges dominate, resembling a tower of melting candles and teeming with fish. With so many species to explore here, Pulau Sipadan truly is a treasure trove of sea life for divers.

Good to know: Trips to Pulau Sipadan depart from dive shops on the nearby islands of Mabul and Kapalai.

402

MALAYSIA

Explore Kuala Lumpur

Today, elegant modern structures and traditional temples reflect Kuala Lumpur's multifaceted origins.

Malaysia's capital city might be relatively young, but it's already got a lifetime of stories to tell. Sitting pretty in the Klang Valley, Kuala Lumpur was established in 1857 as a ramshackle trading post, and has witnessed it all: floods, fires, civil wars. When the city was made the capital of the newly formed Federated Malay States in 1896, a huge population boom followed, and the influence of Malay, Chinese and Indian cultures began to leave their mark. Today, elegant modern structures and traditional temples reflect the city's multifaceted origins: in one day, you can join devotees beneath the towering facade of the Sri Maha Mariamman Temple with its colorful sculptural reliefs of Hindu gods, tuck into roast duck at a Chinatown food stall, and admire the geometric masterpieces of the Islamic Arts Museum. Above it all soar the iconic twin Petronas Towers, once some of the world's tallest buildings. This is what impressive looks like.

Good to know: July and August are good times to visit Kuala Lumpur, as these are the least rainy months.

403

MALAYSIA

See in the Lunar New Year on the island of Penang

Usually falling in January or February, Lunar New Year celebrations are accompanied by the swelling sound of drums, the scent of incense from golden temples, and fireworks glowing against the inky sky. It's on the island of Penang, however, that the most exuberant 16-day party takes place. Things start with a bang as fireworks dance over Kek Lok Si, one of the largest Buddhist temples in Southeast Asia. The celebration only goes up from there, with the grandest night being the ninth, when events move to Penang's bustling city of George Town. Religious icons and ceramic urns filled with wafting joss sticks take over the promenade, and food stalls serve up tasty festive treats like *changshou mian*. Known as "longevity noodles," this dish is said to bestow long life, but there's a catch: you can't bite the noodles, so slurping is a must. By the time the eve of the New Year rolls around, it's back to Kek Lok Si, where towers and pavilions are covered in twinkling lights and Chinese lanterns fly above.

Good to know: While you're in George Town, seek out the famous *Boy on a Bike* street art mural.

SINGAPORE

Snack in Singapore's hawker centers

In a place as polished as Singapore, one of the places to experience authentic day-to-day living is at the city's beloved hawker centers. Beneath whirring ceiling fans, locals, expats, and tourists alike come together in these laid-back food hubs to indulge in tasty street food. Customers eat and drink around large, communal tables, and animated conversations echo through the air. Tucking into favorites like roast pork char siu, congee, or chicken rice—maybe the best-known Singaporean dish—are a must on any visit. Prices are refreshingly low for a city where dining out can be an expensive treat—this even holds true at some of the most celebrated joints like Tai Hwa, a stand based in the Hill Street hawker center. This spot has won a Michelin star for its tasty pork noodles, making it an accessible place to go gourmet. So, pick up a plate (or two), grab a drink, and get a taste of the real Singapore.

Good to know: Make sure to bring some cash—the majority of hawker center stalls don't accept card payments.

WHERE ELSE TO EXPLORE INNOVATIVE GARDENS

THE EDEN PROJECT, UK
Eight spaceship-like domes make up this garden of the future, the transparent covering allowing ultraviolet light to penetrate so the world's most important plants can thrive.

ENEA TREE MUSEUM, SWITZERLAND
The first—and only—tree museum in the world showcases more than 25 regional species, all saved by an enterprising Swiss landscape architect and replanted on parkland.

405

SINGAPORE

Walk through the Gardens by the Bay

There is, arguably, no image more totemic of Singapore than Gardens by the Bay's Supertrees: 160-ft- (50-m-) high latticed metal trunks entwined with rare orchids, vines, and bromeliads. These skyscraper-high masterpieces dance with light every evening, but they aren't the only reason to visit this waterfront complex. This is the government's vision of creating a city in a garden, and since opening in 2012, Gardens by the Bay has embodied Singapore's twin pillars of futurism and environmentalism, embodied in the climate-controlled conservatories and the world's second-tallest indoor waterfall. Add to that carbon-sequestering mangrove plants that help mitigate the effects of global warming, and the prioritizing of rare and endangered plants in the collections, and you're looking at the future.

Good to know: The site is split into three sections—Bay East, Bay Central, and Bay South Garden—all connected via a shuttle.

FLOATING GARDENS OF XOCHIMILCO, MEXICO
Some of the most unusual and ingenious gardens on Earth, this network of artificial islands connected by waterways dates back to the time of the Aztecs. They supply fruit, vegetables, herbs, and flowers for Mexico city.

407

INDONESIA

Watch the sunrise over Java's Borobudur Temple

Ascending to the top of Borobudur, the world's largest Buddhist temple, is eye-opening. Built in the 9th century by the seafaring Shailendra dynasty, it lay hidden for centuries under overgrown volcanic ash and jungle until the temple was rediscovered in the 19th century. Despite being well known today, arriving here still feels like stumbling upon another world. After centuries spent buried, the two million blocks of stone, used to create a pattern of ascending terraces representing the cosmos, are amazingly well-preserved. There are endless tiered steps, seemingly thousands of sculptural reliefs depicting the Buddha, and intricately carved scenes from Javanese mythology to be admired up close. For a memorable view, arrive in the early hours of the morning to see the sunrise over the mist-wreathed jungles of Java's Kedu Plain. The journey to the top of the temple's stairs is symbolic of the path to enlightenment, and, as daylight breaks over the Progo River to the east, you really will feel like you're touching nirvana.

Good to know: Sunrise tours are available from most nearby hotels, which drop groups at the complex in the early morning.

406

SINGAPORE

Feel on top of the world at Marina Bay Sands

Singapore's skyline has impressive buildings galore, but none are as iconic as the Marina Bay Sands Hotel. The distinctive hotel structure is made up of three towers supporting a long, flat rooftop deck, home to myriad luxurious bars and restaurants, as well as *that* famous infinity pool. But even better than the view of this hotel? The view from it. You won't be able to take a dip in its pool unless you're a guest, so head up to the hotel's SkyPark observation deck (ticket in hand) to take in the views or, for a swankier experience, visit the Cé La Vie Sky Bar. Here, you can pull up a seat overlooking the city while sipping a classic Singapore Sling cocktail—the sweet and sour gin, pineapple, and pomegranate concoction developed in this city. Arrive in time for sunset, and you'll see another famed cityscape spot, the Supertree Grove at the Gardens by the Bay, all aglow.

Good to know: The SkyPark is busiest in the early evening, but a Sunset in the Sky ticket will guarantee an undisturbed view.

409
INDONESIA

Dare to take on Java's Mount Merapi

In a country with a whopping 130 active volcanoes, Mount Merapi holds the title of Indonesia's most active. Its name translates to Fire Mountain, a title it has earned as a result of almost 500 years of regular volcanic eruptions. Lying just north of the cultural capital of Yogyakarta, Merapi is an impressive sight on approach, with steam billowing from its symmetrical top and clouds dramatically forming around it all. The mountain also holds great religious significance for the Javanese, who believe that a sumptuous spirit palace lies within the mountain. To reach the top of Merapi, embark on a hike up from nearby Selo. The journey usually begins in the middle of the night at around 1 a.m. and is moderately tough, with loose scree and volcanic cinder underfoot. The early start and aching legs are undeniably worth it, though, when you reach the summit in time for sunrise over the jungles of Java. Two other mighty volcanoes, Mount Meranti and Mount Merbabu, look tiny from the top, confirming Merapi's dominance over the landscape.

Good to know: Guides in Selo can lead you up the mountain and advise on potential closures due to volcanic activity.

408

INDONESIA

Climb up the Ijen Volcano

Indonesia is no stranger to volcanoes, located as it is within the Pacific Ocean's Ring of Fire. Of all the country's molten mountains, the bright, sulfurous Ijen Volcano might just be the most spectacular. Lying in the remote hills of east Java, Ijen is an otherworldly landscape of steaming fumaroles, acid-green crater lakes, and a magical but extremely rare natural wonder known as "blue fire." Snaking down the mountain in the dark like neon lava, this rare sight is actually made of ignited sulfur. To see it in all its smoking glory, head out in the dead of night on an organized hike, passing by the "blue fire" in the dark before reaching the crater just in time for sunrise. Emerging daylight reveals a steaming, bright-green lake of acidic water stretching over the crater. The views here bring to mind Indonesia's nickname—the Equatorial Emerald may be known for its lush rainforests, but the name could just as well refer to the unique landscapes of Ijen.

Good to know: The smell of sulfur here is strong, so buy a gas mask (usually available from vendors in the parking lot).

411

INDONESIA

Explore Komodo Island

There are few wildlife experiences more primordial than walking among prehistoric Komodo dragons. The fabled home of the world's largest living lizard, Komodo National Park covers most of Komodo Island. Stepping onto its shores, you'll feel like you've traveled to the distant past. Its interior is covered in jungles replete with scrubby palm trees and curling ferns. The otherworldly feel is compounded by its genuinely pink beach, colored a rosy hue thanks to the microscopic organisms living in its sands. And, of course, roaming freely throughout the park are the eponymous dragons themselves. Growing up to 10 ft (3 m) long and 150 lb (70 kg) in weight, these are some truly hefty reptiles, and their vicious reputation matches their bulk—these apex predators hunt large deer and water buffalo several times their size. This is the place to live out your Jurassic Park fantasies (without the ghastly consequences).

Good to know: Visits to the island are led by a guide—you can't explore Komodo National Park without one.

The fabled home of the world's largest lizard, Komodo National Park covers most of Komodo Island.

410

INDONESIA

Find what feels good in Bali

Famously a hub of wellness and self-discovery, Bali is *the* place to rejuvenate and unwind among mountain views and sandy beaches. But all its luxury spa retreats have made this Indonesian island incredibly popular, so it's worth knowing where to escape the crowds and ensure your trip *actually* balances your chakras. South Bali's Uluwatu is great for awakening your spirit with some of the best sunset views and a visit to the sacred site of Pura Luhur Uluwatu, a beautiful sea temple to spirits of the ocean. In Central Bali, you'll find a change of scene in the artistic hub of Ubud, packed with galleries, art studios, museums, and shops selling handicrafts and textiles. And if you are feeling up for something a bit livelier, Bali delivers on that front too, with the most frequented spots of Seminyak and Kuta offering some of the island's best nightlife and beaches. Of course, you're in Bali, so don't shy away from enhancing your overall well-being with a body-soothing massage or a healing skin-care treatment. Bali can be whatever you want it to be.

Good to know: Scooters are the favorite way to get around the island, with plenty of rental places available.

412

INDONESIA

Spot manta rays in Raja Ampat

Witnessing a manta ray sweeping through the ocean is a spellbinding experience, and one that Indonesia offers up in bucketloads along its many coastlines. Hot spots include Komodo Alley and Nusa Penida, but if you're looking to spot (or even swim with) these marine animals, visit the warm waters of Raja Ampat. This barely inhabited archipelago of jungle-tufted islands is fringed by pristine coral reefs on which mantas gather, letting smaller sea creatures nibble the parasites from their skin. You're guaranteed to come across mantas at these cleaning stations, enjoying a good grooming amid corals, sponges, and tropical fish. As approachable as they may appear, it's important to keep a distance and avoid splashing them to avoid damaging the protective mucus that covers their skin. What you *can* do is just let yourself be mesmerized by these giant underwater gliders.

Good to know: Manta-spotting season is from September to April; tours depart from the town of Waisai during this time.

413

PHILIPPINES

Island-hop around the Philippines

There are three essential ingredients for an island retreat—sea, sand, and sun—and the Philippines is blessed with each one. A country that is 95 percent isle-based, the Philippines has a wealth of pristine, untouched coastlines, many of which are accessible and blissfully quiet. Among the 7,000-strong archipelago, there are a few centerpiece jewels that can't be missed. A vision of limestone cliffs and aquatic life, the island of Palawan is just a short hop away from stunning El Nido, famed for its soft sands and impeccable surfing conditions. If hidden lagoons, pristine white sand beaches, and captivating coral reefs are what you're after, then the idyllic Coron area is an ideal stop. The island Siargao leads to secluded islets such as Naked Island and Daku Island, where tranquil, untouched seas bearing the freshest seafood feasts await. Wherever your island-hopping journey takes you, there's almost certainly a secluded bit of sand awaiting you.

Good to know: Peak season to travel here is from December to March, so make sure to book any ferries well ahead.

CAMBODIA

Soak up the buzz of Siem Reap

Siem Reap literally means Siam Defeated, referring to the Khmer sacking of the great Thai city of Ayutthaya in the 17th century. Today, there's nothing in the way of defeat about this bustling tourist hub, which has grown from a quiet staging post to one of Southeast Asia's hottest nightlife spots. Though Siem Reap didn't start out as a party town, it has an after-hours scene to rival Cambodia's busiest beach resorts, with most of the action concentrated around Pub Street and its hole-in-the-wall dives and lively clubs. Backpacker bars not your bag? You'll find pockets of tradition at the city's markets. At Psar Chas, silks, silver, and stone carving trinkets are up for grabs, while Pho Langka serves up street food like *lort cha* (pin noodles). No matter where you go, you'll find yourself caught between past and present in the best way possible.

Good to know: Strike a bargain at the markets—opening prices for handicrafts are often way over the odds.

CAMBODIA

Admire the masterpiece of Angkor Wat

Angkor, the historic capital of the Khmer Empire, is one of the most magnificent wonders of the world. It took five million tons of sandstone, 300,000 laborers and a thousand elephants 30 years to build the lavish capital in the 12th century. Made up of more than a thousand buildings, it was the largest city in the world at the time. The web of temples, galleries, courtyards, and chambers today are tangled with vines, while the roots of mammoth silk-cotton trees have wrapped themselves around the stones. Ta Prohm once had a starring role in the 2001 *Tomb Raider* film, but the highlight is undoubtedly Angkor Wat. The best-preserved temple here, it was likely built as a tomb for King Suryavarman II. Its walls are carved with thousands of *apsaras* (celestial fairies) and the main structure is made up of five towers. You may have seen pictures of Angkor, but they'll be no match for gazing up at its crenellated towers in real life.

Good to know: To avoid the crowds, try to get to the temple before sunrise. Be sure to dress modestly to be allowed in.

CAMBODIA

Cruise the Mekong River

Unquestionably one of the world's great rivers, the 3,050-mile- (4,900-km-) long "Mother of Waters" trickles out of the Tibetan Plateau and gathers pace as it runs through China, Myanmar (Burma), Laos, Thailand, Cambodia, and Vietnam before flowing out into the South China Sea. It's a life force that provides the many people who live along its banks with power and food, as well as being a great mode of transportation. Along its waters, watch hot air balloons rise over the horizon, take part in the unique watery bustle of one of the many floating markets and admire the leafy riverscapes along the way. There are cruises available for any length of time, with the most popular stretch running from Phnom Penh to Siem Reap in Cambodia. Take time along the river and indulge in the slower pace—there's always something going on, but never enough bustle to shatter the tranquility of the scenery.

Good to know: Set aside two weeks for a pre-booked cruise, where you can disembark at small towns and hiking spots.

LAOS

Bike the Thakhek Loop

Towering karst peaks, yawning caves, and wild swimming spots galore: the popular 280-mile (450-km) Thakhek Loop is one of Laos' highlights for good reason. Going through the Phou Hin Poun and Nakai-Nam Theun National Conservation Areas, the loop is best explored by motorcycle or bike (if your calves are up to the task). Buck the trend by taking on the route in an counterclockwise direction, beginning at Cave Alley and concluding with the Cool Spring swimming hole and Tham Kong Lo. This impressive karst cave is 4 miles (6 km) deep, with a sacred emerald pool inside thought to reflect the skin of the Hindu god Indra. Feeling adventurous? Tack on a two-day extension along dirt roads to see Xe Bang Fai River Cave or plan to bike the route during the rainy season from May to October, when the landscape is greener, there are fewer people, and the air is clearer. Novice or nervous? Don't miss out: hire an "easyrider," and a local tour guide will drive the bike for you.

Good to know: Visit the Inside Asia website to get a tailor-made tour of the loop arranged.

418

VIETNAM

Slurp some pho

There's soup, and then there's pho. Simultaneously sweet, salty, and spicy, this broth—made from bones (usually beef or chicken) simmered for hours before being mixed with rice noodles, thinly sliced meat, and a few green onions—is the dish that defines this country. The origins of this delicious soup are unclear, but many believe it arose in the northern Nam Dinh province, 60 miles (95 km) south of Hanoi, where a local soup using river crabs was adapted to suit the beef-loving palates of the French, who arrived in the region to build a huge silk-textile factory at the end of the 19th century. When colonial rule ended in 1954, millions of people migrated south and the recipe for pho changed because of the availability of different produce. At classic institutions in the north, pho has thinner noodles, fewer garnishes, and a more savory broth; in the south, it's a sweeter affair, with heaps of bean sprouts, fresh herbs, limes, and chiles. No matter the variation, each bowl is undoubtedly delicious.

Good to know: One of the best pho spots is the family run Bún Cha Huong Liên *(24 Le Van Huu)* in Hanoi.

419

VIETNAM

Trek through the rice terraces of Sa Pa

Tier upon tier of rice terraces reflecting the sky like shards of a shattered mirror, while the conical straw hats of farmers bob up and down as they go about their work: it's pastoral views like these that draw walkers to Sa Pa. This implausibly pretty region is couched amid the craggy mountains in northwest Vietnam, where the hilly slopes have been cultivated in order to grow rice. These towering steps are a sight to behold as you hike at an average elevation of 4,900 ft (1,500 m), spying the pyramid-capped Fansipan Peak, traversing the hanging bridge of Muong Hoa Valley and weaving between bamboo forests. Opt to walk over a few days with a local guide and spend time supporting and learning from the Indigenous communities of the region, like the Hmong, Dao, Tay, and Giay. Along the way, share bowls of pho, purchase handmade crafts, and try a batik fabric workshop as you soak up the gorgeous views.

Good to know: Book a place with Sapa Sisters, a local Hmong-owned trekking group.

420

VIETNAM

Take a cruise on Halong Bay

According to local legend, Halong Bay was formed when a gigantic dragon (*ha long* means descending dragon) plunged into the Gulf of Tonkin and lashed its tail to create a barrier against invaders. And the resulting scenes are stunning. Spread across an immense 600-sq-mile (1,500-sq-km) area, this world-class bay is dominated by more than 1,900 limestone dolomite outcrops, the highest concentration found in the world. Take in the weathered pinnacles and grottoes from the water itself, joining an overnight cruise aboard a traditional junk boat, sailing around with a guide by chartering a private boat, or even by kayaking the placid waters here. Drifting past the evocatively shaped islets and dramatic caves, you'll be transported into another realm entirely.

Good to know: It's possible to charter a private boat from Cat Ba Island, but booking a cruise is the easiest way to see the bay.

WHERE ELSE TO SAIL AROUND A SCENIC BAY

BAY OF KOTOR, MONTENEGRO
What it lacks in rainforests, it makes up for in striking cliffs, mountains, and cozy coves. Montenegro's Boka Kotorska (Bay of Kotor) is a stunning spot where boats and cruises pass through, stopping off in the clear waters and near historic towns.

PHANG NGA BAY, THAILAND
Like Halong Bay, this scenic spot is home to limestone mounds emerging from the tranquil sea. Kayaking is the preferred mode of transportation through these parts, allowing for easy access to the many coves and caverns here.

RAJA AMPAT, INDONESIA
Though not a bay, Raja Ampat (which means "four kings") is a stunning archipelago with many verdant green islands, all surrounded by turquoise waters and some of the world's richest marine biology.

VIETNAM

Sip a Vietnamese coffee in Hanoi

With sweet condensed milk a comforting base to many a caffeinated drink in Vietnam, it's no wonder the local coffee has become globally popular. The country is among the world's largest coffee exporters, and its capital, Hanoi, is the best city to try variations of the classic brew. For a drink that packs a punch, there's nothing better than the *cà phê sua nóng*—its potency is thanks to a winning combination of a dark coffee bean roast and a touch of condensed milk. After something that melts in the mouth? Go for the egg coffee, or *cà phê trung*, where coffee, whipped egg yolk and condensed milk are brought together to make a thick, frothy drink. Or, if iced coffee is your jam, ask for a *cà phê sua chua*, a smooth yogurt-based brew that provides the perfect cool down. It's a tall order deciding what to go for.

Good to know: Plant-based or dairy intolerant? Hanoi and Da Nang have many coffee shops that cater to vegan diets.

Pack your saddlebags and set off on a south-to-north motorcycle trip through Vietnam, a warm wind your constant companion as you zoom through vibrant cities and landscapes.

VIETNAM

Motorcycle in Vietnam

Pack your saddlebags and set off on a south-to-north motorcycle trip through Vietnam, a warm wind your constant companion as you zoom through vibrant cities and landscapes. You can cover much of the country by traveling along the coast from Ho Chi Minh City to the capital, Hanoi, passing historical highlights such as Hôi An, a perfectly preserved 15th-century trading port, and the vast Cù Chi Tunnels, created by the Viet Cong as a hiding place during the Vietnam War. In between lie time-lost villages, where farmers coax water buffalo to till their rice paddies, and natural wonders such as Phong Nha Ke Bang National Park and Hang Son Doong, the world's largest cave. And don't miss testing your tires against the Hai Van Pass, a 13-mile (21-km) section of switchback coastal road best tried at sunset. Skirting (mostly) along the edge of the South China Sea, this stunning route showcases a country much changed since the Vietnam War.

Good to know: If you're a novice rider, take a motor tour for a stress-free way to explore.

423

CHINA

Hike Tiger Leaping Gorge

In northern Yunnan province, on the fringe of the Himalayas, the Jinsha River has carved out one of the world's deepest and most spectacular gorges. Legend has it that a band of hunters chased a tiger down to the river here; to escape, it leapt across the frothing water, giving the gorge its name. With the snow-capped peaks of the Haba massif and Jade Dragon Snow Mountains soaring to over 16,400 ft (5,000 m) on either side, the gorge sets the scene for a thrilling trek—and it's also one of China's most accessible. Over two days, you'll set out across the 18 miles (30 km) of craggy trails, teetering cliffside paths, and gorgeous countryside. Take a breath when you reach the infamous switchback climb, the most challenging point with 28 bends in the trail. Thankfully, though, hillside guesthouses will be there to welcome you at the end of a strenuous day, offering up cold drinks and somewhere to bed down before setting out again the next day.

Good to know: Check the weather and don't trek alone; spells of heavy rain (especially in July and August) can cause landslides.

424

CHINA

See Tibet's Potala Palace

Embraced by the Himalayas, where the air is thin and the landscapes vast, a majestic, ivory-hued edifice looks out over the valley from its rocky perch. Potala Palace, with its inward-sloping walls of wood, stone, and earth, 16 ft (5 m) thick at the base, may look like a fortress at first glance, but the scent of burning juniper incense and the tolling of distant bells reveals that this is a sanctuary of another kind. The palace served as the winter residence of the Dalai Lama from the 17th century until 1959, when the 14th Dalai Lama left to live in exile in India. Inside, there are endless halls, prayer rooms, shrines, and temples, visible only by the dim light of the yak butter candles that throw flickering shadows upon centuries-old frescoes. Staircases worm upward through an impressive 13 floors, worn smooth by the footsteps of saffron-robed monks. Contemplating the surrounding landscape from these heights, it's clear to see that there couldn't be a more fitting setting for this former spiritual center.

Good to know: Non-Chinese travelers can only visit as part of a tour; you'll need both a Chinese visa and a Tibetan Travel Permit.

425

CHINA

Retrace the Silk Road

One of the great overland journeys of antiquity, the legendary Silk Road was a network of trade arteries through desert sands that connected the ancient Chinese capital of Chang'an (today's Xi'an) with many trading hubs dotted along the way in classical Persia, Arabia, and Europe. Nowadays, trains and buses have replaced plodding camel caravans along the 4,300-mile (7,000-km) route. Just as merchants wouldn't try to cover the entire route back in its heyday, most modern travelers tackle just a portion too, and China's section from Dunhuang to Xi'an is one of the most epic, passing through mountainous regions and deserts. But the Silk Road is much more than mere photo fodder. You'll discover that it wasn't just key commodities like silk, spices, and textiles that were traded, but technologies, philosophies, and religions. Travel along it, and you'll see how it helped forge much of the modern world.

Good to know: Entry requirements and regulations vary country to country, so check government websites carefully.

CHINA

Count up the sculptures of the Terra-Cotta Army

When farmers unearthed a soldier's head crafted from clay while digging water wells in 1974, little did they know they had uncovered one of the most significant archaeological finds in history. A tomb containing more than 8,000 life-size sculptures of horses, generals, archers, and infantrymen created to guard Qin Shi Huang Di—China's first emperor—in the afterlife was discovered. Originally painted bright red, black, white, and green, the once-vibrant soldiers were stripped back to their terra-cotta base when the lacquer flaked off after tombs were opened. Not all of the figures have been excavated, but those that were—more than 2,000—are lined up today in neat, dusty rows at Emperor Qinshihuang's Mausoleum. Peer over the eerie assemblage and you'll notice that, among the braided hair, armor, and mustaches, each soldier is unique, thought to be based on a true likeness. It's like witnessing a real army standing at attention.

Good to know: Entrance tickets are capped at 65,000 per day and they sell out quickly; book in advance online.

427

CHINA

Take in the Leshan Giant Buddha

In China's Sichuan province, home of the panda and the mouth-numbing peppercorn, lives a giant. All day long he sits, hands on knees, nestled between cliffs of red sandstone. From bus-size feet to cranial bun, he measures over 230 ft (70 m) in height. His serene face, eyes closed and lips forming a subtle smile, is the height of a four-story building. For well over a thousand years, since the distant Tang Dynasty, the Giant Buddha of Leshan has been devoted to a single task—calming the turbulent river waters before him. He sits at the point where the Min and Dadu rivers meet in a fast-flowing maelstrom that once posed great danger to boat traffic. The Buddha's gaze was intended to appease the river spirits and protect those navigating its waters. Providentially, the removal of such a vast quantity of material during the statue's carving, subsequently deposited into the river, did indeed serve to alter its flow and make the channel safer to navigate—truly a case of divine intervention.

Good to know: For a full account of the Buddha's history and construction, check out the Jiazhou Huayuan museum nearby.

> For well over a thousand years, since the distant Tang Dynasty, the Giant Buddha of Leshan has been devoted to a single task—calming the turbulent river waters before him.

428

CHINA

Scoff Sichuan staples in Chengdu

You'll never forget your first Sichuan red peppercorn. Its citrusy, tongue-numbing taste is so unique that it has its own word—*málà*—to describe it, and so prized that people risked their lives crossing jagged mountains to trade it on the historic Tea Horse Road. Despite the name, they're not peppercorns at all—they're the dried berries of the prickly ash tree. When combined with chili oil, they form the base of Sichuan cooking, one of China's eight major regional cuisines. Managing to be spicy, salty, and sour at the same time, they're showcased in classic dishes such as *dan dan mian*, spicy noodles topped with crispy pork and chopped peanuts, and *chengdu* hot pot, a bubbling cauldron of hot spicy oil served with platters of raw meat and vegetables to cook at the table. Pull up a chair and tuck in—dining on one of these dishes in a cozy local restaurant is close to experiencing culinary perfection.

Good to know: See how Sichuan staples are made at the Museum of Sichuan Cuisine *(8 Ronghua North Alley)*.

CHINA

Climb Tianmen Mountain

Climbing the stairway to heaven's gate is normally considered to be a one-way trip—unless you happen to be in Zhangjiajie, that is. Of the ring of verdant mountains that envelop this small city nestled in the Hunan province, Tianmen Mountain, literally "Heaven's Gate," is a stand-out peak. Its soaring height of 5,000 ft (1,500 m) is impressive in itself, but it's the unique natural wonder lying close to the summit that is the real star here. Cutting clean through the mountain is a limestone karst grotto shaped like a Gothic church window, one of the tallest natural arches in the world at 430 ft (130 m) high and 190 ft (60 m) wide. To knock on heaven's door, you'll need to lace up your boots and climb the epic 999 steps up, but have no fear—nine is a lucky number in Chinese culture, and fortune favors the brave. Want to test your mettle even more? Dare to traverse the nearby Walk of Faith, a narrow cliff-side walkway made of glass and suspended 4,600 ft (1,400 m) above the ground.

Good to know: Skip the hike and board one of the world's longest cable-cars, which starts near Zhangjiajie Railway Station.

CHINA

Meander down the Li River

Sailing on a motorized raft down the clear Li River, you'll pass through landscape that seems lifted straight out of a Chinese scroll painting.

Sailing on a motorized raft down the clear Li River, you'll pass through landscape that seems lifted straight out of a Chinese scroll painting. The shallow Li weaves between sheer-sided, 1,00-ft (300-m) karst peaks, all weathered into intriguing shapes and interspersed with the villages and bamboo groves typical of southern China's rural areas. People here still travel the river on low bamboo rafts, but to glide down it yourself, you'll board a boat at the Zhu Jiang pier. You'll pass the Penholder Peak, a sharp, vertical outcrop that does indeed resemble a traditional Chinese penholder; beautiful scenery at the wooden town and ferry port of Xingping; and lastly Dragon Head Hill, an imposing peak said to resemble the head of a dragon with its gaping jaws wide open. By the time you disembark at Yangshuo, your jaw will be just as wide in awe.

Good to know: In winter, if water levels are too low upstream, tours may start a little farther downstream at Yangdi.

431

CHINA

See the Lantern Festival

On the first full moon of the lunar calendar, the Lantern Festival is celebrated across much of China. This bright festival of lights is the final hurrah after the 15 days of firecrackers, feasting, and gatherings that dominate the Chinese New Year festivities. To mark the holiday, families congregate around paper lanterns inscribed with mythological riddles and eat homemade *tangyuan*, sticky-sweet orbs of rice flour. Grand events like Shanghai's Yuyuan Gardens Lantern Festival attract thousands of revelers, but nothing comes bigger than the celebrations in the unassuming city of Zigong in Sichuan province. Known as the "city of a thousand lights," Zigong transforms into a kaleidoscopic wonderland of fantastical lanterns, crafted in endless shapes and designs. Watch as dragons, fish, birds, and colossal creatures to match that year's zodiac animal occupy the city's streets. The majority of the lanterns are produced by a thriving local industry of specialists, who continue this centuries-old craft. The Lantern Festival is the ultimate expression of light dispelling darkness, bringing people together and encouraging positivity for the year ahead.

Good to know: Make sure to be in Zigong at the end of the Chinese New Year to catch the best of the lantern festivities.

432

CHINA

Stroll through Hong Kong

Sprouting from the seeds of colonialism to dizzying heights of modern wealth and development, Hong Kong has long felt like a destination where anything is possible. When the Union Jack was first hoisted over the Chinese territory in 1841, Hong Kong had a population of less than 8,000 people and was mainly inhabited by farmers and fishers. Fast forward to the present, and this island metropolis is now a special administrative region of China with a population of over seven million people, who live among more skyscrapers than in any other city on Earth. Wherever you look, tradition and the ultra-modern jostle for your attention: glitzy shopping malls tower over incense-shrouded temples, while high-end restaurants sit beside bustling old markets. Whether you're strolling its slick streets or taking in the view of skyscrapers from the green surrounds of The Peak, Hong Kong is a fast-moving city that will impress.

Good to know: Spring and fall are the most comfortable times to visit, when the heat and humidity are more forgiving.

CHINA

BEIJING

Modern China is a powerhouse, and Beijing is at the heart of its activity. The city heaves with innovation and modernity—but those aren't the only reasons to visit. It's also home to China's cultural heritage, where you can step back into the past among dynastic palaces and temples which have stood the test of time.

433

Wander the grounds of the Summer Palace

A marvel of Chinese landscape design, the Summer Palace is a world unto itself. Located on the edge of Beijing, it's where the imperial court would be relocated to escape the stifling summer heat of the city. With its many lakes, islets, artificial hills, and vaulted arch bridges surrounding the palace buildings, it's a luxurious, restful retreat. The complex was eventually home to the 19th-century Empress Dowager Cixi, who was a complex and divisive figure in Chinese history. Stand on the grand 17-Arch Bridge, and you can see one of her controversial legacies on Kunming Lake: Marble Boat, a huge, two-story entertainment pavilion built in the shape of a paddle steamer. By the lake, the colorful Long Corridor is not to be missed: carefully decorated with more than 14,000 intricate paintings, it's a feast for the eyes as you walk through. Many more halls and temples dot the green mound of Longevity Hill, topped with the tall Tower of the Fragrance of the Buddha. Revolution may have swept away millennia of imperial rule, but the Summer Palace still retains its regal air.

Good to know: For the chance to ice-skate on frozen Kunming Lake, visit during the winter months.

434

Walk in imperial footsteps at the Temple of Heaven

The Temple of Heaven is one of the most stunning remnants of China's dynastic history. A bright, round structure set against the often-gray Beijing sky, its intricate decorations and green setting draw crowds by the thousands each day. The Temple of Heaven was designed as a conduit to the divine, like a two-way telephone connecting the Middle Kingdom with the realms above. It was reserved for the emperor, who would depart the Forbidden City at winter solstice in a solemn procession to make offerings at the Round Altar in return for bountiful harvests and a prosperous empire. Walk in and see the Hall of Prayer for Good Harvests where this would take place, with its triple-tiered conical roof glazed in deep blue tiles denoting its divine status. Look to its ceiling and you'll see a gilded dragon and phoenix at its colorful center. Today, the temple teems with all manner of visitors and locals who flow into the grounds to admire the grand structures, go for a walk with friends, or join a tai chi session in the surrounding parkland.

Good to know: The sights open at 8 a.m., but if you come earlier, you'll see locals practicing tai chi in the park's vast gardens.

MUST-VISIT TEMPLES IN BEIJING

Temple of Heaven
Originally the venue for annual winter solstice sacrifices, this temple is Beijing's best-known icon.

Fayuan Temple
Built in 696 CE by Tang Dynasty emperor Tai Zong to mourn fallen soldiers, Fayuan is Beijing's largest Buddhist temple.

White Cloud Temple
Built in 739 CE, Beijing's only Taoist temple houses the China Taoist Association.

Lama Temple
The largest and most spectacular of the city's temples is a working lamasery.

Wanshou Temple
This complex houses the Beijing Art Museum—a collection of historical relics.

Confucius Temple (Kong Miao)
A huge complex of wooden halls and flagstone courtyards.

435

See the Forbidden City

Beijing is inseparable from the Forbidden City, the monumental, compass-perfect palace complex once home to 24 past emperors, their families, and legions of servants. Viewed from above—by climbing the hill installed to thwart bad air from the north—tiers of sloping yellow-tiled rooftops fade into the distance, a masterpiece of scale and symmetry. It's incredible to think that, for almost 500 years, this mysterious complex existed as a gaping void at the heart of the capital city, entirely off-limits and hidden behind 2 miles (3.5 km) of citadel walls. Nowadays, visitors enter the Forbidden City through the central arch of the enormous Meridian Gate, once reserved solely for the emperor. From there, some 900 buildings await, the greatest of which is the Hall of Supreme Harmony, where the "Son of Heaven" presided over ranks of kowtowing officials from his perch on the Dragon Throne. But, for all its antiquity, barely a hundred years have passed since the last emperor departed. Museum it might now be, but the halls still ring with echoes of past glories.

Good to know: Tickets for the Forbidden City, officially called The Palace Museum, should be purchased in advance online.

437

CHINA

Hike the Great Wall of China

Everything about China's formidable wall is, indeed, great, draped dreamily as it is across the north of the country and stretching out for more than 13,000 miles (21,000 km). And it took some might to build the wall, continuously worked on from the 3rd century BCE until the 17th century CE. The wall was mostly built from tamped earth, but, to defend the capital, it was fashioned from granite and brick and lined with ornate watchtowers. Often following the high ridgelines of mountains, it presented a formidable barrier to any would-be invaders. This sturdiness and inaccessibility helped preserve it, though some of it survives in a state of ruin. Today, it's the domain of hikers, who step into history from any of the 15 Chinese provinces through which the vast wall passes. That first sight of battlements crumbling, overgrown, and snaking away over lonely mountains is like nothing else.

Good to know: The unrestored Great Wall around Beijing can be difficult to access, so consider going with a reputable tour.

436

CHINA

Take in the glitz and glamour of Shanghai

Easily China's most cosmopolitan city, Shanghai jostles with Beijing to be the country's leading metropolis—a battle this shining contender appears to be winning. Straddling both banks of the Huangpu River, near the mouth of the Yangtze River, Shanghai is China's largest and most dynamic city, where everything is bigger, faster, and glitzier. Towering over the city from the business area of Pudong is the Shanghai Tower, the city's architectural symbol and China's tallest building. The skyline around it is a loud, proud proclamation of China's modern-day economic miracle in contrast to the Old City opposite, where architecture can trace its heritage back to the Ming Dynasty. Add to that high-speed train routes, famous graffiti walls and the latest street fashions, and Shanghai is the best place to get a feel for the China of the future.

Good to know: Avoid arriving in the first week of October, because it's one of China's most crowded holiday periods.

MONGOLIA

Take in the beauty of Mongolia's landscape

From the Gobi Desert sands to the Siberian frontier, space and solitude reign supreme in Mongolia, one of the most sparsely populated countries on Earth. Piloting a 4WD across an expanse of grass, or gripping the reins of a horse as you skirt the shore of a lapis-blue lake, it can feel like you've got the country all to yourself. These are landscapes so boundless they change only imperceptibly from one moment to the next. Every so often, bone-white yurts, known as *ger*, break up the green uniformity of the grasslands. Away from the capital, Ulaanbaatar, most Mongolians live in these small, felt-lined abodes, tending animals and moving with the seasons; theirs is a way of life hardly changed since the days of the ruler Genghis Khan. Stepping inside to share milk tea and mutton with a herding family, with the stove crackling as the *ger* creaks in the gusty wind, is a memory you'll be reminiscing about for a long time.

Good to know: The best time to visit is between May and August, with the big Naadam Festival taking place in July.

439

SOUTH KOREA

Enjoy a change of pace in fast-moving Seoul

Everybody is talking about Seoul. Why? Riding high on the Korean Wave (Hallyu) of pop culture domination, this city has captured the world's attention with its stadium-filling pop bands, game-changing beauty products, and Netflix smashes—and that's without mentioning the food. South Korea's capital for 600 years, it's home to fully half of the country's population, and is the cultural star the rest of Korea orbits. All that makes for a city that's constantly busy and chasing the new; trends shift at lightning speed, new landmarks shoot up in the blink of an eye, and that coffee shop you fell in love with might be replaced in a flash. But underneath that restless energy lies a traditional core, where hearty bowls of kimchi stew are served in decades-old restaurants and artisans fold *hanji* (Korean paper) in beautiful hanok villages. *Hanbok*, Korean traditional dress, is so loved that it has its own dedicated holiday in October. It's only by visiting that you'll begin to tap Seoul's deep well of excitement and creativity—one that goes far beyond Hallyu.

Good to know: Summers here can be hot, humid, and hectic, so save your visit for the fall.

In Jeju, coral-rich seas splash onto volcanic sand beaches, hidden waterfalls plunge in lush countryside, and dormant volcanoes give way to epic lava tube caves.

440

SOUTH KOREA

Escape to Jeju Island

South Korea is blessed with well over 3,000 islands, but Jeju is a cut above the rest. Lying around 52 miles (83 km) off the south coast, Korea's biggest island is the country's most cherished escape, and it's easy to see why. Here, coral-rich seas splash onto volcanic sand beaches, hidden waterfalls plunge in the lush countryside, and dormant volcanoes give way to epic lava tube caves. Watching over this idyllic portrait is the country's highest mountain, Hallasan. If all this sounds like the archetypal island escape, just wait until you hear a hypnotic whistle sound across the waves. This melodic sound, known as *sumbisori*, is part of the ancient breathing technique used by the island's *haenyeo*, female free divers who swim deep underwater to harvest marine life. Emerging from the volcanic shores, carrying a bountiful catch after their morning dive, the divers whistle after holding their breath for such a long time. And while Jeju is undoubtedly beautiful, it's the *haenyeo* that make this island unique—it's the only place where such divers still make a living. Suffice to say, shellfish plucked fresh from the seabed will never taste quite like it does on Jeju Island.

Good to know: To skip the crowds, avoid traveling during the public holiday periods in South Korea and China.

442

JAPAN

Pass through a tranquil bamboo grove

Fast-growing bamboo is endlessly versatile: it's a delicious springtime snack as much as it is a great renewable building material. However, forest bathing in a grove of this unique plant is where its power can really be felt. The long, papery leaves of the sky-reaching plant filter light to create a dappled effect on surfaces, known in Japanese as *komorebi*. Lengthy bamboo stalks grow all over Japan—usually found on farmland, temple grounds, and even in urban green spaces. One of the most magical places to see it is the Arashiyama Bamboo Grove, on the outskirts of Kyoto. A few minutes in this forest—provided you visit when it's not too crowded—will have you feeling calmer, centered, and close to nature. Walk through and hear a soothing susurrus, made as the slender stalks bend and sway in the wind.

Good to know: Visit during the Arashiyama Hanatoro in December, when it's covered in a green light every evening.

441

JAPAN

Walk the Kumano Kodo

The roads of the Kumano Kodo have been traversed for more than a millennium by pilgrims seeking out ancient sites of worship. Sprawling more than 150 miles (350 km) on Honshu island, this network of trails makes up one of the country's most celebrated and protected journeys. Portions still exist today as they did a thousand years ago, winding through forests, along coastal paths, and occasionally widening into a village where walkers can rest at an inn. The tranquil nature here is a draw, but so are the shrines and temples, of which the three Kumano shrines are the highlights. These sites provide a chance to worship in Kumano faith, combining Shinto, Buddhism, and various local folk beliefs, and see structures dating back as early as the 10th century.

Good to know: The local tourism bureau runs Kumano Travel, which offers information about the different routes.

Sprawling more than 150 miles (350 km) on Honshu island, this network of trails makes up one of the country's most celebrated and protected journeys.

JAPAN

Indulge in culture in Kyoto

Kyoto was Japan's capital for more than a thousand years, from 794 until 1868, and, in many ways, it's still its cultural center. It brims with history—it's home to more UNESCO-listed sites than any other city on Earth—as well as beauty and religious import. There are about 2,000 temples and shrines scattered in Kyoto, including Kinkakuji with its Golden Pavilion and Ryoanji, which houses a famed dry garden. One of the most popular, though, is the Fushimi Inari Taisha, which draws crowds daily. The red, torii-lined path here, which marks the boundary between the everyday and the sacred, is among the most iconic sights in the Kansai region. Wherever you step foot in this city, you're bound to come across some of the elegance and refinement for which Kyoto, past and present, is known.

Good to know: Cycling can be a wonderful way to get around the city; rent an electric bike to help with the few hills.

JAPAN

Drink tea in a traditional teahouse

Frothy, bitter, green, and soul-satisfying, tea goes hand in hand with Japanese culture. The leafy brew has a history in Japan that is thought to go back to the early 800s, when it was first brought from China by Buddhist monks. Since then, the Japanese tea ceremony has been perfected, a ritual that involves ceremonially preparing matcha in order to clear the mind. You needn't partake in hour-long ceremonies to clear your own, though; sipping a brew in a time-honored teahouse is up there with the top relaxation techniques. The best of Japan's teahouses feel like cozy homes, where you're directed to take off your shoes and settle on tatami mats, like at Amazake Chaya in Hakone or Kosoan in Tokyo. Once settled, it's time to choose a tea: perhaps gyokuro, the highest grade of green tea, or a classic matcha, consisting of finely ground powder. With your hands nursing a warm cup, the stresses of the day seem to drift away.

Good to know: If attending a tea ceremony, dress up to show respect and appreciation to your host.

302

445

JAPAN

Scale the scenic trails of Mount Fuji

Visible across the Kantō Plain, Mount Fuji's iconic lilac-gray, sometimes snow-capped peak emerging through low cloud is instantly recognizable. The tallest peak in the country, Fuji-san (as it's known locally) stands at more than 12,300 ft (3,700 m), and straddles the prefectures of Yamanashi and Shizuoka. The mountain is in fact an active volcano—although there haven't been any eruptions since 1707—and, until 150 years ago, it was believed to be so sacred that it was only ever climbed by pilgrims. Today, more than 200,000 people trek the paths of Mount Fuji each year. Some of the easier trails—or stages—don't require a lot of specialized tools, although they do necessitate some preparation. The most popular way to ascend is to hike partway up the night before, rest in one of the mountain huts along the trail, and then finish the climb just before dawn in order to see the sunrise from the peak, with the Fuji Five Lakes gleaming below.

Good to know: The official climbing season is between early June and mid-September, so plan accordingly.

446

JAPAN

See the cherry blossoms

Nowhere celebrates the arrival of spring quite like Japan. In what feels like a blink of the eye, clouds of sakura paint the country a palette of pinks, with 30,000 trees blooming in succession over a few weeks, ornamenting parks, temples, and streets. Locals celebrate with hanami, cherry-blossom viewing picnics that unfold beneath the blooming trees, with some of the best taking place in Tokyo's Shinjuku Gyoen Garden and the town of Yoshino in western Honshu. But it doesn't stop there. The hype extends to sakura-themed snacks, with flavored lattes, burgers, and ice cream making the perfect accompaniment to cherry-blossom viewing parties. As quickly as they arrive, the pink petals soon scatter and the moment is over. If you miss it, there's always next year.

Good to know: Check the Japan Meteorological Corporation's annual sakura forecast online.

WHERE ELSE TO SEE CHERRY BLOSSOMS

WASHINGTON, D.C..
In 1912, Mayor Yukio Ozaki of Tokyo gifted this city 3,000 cherry trees, and the three-week Cherry Blossom Festival over March and April celebrates their blooms.

STOCKHOLM, SWEDEN
In late April, pink flowers dazzle the city of Stockholm, especially along the pretty avenues of Kungsträdgården (The King's Garden).

BONN, GERMANY
Walk down the cobbled lanes of Heerstrasse, nicknamed Cherry Blossom Avenue, in the first two weeks of April for a vivid pink canopy.

VANCOUVER, CANADA
The Vancouver Cherry Blossom Festival is reason enough to visit the city in April, but simply strolling Stanley Park or Queen Elizabeth Park in spring guarantees sakura sightings.

TOKYO

Plucked from the pages of a science-fiction novel, Tokyo is full of gleaming skyscrapers and high-end technology. There's always something happening here, and it's no surprise why—it's a megacity built from many neighborhoods, each with its own draw. Let yourself get lost among its bustling alleys and streets.

Indulge in anime history at the Ghibli Museum

It cannot be overstated how much Japan, or rather, Studio Ghibli, has done for the world of anime. Japanese anime may be more famous in its TV form, but Studio Ghibli's big-screen animated features like *Spirited Away* (2001) and *My Neighbor Totoro* (1988) are some of the country's most loved cultural exports. Whimsical, fantastical, and fully immersive, these films create magical universes that feel real; at the studio's dedicated museum, reality and the magic of imagination collide. "Let's get lost together" is director Hayao Miyazaki's promise with the world he's created inside this quirky mansion, filled with winding staircases, tiny mystery doors, towering character models, and a mock animation room. And, like the best Ghibli films, the magic is in the detail, like the cat taps in the bathrooms that recall Jiji from *Kiki's Delivery Service* (1989), or the stained-glass windows that illustrate scenes from *Princess Mononoke* (1997). For passionate *otaku* (geeks), it's a dream to make a pilgrimage to Japan, and this homage to the studio's work is truly the holy grail (just put your camera away; photography is banned and escapism is mandatory).

Good to know: Advance tickets are essential and sell out fast; they're released on the 10th of the month for the one that follows.

448

Grab the mic at a karaoke joint

Going to karaoke in the land where it was created is something of a rite of passage. With its roots in *utagoe kissa*—singing cafés popular in the 1950s to 1970s—karaoke has become a global phenomenon, but nothing beats experiencing it in Japan. Emerging onto Tokyo's neon-lit streets after eating and drinking in a cozy *izakaya*, it doesn't take much to end up in a private room belting out your favorite tune. Big Echo and Joysound are the most foreigner-friendly in terms of the technology and instructions, but the assistants at any venue will be happy to give you a walk-through of the handheld console that's used to input the songs (and English words almost always accompany the Japanese on screen). In between singing, dancing, and browsing the catalog for the next perfect song, you can use the intercom to order drinks and snacks, which are brought to your room so you don't have to miss one melodic minute.

Good to know: Go to Karaoke Kan *(30-8 Udagawacho)* to see where the karaoke scene in *Lost in Translation* (2001) was filmed.

449

Visit the Tokyo National Museum

Situated in the sprawling Ueno Park on the northeast side of the city, the Tokyo National Museum is home to the world's largest collection of Japanese art and decorative crafts. Dedicated to Asian art—including intricate samurai armor, lacquered treasures, carved religious statuary, and terra-cotta warriors—and run by the Japanese government, the museum is housed in a series of grand buildings that date back to the late 1800s. No two visits here need look the same, with displays changing frequently and almost always around 4,000 objects on display at any one time. First-timer? The Honkan gallery, the museum's main building, is a good place to start for an introduction to Japanese heritage, housing art from ancient finds to modern masters alongside a superb collection of calligraphy, armor, and tea utensils. Don't have time to explore the three other galleries? As if you needed an excuse to return to Tokyo.

Good to know: The free Tokyo National Museum Art Guide app has a free audio guide that can be used on site or at home.

Wander the grounds of the Imperial Palace

The Imperial Palace in Tokyo has been the home of the imperial family since 1868, when Edo Castle, the former home of the Tokugawa shoguns, was commandeered for the emperor and then renamed. Remnants of the old castle are scattered throughout the grounds, which have a moat running around the perimeter. Coupled with the strategically placed keeps, it's a good reminder that this structure was originally built as a fortress. In the spring, blushing cherry trees sweep their branches over the paths, hanging over the water and framing the keeps to make for scenic, postcard-perfect views. The palace perimeter is a popular jogging and cycling route year-round, with a variety of gardens and parks adjacent to it providing the leafy backdrop for a serene stroll. In a city where everything can feel in a permanent state of flux, the palace and its grounds form a green thread of continuity with the capital and Japan's past.

Good to know: While the grounds are always open, you can only enter the Imperial Palace two days a year.

Bar-hop around buzzing Golden Gai

For a quintessentially Japanese night out, you really can't beat an atmospheric *izakaya*—down-to-earth taverns where you eat as you drink. Even better? A whole street dedicated to these institutions. Japan has no shortage of such alleyways, known as *yokocho*, but Tokyo's Golden Gai is famous for good reason. In this labyrinth of six narrow alleys lie more than 200 tiny bars, standing cheek by jowl and stacked on top of one another. In some, there's only room to stand; in others, just a handful of seats welcome you. Part of the Kabukicho red light district, this higgledy-piggledy neighborhood is a battered remnant of the postwar period, surrounded by flashier and more modern architecture that is now the norm in this part of the city. It's a time capsule of a Tokyo that once was, and each bar here is a distinct portal into another world—a library of floor-to-ceiling books might surround you in one, while death metal and horror movies hit you over the head in another. Wherever you end up, visiting several to find your favorite makes for a great night.

Good to know: Some bars can be wary of non-regulars, so look out for "no tourists" or "regulars only" signs on some doors.

452

See a sumo match

With a resounding stomp and a rippling of strong legs, the *rikishi* (professional wrestler) tries to psyche out his opponent. In the national sport of Japan, the actual wrestling time in each bout is often short, the match extended by a great degree of posturing, glowering, and salt-flinging to symbolically purify the ring. All the while, the mighty wrestlers' bulk is on full display, interrupted only by a strategically placed belt and loincloth, with some of the fighters weighing in at more than 330 lb (150 kg). While no one knows exactly when sumo began, it's thought to have started at least 1,500 years ago as a way to delight the gods during harvest rituals and gain their support for a good crop. After all of that pre-bout posturing, the referee gives the nod and the two wrestlers collide into one another with a thud and a crack, sending gasps around the arena. A flurry of slaps and shoves commences before one *rikishi* is thrown to the ground or tumbles out of the ring. The match is over, but the admiration for these wrestlers lingers long after.

Good to know: Three tournaments take place in Tokyo's Ryogoku Kokugikan arena in January, May, and September.

> While no one knows exactly when sumo began, it's thought to have started at least 1,500 years ago as a way to delight the gods during harvest rituals and gain their support for a good crop.

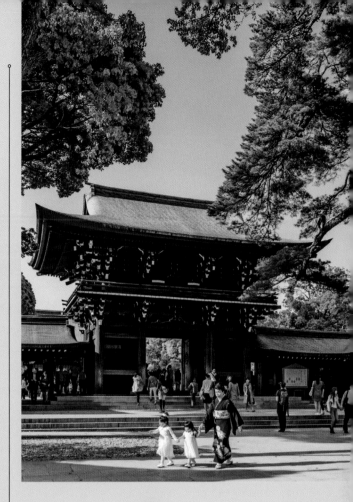

453

Pay a visit to the tranquil Meiji Jingu Shrine

It's preternaturally quiet on the grounds of Meiji Jingu Shrine, a pleasant surprise considering it's located in the center of one of the world's busiest cities. Built across 170 acres (70 ha) of evergreen forest with some 120,000 trees, the lush grounds of the shrine are fragrant with camphor and fringed with ferns, a beautiful setting for one of the most famous and important Shinto sites in Japan. For many, coming here is about quietly praying, purchasing amulets for safety and health, and paying their respects to the Emperor Meiji and the Empress Shōken, who are enshrined here. For others, it's about walking through the largest wooden torii (sacred gate) in Japan. Reaching more than 40 ft (12 m) high and 55 ft (17 m) wide and hewn from the timber of a 1,500-year-old cypress tree, the torii separates the realm of the gods from the human world. Wherever your feet take you, it'll be a prime spot to have a mindful moment.

Good to know: The grounds are open from dusk until dawn, so don't plan your visit to too late in the afternoon.

454

Soak up the atmosphere of Sensoji Temple

Tokyo's oldest Buddhist temple dates back to the year 645, when the city was still a humble fishing village. A statue of the bodhisattva Kannon, goddess of mercy, was found by two fishermen in the Sumida River, and a temple was soon constructed to enshrine the find. The temple has three gates, each flanked by fierce guardians that protect the structure and the statue within. Of these gates, the mighty Kaminarimon (meaning Thunder Gate) marks the entrance to the temple precinct, a riot of activity, and the start of Nakamise-dori street, a busy shopping lane stuffed with snacks, souvenirs, and religious objects. Inside the temple's main hall and around the five-tiered pagoda—both lacquered a distinctive red, black, and gold—the air hangs thick with incense and the prayers of the 30 million visitors who come here every year seeking succor. Arrive for new year celebrations or on festival days, and you'll see the streets throng with visitors chanting, praying, and celebrating in festival dress.

Good to know: Bring a few coins when visiting for incense offerings, fortunes, or amulets.

Take in the views from Tokyo Tower

Its claim to fame as Japan's tallest structure has been usurped by upstarts in recent years, but Tokyo Tower still has a place in Tokyoites' hearts as one of the most iconic of the city landmarks. Modeled on Paris's tall Eiffel Tower and sporting a bright orange and white design, it's hard to miss on the city's skyline today. It was in fact built as a communications tower in 1958, made of steel and scrap metal melted down from US tanks after the end of World War II. Standing at a whopping 1,091 ft (333 m) tall, this soaring structure was at one point a striking symbol of Japan's postwar boom and new technological developments—it was the sole broadcasting tower for the Kantō region when first opened. FM radio signals continue to be broadcast from here today, though newer digital broadcasts have moved. From the two observation decks—the Main Deck at 492 ft (150 m) and the Top Deck at 820 ft (250 m)—an endless panorama of Tokyo and Mount Fuji unfolds, making for breathtaking views.

Good to know: Head up the 600 steps to the main observation deck, halfway up the tower, to get a feel for its height.

455

Sample some of the world's best sushi

Today, sushi is a ubiquitous dish around the world. Often reworked to suit local tastes when prepared outside of Japan, sushi in the capital city is made according to the long-standing traditions that make this dish so special. It was first prepared in Tokyo in the 1800s as raw fish served on a bed of vinegared rice, eventually evolving into the bite-size format most familiar to diners today. Find a good sushi restaurant—easily done in a city with the most Michelin-starred restaurants in the world—and settle into a carefully curated dining experience. With a skilled sushi chef at the helm, you'll likely be presented one sushi dish at a time, amounting to a mouthful or two. Freed from other distractions on your plate, you can focus on the presentation and flavors of each ricey mouthful. Expect very fresh, seasonal seafood; perfectly prepared rice; and unique flavor combinations served up in a minimalist setting—when it comes to sushi, simplicity is never boring.

Good to know: For sushi on a budget, head to a restaurant where you can pluck plates from a conveyor belt.

JAPAN

Unwind with a dip in an *onsen*

With more than 100 active volcanoes and more than 27,000 thermal springs, Japan has developed a unique bathing culture that makes the most of the natural wonders it's been blessed with. Using naturally hot water from these springs, *onsen* invite people to bathe in restorative waters. Depending on the spring, various minerals will likely be present in the waters, each offering different healing and soothing properties, from relieving high blood pressure to treating the likes of arthritis and joint pain. Some indulge in an *onsen* while staying at a *ryokan*, a traditional inn, while others visit a spa for a day; for something truly unforgettable, though, visit a *rotenburo* (an open-air bath), which may offer spectacular views you couldn't access any other way. The winter season makes a particularly beautiful setting, with forest, mountain, or ocean views unfolding as you bathe, helping you truly commune with nature.

Good to know: Bathing etiquette dictates that you wash your body before getting into communal pools.

JAPAN

Hop on board a speedy bullet train

Hurtling past rice paddies, snow-capped mountains, and lush tea fields at speeds of 200 mph (320 kph), the *shinkansen* (or bullet train, as it's known) is the best way to travel across Japan. With a network crisscrossing most of the country, the rail service allows smooth, efficient, and comfortable transit between most of Japan's major cities. Since 1964, it has carried over six billion passengers, with a daily capacity of around 229,000 people. Not one to sit on its laurels, operator JR Central is also working on the Chuo Shinkansen, a maglev train that will travel at a speed of 300 mph (500 kph), connecting Tokyo and Osaka in just over an hour. And, in spite of the breakneck speed and number of passengers, all is peaceful on board, the seats spacious. Japan does speed and efficiency like nowhere else, so sit back, tuck into a "train lunch box" or sushi and watch Mount Fuji sail serenely past your window.

Good to know: Purchase a Japan Rail Pass, which covers journeys on any *shinkansen* except Nozomi services.

JAPAN

Spend the night in a ryokan

Visiting a traditional Japanese inn—or *ryokan*—is a must-do Japanese experience. More than just a place to lay your head after a whirlwind day of sightseeing, these guesthouses offer a taste of Japanese hospitality and culture; some are family-run with a handful of rooms, others are huge hotel-like spots. Regardless, rooms are always beautiful, adorned with sliding paper doors and decorative scrolls. Guests spend their time drinking pots of tea (as opposed to cups of coffee) and tucking into sumptuous multicourse *kaiseki* (Japanese gourmet) meals, washed down with plenty of sake. Many inns also have on-site *onsen* to relax in and offer traditional *yukata*, soft, cotton robes perfect for post-bath lounging. Come nightfall, guests sleep on a futon bed laid upon a tatami, rectangular padded straw-and-rush mats used for flooring and providing a soft surface on which to rest. It's the ideal setting for reflecting on your day.

Good to know: For information on how to make a booking, visit the Japan National Tourism Organization website.

OCEANIA

AUSTRALIA

See Uluṟu

Standing proud on a desert plain in the Northern Territory, iconic Uluṟu (once known as Ayers Rock) is the world's largest monolith and the spiritual heart of Australia. The rock is part of the larger Uluṟu-Kata Tjuṯa National Park, jointly managed by the Aṉangu people, its traditional custodians. Stay in the "Red Centre" for at least a few days to truly experience Uluṟu's myriad faces. Rise early to a chorus of birdsong and see the rock change colors as the sun slowly lifts over the plain; you can return in the early evening to witness the sun setting Uluṟu ablaze with fiery shades of orange. By day, learn about Aboriginal culture and rock art on guided tours of the region; hike, cycle, or segway along the 6-mile (10-km) Base Path; or take a bush food class. At night, dine under the stars as you watch the spectacular Wintjiri Wiru, an immersive storytelling light show, and see the "Field of Light" art installation, which illuminates the surrounding desert with over 50,000 stems of shimmering light.

Good to know: Fly to nearby Yulara on the outskirts of the national park or take a four-hour drive from Alice Springs.

462

AUSTRALIA

Meet the quokkas at Rottnest Island

A short ferry ride from Western Australia's capital city of Perth whisks passengers to Rottnest Island, known as Wadjemup in Noongar. The coastline here is dusted in white sand, the waters range from baby blue to deep cobalt, and salt lakes change from pink to red depending on the time of day. But it's not just the island's beauty that draws visitors to these sublime shores—a trip to Rottnest also offers a chance to meet a quokka, a friendly, cat-size marsupial. And who wouldn't want to meet the world's happiest animal? They can only be found in places in Western Australia where there are few predators, like Rottnest Island. When 17th-century Dutch sailors landed here, they mistook the quokkas for giant rats, so called the island "Rat's Nest"—and the name stuck. The seemingly grinning quokkas bound around the island searching for shrubs and can be spotted in shady areas escaping the heat. Look closely and you might even see a little joey peering curiously out of its mother's pouch.

Good to know: Stay on the island overnight—quokkas are most active once the sun sets.

461

AUSTRALIA

Marvel at the Outback

The head-spinningly vast Outback is home to some of the most celebrated landscapes on Earth. Visit at sunset, when the ocher-colored dirt turns to fiery amber, and you'll quickly see why. Seemingly endless, this gargantuan patchwork of desert and subtropical savanna is Australia's glorious heartland, forming more than 80 percent of the country's interior. The Outback is a land of scorched extremes: you can explore the sacred sandstone monolith of Uluru, gaze out over the plunging gorges and vertiginous cliffs of the Kimberley region, or climb the prehistoric peaks of the Bungle Bungle Range. Though it seems beautifully desolate, the Outback has been home to Aboriginal Australian cultures for around 60,000 years. Ancient petroglyphs (rock carvings) and rock paintings are testament to the vision of these peoples, revealing the close kinship between humans and landscape. Perhaps the best way of exploring this vast desert wonderland is by touring the landscape with an Aboriginal guide—there are few better ways of connecting with this vast land and its ancestral communities.

Good to know: Food, water, and phone reception can be sparse in the Outback—plan accordingly.

> Seemingly endless, this gargantuan patchwork of desert and subtropical savanna is Australia's glorious heartland.

463

AUSTRALIA

Road trip along the Great Ocean Road

There's something elemental about driving the Great Ocean Road, which follows what may just be Australia's most beautiful stretch of coastline. Spanning 150 miles (240 km) across Victoria, from the sleepy surf hub of Torquay to the small town of Allansford, it winds past eucalypt forests, world-class surf spots, coastal hiking trails, and spectacular natural wonders. And there's no bad time of year to do it. When it's warm, this road trip can feel like traveling through an idealized version of an Aussie summer, with wild waves crashing upon endless expanses on golden sand. When the wind blows, it's easy to see why there have been so many shipwrecks here, and striking rock formations such as the limestone Twelve Apostles attest to the ocean's erosive power. A coastal hiking trail follows most of the road, so don't miss the opportunity to park up and stretch your legs; you might just spot wallabies, kangaroos, and echidnas on your adventures. And be sure to take turns as you drive—part of the joy of this route is simply taking in those views.

Good to know: Plan around four to five days to complete the road trip at a leisurely pace.

464

AUSTRALIA

Get to know koalas on Kangaroo Island

There's an irony to visiting Kangaroo island to see koalas, but Australia loves its humor. Arguably among the world's coolest marsupials, koalas are one of the country's best-loved animals and an absolute must-see when down under. To guarantee a special encounter, head to one of the private animal reserves on South Australia's Kangaroo Island. Taken here from the mainland more than a century ago to help protect their population, the koalas are now larger and have longer, tuftier ears than their cousins across the water, but they are every bit as photogenic. At the Kangaroo Island Wildlife Park, visitors can get right up close to watch koalas dozing (they sleep for up to 20 hours a day), munching lazily on eucalyptus leaves, or clumsily shuffling between tree branches. For more of a wilderness experience, join a guided walk at Hanson Bay Wildlife Sanctuary, where you can see koalas in the wild, as well as kangaroos, echidnas, and a range of birds. Alternatively, try your luck spotting koalas hiding in the red gum trees along Cygnet River. They're usually more active at dusk, so watch as the sun goes down.

Good to know: Whether you take the ferry or fly over, you'll need a car to explore Kangaroo Island.

AUSTRALIA

Snorkel the Great Barrier Reef

Grab your mask and snorkel to dive into the world's largest coral reef system. Big enough to be seen from space, the Great Barrier Reef is estimated to comprise more than 2,500 individual reefs of coral and is home to more than 1,500 species of fish. Its seagrass beds are safe havens for peaceful dugongs, while sand banks and islets provide refuge for migrating sea birds and nesting sea turtles. In the deeper, darker blue, humpback whales cruise along the "Humpback Highway" to mate and give birth in its warm waters before returning to Antarctica—the best time to see these gentle giants is from June to November. To get a deeper look at all the marine life and seascapes, sign up for a scuba diving course and make a liveaboard yacht your base. Falling asleep under a starry sky and waking to technicolor corals? Bliss.

Good to know: Ensure you snorkel responsibly by booking a tour with a dedicated reef expert.

AUSTRALIA
SYDNEY

Golden sands lapped by azure ocean waters. World renowned harbor architecture. An inclusive, diverse, and welcoming culture that prides itself on wild celebrations. Sydney has long been the destination par excellence for all kinds of globetrotters, and with very good reason.

Admire the Sydney Opera House

Instantly recognizable all over the world, this architectural icon has become a symbol of Sydney. And it's little wonder it garners so much attention: there are few buildings with as distinctive a design as the Sydney Opera House. Though popularly known as just the "Opera House," it is, in fact, a complex of theaters and halls linked beneath its famous shells. It's these staggered white panels, which look like billowing sails, that have helped propel the building—and its home city—onto the front cover of endless tourism brochures, and make its long, complicated birth even more worthwhile. In 1957, Danish architect Jørn Utzon won a competition to design a performing arts center in Sydney, beating 232 other entries. Construction began in 1959, proposed to be completed in four years with a $7 million budget, but resolving the challenges of its complex design meant it instead took $102 million to build and didn't open its doors to visitors until 1973. Considering its status as one of the world's most recognizable buildings today, perhaps it was worth the extra time and expense.

Good to know: Don't just admire the exterior—be sure to buy a ticket for an opera performance or ballet show inside.

Climb Sydney Harbor Bridge

The greatness of Sydney Harbor Bridge is best expressed in numbers: 1,400 workers were involved in its construction, more than 150,000 vehicles cross the bridge each day, and it takes 1,332 steps to reach the top, where you'll have a front-row view of icons like the Sydney Opera House. Affectionately known as "The Coathanger" thanks to its distinctive shape, the bridge has been the backbone of Sydney Harbor since 1932, linking the southern and northern sides. While trips run at various times of day, opt for the sunset climb to witness the dropping sun glimmering against the skyscrapers of the city's Central Business District. Alternatively, take a tour led by a First Nations Storyteller to hear about Aboriginal landmarks and original stories of Sydney and its beautiful surroundings. If the three-hour climb isn't enough, the bridge has a relatively flat pedestrian path which you can walk slowly, marveling at the Sydney skyline for as long as you'd like.

Good to know: BridgeClimb Sydney has staff who provide extra support for climbers who have a fear of heights.

MUST-DO SYDNEY FESTIVALS AND EVENTS

Sydney Gay and Lesbian Mardi Gras
A fun-filled festival ending with a huge parade in March.

Lunar New Year
Fireworks, lanterns, and lion dancers take over the streets in February.

Sydney to Hobart Yacht Race
Sydneysiders line the harbor in December to watch yachts compete for first place.

NAIDOC Week
The National Aboriginal and Islander Day Observance Committee Week celebrates Torres Strait Islander and Aboriginal cultures in July.

Vivid Sydney
Expect epic light installations, music, and talks between May and June.

Manly International Jazz Festival
Australia's largest community-based celebration of jazz sees performances take over various venues in Manly in October.

Celebrate the Sydney Gay and Lesbian Mardi Gras

What began as a protest march against gay and lesbian discrimination in 1978 has grown into *the* LGBTQ+ Pride party to end all Pride parties. This legendary two-week-long festival brings cabaret and comedy, drag and dance to the city every year in March, with the Sydney Opera House displaying the Progress Pride flag, rainbow murals covering once-barren building walls, and some roads even receiving a splash of paint for the occasion. Art workshops, performances, mini festivals, and conferences take over during the two weeks, but it's the Mardi Gras Parade that's the talk of the town, and has everyone dressing to the nines. This huge sequin-and-glitter-filled parade sees more than 200 floats take over Oxford Street, including the beloved 78ers, the first Sydney Mardi Gras marchers, many of whom were arrested in 1978. Show your support by getting glammed up and shimmying down the parade route in your finest.

Good to know: Bring snacks and wear comfy shoes during the parade—you'll be standing for hours.

469

AUSTRALIA

Swim at Bondi Beach

A languorous afternoon spent on Bondi Beach? That'll do nicely. Come summertime, hundreds of colorful towels, umbrellas, and buckets accent the golden swath of sand at Sydney's iconic beach resort, while surfers visit from far and wide in search of the perfect wave. Made famous worldwide by the reality TV show *Bondi Rescue*, Bondi has become a poster child for Sydney's thriving beach culture, and it offers the definitive beach experience: see and be seen at the outdoor gym, get an adrenaline fix at the skate park, or cool off with an ocean dip and you'll quickly see why so many yearn for Sydney's golden sands. But of all the iconic activities to take part in here, a swim at the Bondi Icebergs pool on the beach's southern end tops them all. Open since 1929 as a way for local life savers to maintain their fitness during the winter, Bondi Icebergs remains a year-round public access hot spot, home to two outdoor pools and a sauna. So throw down that towel and get your lengths in.

Good to know: Bondi's gentle waves are perfect for beginners, so inquire at the surf schools dotting the beachfront.

AUSTRALIA

Explore the world's oldest rainforest in Daintree

Time travel over 130 millions years into the past, to when dinosaurs still roamed Earth, on a visit to the Daintree Rainforest. There are few more biodiverse places in the world: the forest supports more than 3,000 plant, 100 mammal, 100 reptile, 50 amphibian, and nearly 400 bird species. Tread lightly along its trails and you might spot a cassowary, a 5½-ft- (1.7-m-) tall bird with a radiant blue head and dangling red wattle. The cassowary acts as de facto custodian of the Daintree, eating fruits that other critters are too small to consume and spreading their seeds across the forest floor. Cruise the rivers to spy saltwater crocodiles basking on the shore; hike with an Aboriginal custodian of the land to learn about the relationship between the forest and its people; and venture out at night to spot bandicoots, owls, and frogs. When you've had your fill, venture to the coast, where sandy beaches and coral reefs await.

Good to know: Though you can expect some rain all year, the driest time to visit is from May to September.

471

AUSTRALIA

Set sail on the Whitsunday Islands

Australia is home to many stunning holiday destinations, and the Whitsunday Islands are up there with the best of them. Not only is Whitsunday Island itself home to Whitehaven Beach, said to be one of the world's best beaches, but this entire archipelago off the Queensland coast is made up of 74 jewellike islands and islets, all ripe for exploration. Around 66 remain uninhabited, with a boat being the only way to reach many of them. Each island has its own appeal: Hamilton Island is dotted with hiking trails and luxury resorts, Hook Island offers rugged beauty and unrivaled snorkeling, and Langford Island is home to vibrant coral reefs and manta rays. Between mastering the points of sail, an entire day can easily slip by going on an underwater safari, keeping an eye out for clown fish and giant clams. And at night? Well, you'll be far away from any semblance of city living, so close your eyes and let the water tapping against the hull lull you to sleep.

Good to know: Time your trip to coincide with humpback whale migration season, from June to October.

The Milford Track was named "the finest walk in the world" by *The Spectator* magazine back in 1908, and it's a claim that still holds true more than a century later.

472

NEW ZEALAND

Hike the Milford Track

The Milford Track was named "the finest walk in the world" by *The Spectator* magazine back in 1908, and it's a claim that still holds true more than a century later. The most famous of New Zealand's "Great Walks," this multi-day route serves up beautiful landscapes in spades as you journey into the heart of the remote Fiordland National Park. After a boat trip across Lake Te Anau, you'll begin walking into a damp, mossy forest, through alpine carpet and majestic mountains before a boat takes you to the track's namesake, Milford Sound. This stunning fjord, with inky waters and forest-covered cliffs, offers the perfect crescendo to a hike that leaves little doubt that the Milford Track is one of the world's finest walks. One thing to note before you head off: at some point it'll probably rain, so make sure you pack your raincoat. Fiordland is, after all, one of the wettest regions in the world, but that only adds to the dramatic scenery.

Good to know: It's not possible to hike without prebooking and paying to stay in a Department of Conservation-run hut.

NEW ZEALAND

Test your limits in Queenstown

If your bucket list is brimming with epic adventures like jumping out of a plane, head to Queenstown, the "Adventure Capital of the World." Tucked in New Zealand's Southern Alps between snow-capped Coronet Peak and the jagged slopes of The Remarkables, Queenstown emerged as a world center for extreme sports during the 1970s. As tourism boomed, entrepreneurs found innovative ways for visitors to experience the area's stunning natural playground, developing the likes of para-gliding and bungee jumping. Things have become more extreme today, and you'll find just about every kind of adrenaline-inducing activity you can shake a ski pole at. Want to plunge off a hill? Paraglide from Bob's Peak above Lake Wakatipu. Up for plummeting from a daredevil height? Bungee jump from Kawarau Bridge, where the drop dips you into the water. Always wanted to speed through narrow gorges and thundering rapids? Whitewater raft over Shotover River. It's time to get your pulse racing.

Good to know: If you can't decide on an activity, book onto a multi-day tour with a company like Haka Tours and try them all.

NEW ZEALAND

Spot yellow-eyed penguins

South Island's beautiful 15-mile- (24-km-) long Otago Peninsula is home to the incredibly rare yellow-eyed penguin. *"Hoiho"* in te reo Māori, this is the world's most endangered penguin, with only around 225 pairs left in New Zealand. The best way to see these delightful creatures is in the company of an in-the-know guide, who'll ensure you don't miss them silently tumbling in on the evening waves or waddling their way to their shore nests. A guide will also help you maintain a respectful distance, focusing on the birds through binoculars so they can carry on their gallivanting untroubled by human presence. Take a tour, and you'll learn about the penguins' unique habits and history, and perhaps see other incredible local bird and marine life, such as cormorants, little blue penguins, sea lions, and royal albatrosses (this is the only mainland albatross colony in the Southern hemisphere, after all).

Good to know: During the nesting season, view penguins at close range from hides at the award-winning Penguin Place.

476

NEW ZEALAND

Stargaze in Aoraki

You've never seen stars quite like this before. Certified the world's first gold-tier reserve, the remote Aoraki Mackenzie International Dark Sky Reserve offers some of the very best stargazing on the planet. Come sundown, the night puts on a majestic show, and you'll enjoy the perfect cosmic vista: trace mystic constellations as meteoroids cascade across the darkness, or look out for distant planets shining with crystal clarity. It's possible to embark on a DIY stargazing experience at the reserve, but budding astronomers will get a lot more from a visit on an organized tour. Astronomy plays an important role in Māori culture, both as a tool for navigation and as the source for rich and complex Māori mythologies. Learn about this stargazing heritage on the Dark Sky Astronomy Experience at Lake Tekapō, within the Aoraki reserve, then join the professional research observatory at the summit of Mount John for night sky tours using both the naked eye and a range of high-powered telescopes. Get ready to lose yourself in the sublime immensity of the cosmos.

Good to know: Check the lunar calendar; the best time for stargazing is closer to the new moon.

WHERE ELSE TO GO STARGAZING

IRIOMOTE-ISHIGAKI NATIONAL PARK, JAPAN
The first place in Japan to receive an International Dark Sky Places accreditation, Iriomote-Ishigaki is the perfect place to see up to 84 constellations (weather depending, of course).

MAUNA KEA, HAWAII
Perhaps Hawaii's most famous stargazing spot, Mauna Kea is home to the world's largest research observatory, the Mauna Kea Observatory. Being so close to the equator, it's also a prime spot to see roughly 85 percent of all Earth's stars.

NEW MEXICO
Thanks to its high altitudes and low light pollution, this state promises views of Venus, Mercury, and the Milky Way. Follow the New Mexico True Dark Skies Trail for your best viewing chances.

475

NEW ZEALAND

Marvel at the Southern Lights

Like their northern hemisphere counterparts, the Southern Lights (or aurora australis) see the night sky awash with dancing lights of green, blue, purple, and red, as the sun's solar wind strikes Earth's magnetic field. To witness the display is an inspiring and humbling experience that's sure to remind you of Earth's tiny place in the universe. Bring your camera and tripod and expect to be out after midnight to witness this incredible natural phenomenon for yourself. Visible from the southern parts of New Zealand, Antarctica, and sometimes Tasmania in neighboring Australia, the aurora can be spotted at any time of year. For the best chance, however, time your visit between March and September, and travel as far south as you can. The sparsely populated Stewart Island/Rakiura is a good place to try, as is Lake Tekapō, part of the Aoraki Mackenzie International Dark Sky Reserve. Just head far away from the cities and get ready to take in the vast night sky as it springs into dazzling life.

Good to know: Aurora alerts are issued via NASA when space weather activity heats up.

477

NEW ZEALAND

Road trip from Christchurch to Blenheim

There are many reasons to stay in Christchurch, but there's a reason to leave too, and that's this road trip north to the town of Blenheim. Stay a couple of nights in Kaikōura, the perfect place to break up your trip, to take whale-watching tours, swim with dolphins, and watch New Zealand fur seals lazing on the shoreline. And birdwatchers, pack your binoculars: Kaikōura is also a center for seabirds, from penguins to petrels. Leave time to detour via Hanmer Springs, a small mountain hamlet with thermal springs and plenty of outdoor activities. As you continue to Blenheim, admire the mountains to your left and the Pacific Ocean on your right. Then wrap the road trip up with a boat tour of the Marlborough Sounds and a cycling tour of the wineries around Blenheim. Ignore the ETA on your GPS: a road trip up Highway 1 will take longer than you think—passing other cars is almost impossible and you'll need time to stop for photographs of those views along the way.

Good to know: A one-way car rental from Christchurch means you don't need to circle back down.

> There are many reasons to stay in Christchurch, but there's a reason to leave too, and that's this road trip north to the town of Blenheim.

478

NEW ZEALAND

Attend a hāngī

Enjoying a Māori hāngī—a feast of meat and vegetables cooked on hot stones underground—is a perfect way to enrich your understanding of Māori culture. The significance of the hāngī extends well beyond food preparation: it's a harmonious social ritual used to bridge the divide between peoples. The use of underground earth ovens is common across the Pacific, with *umu* used in Samoa and Tonga, *lovo* in Fiji, and *ahima'a* in Tahiti. Choosing the right stones and tending to them as the food roasts is an art passed down the generations. You can enjoy the ritual on a guided tour at the Waitangi Treaty Grounds or by joining one of the Māori-owned and run ventures in Rotorua. After a welcoming ceremony (*pōwhiri*), you'll feel the full force of the iconic Māori *haka*. This is usually followed by group singing (*waiata*) and *poi* dances. While you're absorbed by these powerful cornerstones of Māori culture, the hāngī will be slow-cooking over hot stones underground. Once the tender-cooked cuisine has been perfectly roasted, tuck in with a deeper appreciation and understanding of the country's ancestral culture.

Good to know: In Rotorua, you can enjoy a hāngī that's been roasted using the land's geothermal properties.

NEW ZEALAND

Hike Te Araroa
(The Long Pathway)

For bucket list travelers with time on their hands, this epic 1,900-mile (3,000-km) walk runs from Cape Reinga at the very top of New Zealand's North Island to Bluff at the tip of the South Island. You'll need at least four months to hike the whole Te Araroa (The Long Pathway) at an average of 16 miles (25 km) each day, but if you can set aside three months per island, you'll have time to stop in some of the places you'll fall in love with along the way (not to mention to rest or ride out inclement weather). Te Araroa traverses every kind of New Zealand landscape: farmland, forests, mountains, volcanoes, rivers, lakes, and white-sand beaches, plus cities like Auckland, Hamilton, and Wellington. It might be as simple as placing one foot in front of the other, but this demanding and extended adventure will guarantee a lifelong love affair with New Zealand.

Good to know: Te Araroa is best walked from north to south between October and April—or tackle it a section at a time.

480

NEW ZEALAND

Go caving at Waitomo

It may take a few moments for your eyes to adjust as your boat glides into the subterranean depths of the Waitomo Glowworm Caves. Slowly, the ethereal spectacle unfolds: thousands of luminescent glowworms dotting the cave roof like stars in the night sky. These vast limestone caves and their incandescent population of *Arachnocampa luminosa* have been amazing visitors since they were first opened in the 19th century (though the caves have been revered by the Māori for far longer). Later, as you wander through the cave system with your tour group, you'll learn about the spectacular history and cultural legacy of the caves. Ready to take this experience to the next level? It's time to get outside your comfort zone and rappel, rock climb, or even black-water raft into the bowels of this underworld. Claustrophobic? Vertigo-prone? Afraid of the dark? Maybe give this part a miss. For everyone else: adventure awaits.

Good to know: Book onto a tour, which vary by budget and level of difficulty.

481

NEW ZEALAND

Set-jet around Hobbiton

It was Peter Jackson, arguably, who put New Zealand on everyone's travel bucket list, with his Oscar-winning *Lord of the Rings* trilogy showcasing the country's epic natural beauty. And while adventures in "Middle Earth" can be had on both islands, to channel your inner Bilbo Baggins you'll want to visit the magical village of Hobbiton. The Hobbiton™ Movie Set Tour sweeps visitors into the world of Tolkien, offering the chance to explore the lush green pastures of the Shire and the cozy nooks of a Hobbit home. If time allows, the evening Banquet Tour is the most immersive way to experience Hobbiton, with a feast of top-quality New Zealand fare served at large banqueting tables in the Green Dragon Inn. After eating, drinking, and merry-making with fellow fans, top the night off with a storytelling session at the Party Tree, the tallest in the Shire. By the end of the tour, you'll feel a little closer to the magic of Tolkien's creation and the country that brought it to life.

Good to know: This is a popular stop on the journey from Auckland to Rotorua, so book ahead.

482

NEW ZEALAND

Unwind in one of Rotorua's thermal pools

Popular well before the wellness trend, the thermal pools and bubbling mud baths of Rotorua have been drawing visitors for more than a century. Hailed for their healing properties, these geothermal wonders are a result of powerful volcanic activity below ground. The thermal pools offer restoration of countless varieties: you can choose a secret hot tub surrounded by lush tree ferns and wood decking, or opt for an ultra-luxurious outfit offering spa treatments using Indigenous herbs, mud baths, and traditional Māori massages. One lakeside hot pool even has its visitors arriving by jet boat or seaplane. After a day spent indulging in some of the more high-octane experiences on offer in Rotorua—mountain biking, kayaking, and even luging down the side of a hill—an afternoon soaking in the naturally heated waters of Rotorua is all the more relaxing. The pools aren't only renowned for their health-enhancing charms, however: Rotorua is referred to as "sulfur city" for the naturally acrid scent of the geothermal gases. Once you sink into the warming waters, we're certain you'll be able to forgive the distinct aroma.

Good to know: The Polynesian Spa is the most renowned here, offering a mineral pool overlooking a heated freshwater pool.

483

NEW ZEALAND

Visit Auckland

Perched on an isthmus and shaped by its meandering harbor and the now-dormant volcanic peaks that surround it, Auckland isn't your average metropolis. In New Zealand's largest city, you can spend the day gallery- and museum-hopping and feasting at stylish restaurants in the urban center, or change the pace and head west to subtropical rainforest hems and sweeping beaches. The best trips start with those museums, like the moving Auckland War Memorial Museum, built to mark the end of World War I as a memorial to fallen soldiers; today, it covers the fascinating history of New Zealand's landscapes and people. When fresh air calls, head to Waitemata Harbor, where regattas bob on the water, testimony to New Zealand's success as a sailing nation. As the day draws to a close and you're soaking up the views from the soaring Sky Tower, the knowledge that you're only an hour's drive away from stunning beaches and bush tracks to explore the following day is as good as it gets. This buzzing city really does have it all.

Good to know: One of the nicest (and least expensive) ways to cruise around Auckland Harbor is to hop on a local ferry.

> Perched on an isthmus and shaped by its meandering harbor and the now-dormant volcanic peaks that surround it, Auckland isn't your average metropolis.

484

FIJI

See the Sigatoka Sand Dunes

Rippling along the wild shoreline of Viti Levu's southwestern coast, the peppery sand dunes of Sigatoka are a true visual feast. These intricate geological masterworks were sculpted over thousands of years as sediment from the Sigatoka River was washed ashore and swept into soaring dunes by coastal winds. The natural features of these landscapes are mesmerizing enough, but Sigatoka is culturally significant too. One of Fiji's oldest recorded prehistoric sites, the shifting sands continue to yield evidence of the past, with human bones, pottery, and stone tools emerging from below the surface. Two walking trails immerse you in this UNESCO-listed wilderness. As you walk, keep an eye out for endemic birds, including the Fiji goshawk and the many-colored fruit dove. Allow two hours for the longer trail; you'll want time to clamber up the dunes, stopping often to marvel at the soul-stirring views of the coast.

Good to know: Most buses traveling between Nadi and Sigatoka can drop you at the Sigatoka Sand Dunes visitor center.

This is feasting, Fiji style, and it's worth crossing an ocean to get involved.

485

FIJI

Tuck into a hearty *lovo* feast

No trip to Fiji would be complete without a *lovo*. This generous meal takes its name from the underground oven used to prepare it, which is typically fired up on special occasions and used to cook food in large quantities. And if you count every day of your vacation as a special occasion (as you should), you'll be pleased to discover that *lovo* feasts are a weekly tradition at many of the island nation's resorts. There's an art to a good *lovo*. First, a shallow pit is dug in the ground and lined with rocks to keep the heat in. A fire is then built in the hole and burned down until only the coals remain. Then a variety of meats and vegetables are marinated in fresh coconut milk and spices and wrapped in foil and banana leaves. Finally, the food is placed inside the covered pit and left to slow-cook for several hours, absorbing the smoky flavors of the fire. This is feasting, Fiji style, and it's worth crossing an ocean to get involved.

Good to know: Time a resort stay to coincide with its weekly *lovo* dinner day. And consider skipping lunch.

486

FIJI

Beach-hop around Fiji's islands

Studded with coconut palms, fringed by coral reefs, and lapped by the tropical waters of the South Pacific, Fiji was made for beach-hopping. And with more than 330 glorious islands to choose from, you're spoiled for choice. Our suggestion? Invest in a Bula Pass, which gives you the ultimate freedom to cruise between golden sands on a luxury catamaran. This trip is all about kicking back, so leave the planning to a minimum. One minute, you might be living out your Hollywood fantasies on a day trip from the lower Yasawa islands to the beaches of Monuriki island, which set the scene for the 2001 Tom Hanks film *Castaway*. The next, you can put your feet up with a cocktail on Natadola Beach, a crescent of white sand at the southwestern tip of Viti Levu, Fiji's main island. Despite the islands' swoon-worthy tropical beauty, you'll rarely have crowds to contend with. Instead, you can enjoy the illuminating company of marine turtles, rays, docile sharks, and starfish just a short swim from the beaches. Life is rarely this relaxing.

Good to know: Get your Bula Pass online, choosing from a duration of 5 to 15 days of island-hopping.

WHERE ELSE TO WITNESS FIREWALKING

THIMITHI FESTIVAL, TAMIL NADU, INDIA

Every year, this Hindu festival sees devotees walk over a pit of fire that's nearly 9 ft (2.7 m) in length, cooling their feet in a pit of cow's milk at the end.

NORTHERN GREECE AND SOUTHERN BULGARIA

In several villages across these two regions, the Anastenaria ritual sees participants walk barefoot on glowing coals. The origins of this ritual are debated, but many believe it to celebrate refugee ancestors who entered the regions after the Balkan Wars.

PASO DEL FUEGO AND LAS MÓNDIDAS FESTIVAL, SPAIN

Held in the town of San Pedro Manrique, locals celebrate the beginning of summer by dancing across coals every Midsummer night's eve on June 23.

487

FIJI

Watch a Fijian firewalking ceremony

Observing a firewalking ceremony is always an intense and stirring affair. Many moons ago, spirits are said to have bestowed the gift of firewalking upon a member of the Sawau tribe, and the powerful practice is maintained to this day by Sawau peoples. Imagine the smell of burning coconut husks filling the air as a troupe from Beqa Island prepare the fire pit, removing burning material so only the red-hot rocks remain. They've been preparing for days, abstaining from earthly pleasures to discipline the mind and please the spirits. At the signal of a ceremonial priest, the chanting firewalkers enter the arena and step, without flinching, across the heated stones. When each has crossed the fiery pit, the ceremony ends with more chanting and the sacrifice of the firewalkers' fern anklets to the pit. In the coming days, the anklets are recovered, ground and mixed into an earthy tonic that is consumed to complete the ritual. The ceremony is a feast for all the senses: prepare to be moved.

Good to know: Beqa is the place to witness this ceremony, but you can also see firewalking performed at resorts on Viti Levu.

488

FIJI

Dive into Fijian waters

It's difficult to resist the allure of a place described by legendary oceanographer Jacques Cousteau as the soft coral capital of the world. It's a title that continues to ring true at dive sites across Fiji, including Pacific Harbor, Beqa Lagoon, and the waters off the Suncoast, all on the main island of Viti Levu. But that's just the beginning. Fiji's balmy seas, vibrant coral reefs, and good underwater visibility combine to make it one of the South Pacific's most memorable diving destinations, with a huge variety of sites to explore below the surface. Marvel at the majesty of the Great White Wall in the Somosomo Strait off Taveuni, Fiji's third-largest island. Or base yourself on Kadavu island to bask in the underwater splendor of the Great Astrolabe Reef, with its submerged pinnacles, colorful coral gardens, dramatic drop-offs and a shipwreck primed for critter-hunting. It will only take a short foray into these waters for you to see exactly what Cousteau meant: coral reefs don't often come as abundantly alive as this.

Good to know: Underwater visibility tends to peak between July and December, when the water is cooler.

COOK ISLANDS

Explore the dreamy Cook Islands

This charming archipelago of 15 jewel box islands distills the tropical island dream down to its essence: think twinkling lagoons, sunset boat rides, and lush green hills. Islanders are proud of the fact that no hotels here stand taller than a coconut tree—you'll find no sprawling resorts or towering apartments, and very few crowds. The main island of Rarotonga is small (it takes less than an hour to drive a lap), but it's a land brimming with adventure. Trek to volcanic peaks, scuba dive and snorkel with reef fish, and then feast on the ocean's fresh bounty. Incredibly, each of the Cook Islands is smaller and more charming than the last: there's the lush beach-fringed Mauke; the cave-laden Mitiaro; and the 18-million-year-old Mangaia, which is thought to be the most ancient island in all of the Pacific.

Good to know: Since domestic flights can be irregular, book travel before committing to accommodation.

490

FRENCH POLYNESIA

Visit Tahiti

If you can only visit one island in French Polynesia, make it the shimmering wonderland of Tahiti. Not only is it the largest, accounting for almost one-third of the region's landmass, it's also the most bustling, offering a glorious medley of French Polynesia's countless charms. You might picture the island as a place of deep blue lagoons and undulating mountains (and, in large part, you'd be right), but Tahiti is also spectacular for its rich cultural scene. The varied wonders of Polynesian and French culture meet and merge in the energetic capital of Pape'ete, home to boulevards redolent of central Paris, renowned museums housing rare pearls, and a chic harbor thronged with bars. When exploring the city's deservedly famous Sunday markets, be sure to try Tahitian Poisson Cru, French Polynesia's national dish, consisting of raw fish, vegetables, and coconut milk. To get closer to the island, rent a scooter and cruise through the coastal neighborhoods. Unsurprisingly for a land this beautiful, life is mostly lived outside: you'll see friends playing bingo, hikers taking to the hills, and intrepid surfers making for the epic waves of Tahiti Iti.

Good to know: The best way to explore the island is by renting an electric scooter from a company like Hello Scoot.

> If you can only visit one island in French Polynesia, make it the shimmering wonderland of Tahiti.

491

FRENCH POLYNESIA

Be enamored of Bora Bora

There's good reason why honeymooners venture to this South Pacific island after exchanging their vows: few places in the world do luxury quite like Bora Bora. Here, raised bungalows teeter above an aquamarine lagoon, cold drinks are served at the swanky Bora Bora Yacht Club, and the white sands of Matira Beach welcome a day of lounging. But Bora Bora is so much more than a romantic oasis. Protected by a barrier reef, the island harbors an adventurous underbelly beneath its pristine waters. Scuba dive with manta rays, snorkel with blacktip reef sharks, and admire the island from the water on a lagoon tour. On dry land, take a quad journey to defunct World War II canons and climb the volcano of Mount Pahia. All that activity makes indulging in some R&R all the more rewarding.

Good to know: You'll need to organize a connecting flight to Bora Bora Airport from Tahiti.

492

FRENCH POLYNESIA

Dive the Tuamotus

The Tuamotu atolls stretch over French Polynesia's waters like a pearl bracelet. Remnants of ancient volcanoes, these thin islets have shorelines teeming with marine life, providing some of the best snorkeling and diving experiences on Earth. Explore the passes of Fakarava to find the largest gathering of gray reef sharks in the world; dip beneath the turquoise lagoon of Tikehau to explore a vast coral reef nurturing sea turtles and manta rays, and visited by inquisitive dolphins. The atolls are a bustling celebration of the ocean's biodiversity, but the joys of the Tuamotus aren't confined to the water. On the island of Rangiroa, you can sample a glass of the world's only atoll-grown wine, then cycle past tropical forests and golden beaches. A perfect end to a day's diving.

Good to know: Get the Air Tahiti Multi-Islands Pass for an economical way to island-hop the Tuamotus.

493

FRENCH POLYNESIA

Island-hop the Marquesas Islands

The Marquesas Islands are made up of 12 volcanic islands located more than 900 miles (1,450 km) northeast of Tahiti. These tranquil, ocean-lapped wonders stretch the word "remote" to its limits: no other island group on Earth is located this far from another continent, and only six are inhabited. But great things come to those who travel. There's amazing animal encounters to be had as you explore the soaring slopes and golden sands, where endemic species like the Marquesan kingfisher live. There's unique rugged beauty to appreciate, especially on the island of 'Ua Pou, which undulates to such a degree that there is no stretch flat enough to build a runway. And there's the very best of island living to sample on Nuku Hiva and Hiva Oa, where boat tours lead to the idyllic Vaipo waterfall, local markets sell traditional wooden tikis, and Marquesan dance rehearsals play out in town. Even better, you'll find few tourists here—a great thing indeed.

Good to know: In order to reach the islands, first fly to Tahiti, then take a 3½-hour flight to Nuku Hiva.

SOLOMON ISLANDS

Visit Skull Island

At Skull Island, known locally as Nusa Kunda, the clue is in the name: this verdant atoll is home to an eerie collection of carefully preserved human skulls, some more than 300 years old. It might sound morbid, but the island affords fascinating insights into traditional Melanesian culture. Skulls were collected for multiple reasons, some as symbols of wartime victory (those belonging to people killed in battle often have visible punctures and fractures revealing their grisly cause of death) and others as a means of honoring former chiefs and beloved community members. Beside the preserved skulls are the final resting places of renowned chiefs, many adorned with shell money that was once used as currency in the Solomon Islands. The only way to access the island is by boat, with local guides typically performing a short ritual or prayer before stepping ashore. Christian missionaries might have disapproved of these skulls, destroying them as they ventured through the Solomon Islands, but today they serve as a reminder of a powerful and spiritually significant cultural custom.

Good to know: The best way to reach Skull Island is to fly into Munda Airport and then take a 30-minute boat ride.

PAPUA NEW GUINEA

Party at the Mount Hagen Show

With the thump of a Kundu drum, the most exciting party in the Pacific has begun. One of Papua New Guinea's most significant cultural events, the Mount Hagen Show, known locally as a "sing-sing," takes place in the city of Mount Hagen every August, and is a joyous event that unifies peoples from more than 800 regional groups. Bringing together distinct languages, foods, and cultural customs, this is more than a glorious celebration of diversity and tradition—it's the perfect opportunity to deepen your understanding of the region's Indigenous cultures. Since the festival's founding in the 1960s, it's been about preserving and celebrating the region's once fading traditions, and the level of pride on show here— from the performances to the arts and crafts on display—is infectious. Ancestral storytelling sheds light on myths, beliefs, and rituals, while thousands of painted warriors in a sea of head-dresses stomp their feet to rhythmic beats and sing mesmerizing low chants.

Good to know: Book your accommodation at least six months before the Mount Hagen Show, because rooms sell out fast.

496

PAPUA NEW GUINEA

Catch a wave at Vanimo

Unridden waves break along Papua New Guinea's northern coastline, a destination yet to hit the mainstream surfari scene. You won't find these waves plastered on the pages of surf magazines, all over social media, or accurately forecast on major surf websites. No, surfing in Papua New Guinea is one for those who go it alone. New surfers will find forgiving waves at the region's sandy beach breaks, while those with more experience can instead make for the reefs. But how do some of the world's best swells manage to remain so uncharted, you ask? It's all down to Papua New Guinea's surf-management plan, which requires surfers to pay a small fee to ride the waves, with the money going toward keeping the land as pristine as possible. Knowing you're one of the first to cruise along a soaring horizontal tunnel while also supporting the local wave-riding community is pretty awesome.

Good to know: Bring your own surfboards, because rentals are limited in these parts.

497

PALAU

Wonder at the Badrulchau Stone Monoliths

On the northern end of Babeldaob Island, a cluster of 24 mysterious basalt monoliths about 3 ft (1 m) wide and up to 10 ft (3 m) tall are thought to have been the former building blocks of a *bai*—a meeting house—built around 150 CE. Each stone block is square, and many of them have etched faces. While their precise history is unknown, Badrulchau legend states that the monoliths were crafted by the gods during a time of universal darkness. The gods worked together to construct the stones, but Medechii Belau—who was something of a trickster—fell behind in his work, so he turned a coconut into a rooster, which crowed to signal the approaching dawn, causing the rest of the gods to abandon their work and leave behind the rocks you see today. The best time to walk around the monoliths, the oldest archaeological site in Palau? That'll be dawn, of course.

Good to know: The Badrulchau Stone Monoliths are easily visited as part of a full-day road trip around Babeldaob Island.

WHERE ELSE
TO INDULGE IN
A MUD BATH

**HELL'S GATE
GEOTHERMAL
PARK AND MUD
BATH SPA,
NEW ZEALAND**
There's nothing
hellish about
taking a dip here,
the only thermal
park in the country
owned by the
Māori. Pools of
boiling mud treat
different ailments,
from white mud
that relieves burns
to gray mud that
exfoliates.

**BORYEONG
MUD FESTIVAL,
SOUTH KOREA**
If a massive mud
festival sounds like
your kind of party,
head to this city in
July. Mud pools
and mud slides are
a riot, but it's
throwing mud (rich
in minerals) at
strangers that's
the most fun.

**DALYAN MUD
BATH, TÜRKIYE**
In Marmaris
on Türkiye's
southwest coast,
you can cover
yourself in soft dirt
before cleansing
off in a sulfur pool.
Legend says
Cleopatra visited
this area, so follow
suit and pamper
like royalty.

498

PALAU

Dip in the Milky Way Lagoon

With a name like the Milky Way, this lagoon is guaranteed to be out of this world. Lying in the tiny country of Palau in the western Pacific Ocean, the Milky Way Lagoon is tucked between a cluster of limestone islets, each one a coral reef relic that has emerged above the sea's surface over eons. Many are bedecked with tufts of resilient vegetation and fringed with biodiverse mangrove roots reaching deep into the water, while fine clay at the bottom of the lagoon gives it a cloudy hue, making it feel like you're drifting through another galaxy. The lagoon can be explored by boat or kayak, but to really experience its wonders (and its sublime tropical warmth) you'll want to hold your breath and plunge to the bottom to scoop up soft clay. Return to the surface, slather the mud onto your skin and let it dry in the gentle Pacific sunlight before rinsing it off with a quick dip in the sea. Legend states that a mud bath at the Milky Way Lagoon removes ten years of aging, a theory you can test out in person. It's worth a try, right?

Good to know: Plan a trip to Milky Way Lagoon early in your visit in case it needs to be deferred due to inclement weather.

341

500

PALAU

Dive the Blue Corner Wall

The ocean might make up around 70 percent of the Earth's surface, but only 5 percent of the blue expanse has been explored by humans. Blue Corner Wall is one such chartered place. This hugely biodiverse section of Palau's barrier reef is blessed with strong currents, which funnel creatures toward it like an oceanic super-highway and make for one of the world's most epic diving experiences. Plunge into the depths of the water and fin alongside reefs encrusted with hard and soft corals, searching for colorfully named macro-life like nudibranchs, crustaceans, anemonefish, and lionfish. Reef fish dart in between lacelike Gorgonian fan corals, while sea turtles, eagle rays, and manta rays race through the depths in search of food and shelter. If you're lucky, you might spot a whale shark, hammerhead, or bull shark—in 2009, the Palau government declared Palau's waters the world's first shark sanctuary. It's waters like these that are a firm reminder that we're far from alone on this planet.

Good to know: If you plan to dive multiple times daily, a scuba liveaboard trip is worth booking.

499

PALAU

Swim in Jellyfish Lake

Have your underwater cameras ready. Hidden amid a tangled mangrove forest, Jellyfish Lake is a remnant from the last Ice Age, and is fed by sea water trickling through cracks and crevices in the island's limestone. With the only major predator being a sea anemone, millions of golden and moon jellyfish inhabit these waters, gliding almost weightlessly through the depths. Fear not: their stings are harmless to humans, meaning this is one of the few places where you can safely swim among these delicate creatures. With their intricate tentacles and translucent bells, the jellyfish act like alien guides on your ethereal underwater adventure. The jellyfish of Jellyfish Lake are devoted sunseekers: as the day goes on, they follow the sun's rays across the lake. Seeing the sunlight streaming through the depths of the lake and catching their translucent bodies is one of nature's strangest and most astounding spectacles.

Good to know: The lake's ecosystem is fragile; rash guards and leggings for sun protection minimize harsh sunblocks.

INDEX

Flowers (cont.)
Rose Valley (Bulgaria) 200
tulips, Bollenstreek (Netherlands) 162
Valley of Flowers National Park (India) 251
Football, Caesars Superdome, New Orleans (USA) 33
Forbidden City, Beijing (China) 295
Fourth of July (USA) 44
Freetown (Sierra Leone) 219

G

Galápagos Islands (Ecuador) 88
Gambia River (The Gambia) 219
Ganges River (India) 254
Gardens by the Bay (Singapore) 275
Gelato, Florence (Italy) 181
Georgia 205
Gettysburg National Park, Pennsylvania (USA) 46
Ghibli Museum, Tokyo (Japan) 304
Giant's Causeway (Northern Ireland) 121
Girl with a Pearl Earring (Netherlands) 163
Giverny (France) 151
Glacier Express (Switzerland) 166–7
Glastonbury Festival (England) 130
Going-to-the-Sun Road, Montana (USA) 15
Golden Circle (Iceland) 113
Golden Gai, Tokyo (Japan) 306
Golden Gate Bridge, San Francisco (USA) 19
Golden Temple, Amritsar (India) 248
Gold Rush history 26
Golf, St. Andrews (Scotland) 124
Gorillas (Rwanda) 229
Gospel music, Harlem, New York City (USA) 52
Graceland, Tennessee (USA) 39
Granada (Spain) 144
Grand Canyon, Arizona (USA) 29
Grand Central Terminal, New York City (USA) 55
Grand Palace, Bangkok (Thailand) 267

Grand Prismatic Spring, Wyoming (USA) 16
Grand Teton National Park, Wyoming (USA) 16
Great Barrier Reef (Australia) 317
Great Blue Hole (Belize) 76–7
Great Migration (Kenya) 231
Great Mosque, Córdoba (Spain) 143
Great Ocean Road (Australia) 316
Great Sand Dunes National Park, Colorado (USA) 221
Great Smoky Mountains (USA) 39
Great Wall of China 296–7
Greenland 210
Grenadines 85
Griffith Park, Hollywood, California (USA) 23
Grumari beach, Rio de Janeiro (Brazil) 93
Guggenheim Museum, New York City (USA) 49
Guinness (Ireland) 117

H

Hackesche Höfe, Berlin (Germany) 171
Hagia Sophia Grand Mosque, Istanbul (Türkiye) 203
Haight-Ashbury Clock, San Francisco (USA) 19
Halong Bay (Vietnam) 285
Hamburg (Germany) 174
Hāngī (New Zealand) 326
Harlem, New York City (USA) 52
Hauptbahnhof, Berlin (Germany) 171
Havana (Cuba) 79
Hawai'i Volcanoes National Park (USA) 10
Hawker centers (Singapore) 274
Hell's Gate Geothermal Park and Mud Bath Spa (New Zealand) 341
Helsinki (Finland) 208
Hill Country (Sri Lanka) 255
Himalayas (Nepal) 258
Hobbiton (New Zealand) 330
Hokkaido (Japan) 159
Holi (India) 252–3
Hollywood, California (USA) 22, 23
Hong Kong (China) 293
Horseshoe Bend, Grand Canyon, Arizona (USA) 29
Hôtel de la Marine, Paris (France) 153

Hot springs
Budapest (Hungary) 196
Grand Prismatic Spring, Wyoming (USA) 16
onsen (Japan) 310
Rotorua (New Zealand) 330
Pamukkale Hot Springs (Türkiye) 205
Huacachina (Peru) 221
Humayun's Tomb (India) 250
Hvammsvík (Iceland) 114
Hvar (Croatia) 159

I

Ibiza (Spain) 147
Ice hockey (Canada) 62
Idemitsu Museum of Arts, Tokyo (Japan) 305
Igloos (Finland) 206
Iguazú Falls (Argentina) 104–5
Ijen Volcano (Indonesia) 278
Imperial Palace, Tokyo (Japan) 306
Incas (Peru) 95–6
Inca Trail (Peru) 95
Inside Passage, Alaska (USA) 13
Interrail across Europe 140
Inverdoorn Game Reserve (South Africa) 223
Ipanema beach, Rio de Janeiro (Brazil) 93
Iriomote-Ishigaki National Park (Japan) 325
Island-hopping
Bahamas 81–2
Cook Islands 335
Fiji 332–3
Greece 202
Grenadines 85
Maldives 257
Marquesas Islands (French Polynesia) 337
Philippines 280
Whitsunday Islands (Australia) 323
Istanbul (Türkiye) 203

J

Jacobite Steam Train (Scotland) 122
Jamaica 82
Jardin Majorelle, Marrakech (Morocco) 216
Java (Indonesia) 277–8
Jeju Island (South Korea) 299
Jellyfish Lake (Palau) 342
Jemaa el-Fna, Marrakech (Morocco) 216
Joatinga beach, Rio de Janeiro (Brazil) 93

Jungles
Amazon Rainforest (Brazil) 91
Borneo (Malaysia) 271
Tikal (Guatemala) 76

K

Kahlo, Frida 71
Kaieteur Falls (Guyana) 90
Kainuu (Finland) 207
Kalemegdan Park (Serbia) 196
Kangaroo Island (Australia) 316
Karaoke (Japan) 305
Kathmandu (Nepal) 259
Kaua'i, Hawaii (USA) 11
Kayaking
Denali National Park (USA) 12
Yukon River (Canada) 58–9
Kejetia Market (Ghana) 218
Kentucky Bourbon Trail (USA) 36
Kew Gardens (England) 270
Khao Sok (Thailand) 270
Kilimanjaro (Tanzania) 230
Kirishima-Kinkowan National Park (Japan) 10
Klondike (Canada) 26
Koalas, Kangaroo Island (Australia) 316
Koh Pha Ngan full moon parties (Thailand) 268
Komodo Island (Indonesia) 279
Kona, Hawaii (USA) 84
Ko Phi Phi (Thailand) 271
Kraków (Poland) 79, 198
Kruger National Park (South Africa) 224
Kuala Lumpur (Malaysia) 272
Kumano Kodo (Japan) 300
Kyoto (Japan) 301

L

Lagos (Nigeria) 218
Laikipia Wilderness Camp (Kenya) 257
Lake District (England) 128–9
Lake of Stars (Malawi) 228
Lama Temple, Beijing (China) 295
Lantern Festival (China) 293
Lapland (Finland) 207, 210
Lapland (Sweden) 257
Las Móndidas Festival (Spain) 334
La Sorbonne, Paris (France) 153
Las Vegas, Nevada (USA) 27
La Tomatina Festival (Spain) 146
Lavender, Provence (France) 159
La Seo, Zaragoza (Spain) 142

Acknowledgments

The DK travel team would like to thank the following contributors for their words:

Rudolf Abraham is an award-winning travel writer, photographer, and guidebook author specializing in central and southeast Europe. His work is published widely, including in *The Guardian* and *National Geographic Traveler*.

Latifah Al-Hazza is a Kuwaiti-American travel writer who spends her time between Kuwait and the US. Her work can be read in *Vogue Arabia*, *Harper's Bazaar Arabia*, *Travel + Leisure*, and *Forbes*, to name a few.

Paul Bloomfield is a writer and broadcaster based in the West Country of England. He writes on hiking, history, and wildlife for the likes of *The Times*, *The Telegraph*, and *Wanderlust*. He hopes to swim with humpback whales one day.

Nicola Brady is a travel writer based in Dublin, whose work has been in the *Irish Independent*, *Condé Nast Traveler*, *The Times*, and more. She's trekked with gorillas in Uganda and hidden from pythons in Myanmar, but next up on her bucket list is seeing orcas, wherever that may take her.

Jamie Ditaranto is a travel writer who has lived in Mexico, Italy, Portugal, New Zealand, and Brazil, but now calls Barcelona home. Her work has appeared in *National Geographic*, *Travel + Leisure*, and more.

Pavlo Fedykovych is an Uzhhorod-born, Poland-based travel writer. His work has appeared in *The Independent*, *Time Out*, and Fodor's among others. Globe-trotting is his lifestyle, producing music his passion, and writing his calling.

Ben Ffrancon Dowds is a Welsh nonfiction writer and literary translator based in the Cayman Islands. As well as contributing to travel guides to France, Spain, and the Caribbean, he writes textbooks and children's books.

Emma Gregg is an award-winning, UK-based travel journalist who has visited all seven continents. But it's Africa that keeps calling her back. Emma has written for Rough Guides, *National Geographic Traveler*, *Travel Africa*, and many others.

Rebecca Hallett is a Newcastle-based travel writer, who's coauthored several Japan guidebooks. Her work, which mostly focuses on the UK and Japan, has been published in *The Times*, *The Telegraph*, *National Geographic Traveler*, and plenty more.

Paula Hotti is a Finnish travel journalist, writer of detective fiction, and a fan of overland journeys. She has authored guidebooks for Lonely Planet and Rough Guides. When not plotting fictitious murders, she's planning new train trips and dreaming of circling the globe overland.

Kana Kavon is a US-based travel writer whose work centers on Latin American culture and destinations. She authored the children's title, *The 50 States: Amazing Landscapes. Fascinating People. Wonderful Wildlife.*

Stephen Keeling is an award-winning travel writer based in New York City. He worked as a financial journalist in Asia before writing his first travel book in 2005. Since then, he's worked on guides to locations in Europe, Asia, and across the Americas.

Daphné Leprince-Ringuet is a writer and journalist based in Paris. She loves traveling around her homeland and has written about many French regions—but her heart belongs to Brittany's exhilarating seascapes and hearty food.

Shafik Meghji is an award-winning travel writer, journalist, and author of *Crossed Off the Map: Travels in Bolivia*. He has coauthored more than 45 guidebooks and writes for publications such as *BBC Travel* and *Wanderlust*, specializing in Latin America and South Asia.

Thomas O'Malley is a British writer covering travel in China, Japan, Hong Kong, Taiwan, and Mongolia. He is a guidebook author and reports on China travel for *The Telegraph*. He lived in Beijing for 12 years, during which time he gained considerable expertise in Great Wall hiking and Peking duck consumption.

Paul Oswell is a an award-winning, British travel journalist based in New Orleans. He is the author of *Bucket List: North America* and has reported for publications including *Condé Nast Traveler*, *Travel + Leisure*, and *The Guardian*.

Chantae Reden is a travel writer based in Fiji. She is the guidebook author of *Moon Bali and Lombok* and *Moon Tahiti and French Polynesia*, as well as the founder of The Salt Sirens, a website about ocean adventures. When she's not at her laptop, you'll find her free diving, surfing, and hiking throughout the South Pacific.

Sarah Reid is an award-winning Australian travel writer with a passion for positive-impact travel. Her work appears in *BBC Travel*, *Condé Nast Traveler*, *International Traveler*, Lonely Planet, *National Geographic Traveler*, and more.

Anna Richards is a British writer living in Lyon, France. She's the author of *Paddling France* for Bradt Guides. Her work, almost entirely about the country she calls home, has appeared in *The Guardian*, *The Telegraph*, *The Times*, and others.

Daniel Robinson is a Baltimore-based writer, who has authored travel guides for DK, Lonely Planet, and others; his work has appeared in 10 languages. When not covering the Middle East, he enjoys rain forest trekking in Borneo and dining in Singapore's hawker centers.

Kristen Shoates is a writer and brand strategist based in Nashville, Tennessee. She loves going off the beaten path, and has written for *The Infatuation*, *The Nashville Guide*, and DK's *Nashville Like a Local* and *Go Here Instead*.

Daniel Stables is a travel writer based in Manchester, England. He writes travel articles for *National Geographic* and the BBC, and has authored or contributed to more than 30 travel books on destinations worldwide. He also hosts a podcast, Hungry Ghosts, about food and travel.

Selena Takigawa Hoy is a Japanese-American writer living in Tokyo. She has written for *Travel + Leisure*, *National Geographic*, *BBC Travel*, and others. You can find her soaking in an onsen and nerding out on traditional crafts in rural Japan.

Emma Thomson is a UK-based travel writer and author of *Quiet Escapes*, and was the BGTW Travel Writer of the Year in 2019 & 2022. She has walked the Skeleton Coast in Namibia and traced the Silk Road, but swimming with whales in Tonga is now top of her bucket list.

Lisa Voormeij is originally from The Netherlands and now splits her time between the West Kootenay region of British Columbia and Mexico. She has contributed to more than 60 DK books.

Tasmin Waby has spent most of her life in Australia and the UK, despite her parents hailing from New Zealand. Her food and travel writing has been published in *The Age*, *Australian Gourmet Traveler*, *Culture Trip*, and more.

Luke Waterson is an award-winning culinary, adventure and sustainability travel writer specializing in the UK outdoors, Scandinavia, and Latin America. He writes regularly for DK, Lonely Planet, the BBC, *The Telegraph*, and more, and is also a novelist. He can be found on multi-day hikes, usually off-trail and far from the nearest 4G coverage.

Danielle Watt is a writer, photographer, and filmmaker based in Edinburgh, Scotland. She can usually be found scribbling away in one of the city's coffee shops, checking out local gigs, or heading off on an adventure with her husband and her wee dog, Winnie.

Wendy Watta is a Kenyan writer living in Nairobi. Her work has appeared in *Condé Nast*, Lonely Planet, Fodor's, and more. Whether kayaking in Senegal or trekking in Ethiopia, she's always ready for a trip.

Barbara Woolsey is a Canadian journalist with Filipina, Irish, and Scottish roots, living between Berlin and Bangkok for over a decade. Besides writing for Lonely Planet, DK, and others, she DJs in Berlin clubs from KitKat to KaterBlau.

The publisher would like to thank the following for their kind permission to reproduce their photographs:

(Key: a-above; b-below/bottom; c-center; f-far; l-left; r-right; t-top)

123RF.com: Adamico 74-75bc, Agamiphoto 74cr (Bird), Anatoliygleb 8br (Skiing), Blacklistmauer 8ca, Borchee 212cla (Zebra & Cars), Dndavis 8-9br, Eakmoto 75bl, Ekaterinabelova 74clb (Beach), Elisalocci 74c, Enciktat 8clb, Epicstockmedia 312tr, Epokrovsky 212cra, Flippo 8tl (Clapboard), Grazziela 110tc (bouquet), Hanoiphotography 244clb, Haveseen 8tl, Imagex 8br (Trees), Javarman 74cb, Matej Kastelic 301t, Kavram 212-213c, Lev Kropotov 244cra, Lobachad 212b, Maridav 8br, Matthiasbachmaier 74crb, Mehta123 244cr, Membio 74-75c, Nexusplexus 8tc, Nikokvfrmoto 212cla, nk2549 244c, Onlineexpress 74cb (Iceberg), 212crb (Penguins), Oskanov 74ca, Pakhnyushchyy 74-75, Ripiopv 74cla, Rowansims 312bl, Rudiernst 74bc (Car), Sclow1105 244bc (Flower), Shaffandi 8-9c, Shalamov 74bl, Slepitsky 244crb (Tents), Somchaij 8cb, Soysuwan123 312tl, Ssotangkur 8cr, sssccc 212tc, Surachetsh 244br (Noodle), Themess 110clb, Thvideo 212br (Boat), Trendobjects 75cla, Vsurkov 74tc

4Corners: Jordan Banks 107br, Antonino Bartuccio 190t, 190b, Francesco Carovillano 151tl, Estock 184br, Justin Foulkes 54br, 73bl, 132br, 133t, 158bl, 195tl, 240br, Hans-Peter Huber 175tl, Susanne Kremer 112, 195br, Claudio Leolini 154tl, Maurizio Rellini 113tr, 275t, Massimo Ripani 115t, Luca Da Ros 11b, Reinhard Schmid 191bl, 201tl, Richard Taylor 126br, Luigi Vaccarella 121bl

Alamy Stock Photo: Aquascopic 272bl, Gonzalo Azumendi 147tr, D. Holden Bailey 342br, Mark Bassett 305tl, Johannes Vermeer, Girl with a Pearl Earring, 1665, photo Berngardt 163br, Blickwinkel 237tl, Nonglak Bunkoet / Legrand 150br, Cavan Images 88tl, 225b, Charles O. Cecil 229tr, Marcia Chambers 71tl, Daniel Chetroni 200tl, Neale Clark / Robert Harding 63tr, Dennis Cox 31br, Dbtravel 248tl, Danita Delimont 249b, Pham Dinh Duc / Xinhua 286br, Greg Balfour Evans 131br, Fotomaton 136tr, Geoffwiggins.com 214tr, Connie Glass 117br, Martin Harvey 221bl, Juergen Held / Travelstock44 171tl, Susan Heller 66br, Gavin Hellier / Robert Harding 242bl, Afriadi Hikmal 279br, Christopher Hill Photographic / Scenicireland.com 118-119, Kate Hockenhull 274t, Clarence Holmes Photography 44tl, Hufton+Crow-

VIEW / Architect: Heatherwick Studio, 2017 223tr, Imaginechina Limited 291bl, Anton Ivanov 71br, Ayesha Jassat / Stockimo 243bl, Suzuki Kaku 340tr, Jamilya Khalilulina 30br, Markus Mainka 311br, Iain Masterton 242tr, Perry van Munster 142tr, Louise Murray / Robert Harding 338tl, Sérgio Nogueira 226br, Anne-Marie Palmer 80tr, Frilet Patrick / Hemis.fr 40br, Douglas Peebles Photography 334tl, George Philip 124tl, Dave Primov 218tl, imageBROKER / Chris Putnam 42br, Vivek Renukaprasad 251tl, Mike Robinson 332tl, Rolf_52 38tl, Rudi1976 174br, Michael Runkel / Robert Harding 66tl, 299tr, Ivan Rwatschew 287tl, Dan Santillo NZ 326tr, Kevin Schafer / Minden Pictures 90bl, Alex Segre 305br, ShawStock 137bl, Lux Tonnerre 341b, Topcris 73tr, Tuul / Robert Harding 234bl, Suranga Weeratuna 255bl, Edward Westmacott 49bl, Dawid Kalisinski / Zoonar 292bl

Amtrak: 20-21
Alden Anderson: 283tr
Arctic SnowHotel & Glass Igloos: 206br
AWL Images: Mauricio Abreu 247bl, Jon Arnold 127br, 238br, J. Banks 39tl, 41br, Marco Bottigelli 120t, 147bl, 279tl, 306tr, ClickAlps 10br, 22, John Coletti 37tr, Matteo Colombo 176tr, 275b, 284tr, 290b, 308b, Alan Copson 27br, 42tl, Kav Dadfar 262t, Cahir Davitt 186bl, Danita Delimont Stock 47b, 69, 222, Shaun Egan 121tr, Michele Falzone 102t, 104tl, 205bl, Neil Farrin 144b, Jeremy Flint 169b, 292tr, Paul Harris 114tl, Gavin Hellier 130tl, Hemis 78b, 151br, 153tr, 154br, 160br, Francesco Iacobelli 184tl, J. Banks 235b, Karol Kozlowski 78tl, 79tl, 79br, 136bl, 137tr, 208bl, 239b, 241, Nick Ledger 196bl, Julian Love 216, Tim Mannakee 203br, 246, Stefano Politi Markovina 175bl, 177b, Jan Miracky 28b, 260-261, James Montgomery 290t, Christian Mueringer 132tl, Richard Nowitz 124br, Leonardo Papera 180br, Nigel Pavitt 227tl, 231br, Ben Pipe 99bl, Maurizio Rellini 183bl, Jonathan and Angela Scott 262b, Steve Vidler 133b

Belmond Ltd.: Richard James Taylor 98tr
Belmond Management Limited: Maureen Martinez Evans 160tl
© DACS 2024: Picasso Pablo, Guernica, 1937 © Succession Picasso 145tr
Depositphotos Inc: Imagecom 8cl, Peter77 110tc, Valery121283 110cb, Vladsilver 74clb, Warat42 212c, Cezary Wojtkowski 254tr
Dorling Kindersley: Cotswold Wildlife Park / Gary Ombler 212-213c (flamingo)
Dreamstime.com: 9parusnikov 110cr, Adwo 316tr, Acelya Aksunkur 19bl, Leonid Andronov 57tl, Andrey Armyagov 212bl, INigo Arza Azcorra 256br, F Baarssen 201br, Rui Baião 95tr, Benkrut 331tr, Lukas Bischoff

205tr, Darryl Brooks 189tl, I Putu Budiastawa 278tl, Oksana Byelikova 26t, Castenoid 176bl, Klanarong Chitmung 331bl, Valentyna Chukhlyebova 313clb, Jonathan Cohen 122bl, Sorin Colac 143tr, Harry Collins 231bl, Cowardlion 304, Panuwat Dangsungnoen 310t, Ivo De 105, Dimarik16 84b, Erin Donalson 312br, Dorinmarius 141t, Enfig74 45b, F11photo 40tl, 101br, 308t, Sergii Figurnyi 196tr, Fotorince 198tr, Gunther Fraulob 17tl, Zoltan Gabor 193, Vladislav Gajic 187tr, Giuseppemasci 182, Diego Grandi 172tr, Happystock 277br, Amy Harris 312clb, Bradley Hay 244cla, Maurie Hill 26b, Hlphoto 312cb, Idmanjoe 268tl, Eric Isselee / Isselee 312bl (Koala), Isselee 312crb (Clownfish), Jdphotos1 61tl, Jojjik 110bl, Kacas 189br, Keolafirsov 224tr, Andrey Kobylko 207tl, Jesse Kraft 94t, Tjeerd Kruse 254bl, Dalia Kvedaraite 207br, Iuliia Lavrinenko 140tl, Pierrick Lemaret 265tl, Puripat Lertpunyaroj 324tl, Betty Leung 221tr, Miroslav Liska 17br, Manfredxy 244cr (Blossoms), Manjik 277tl, Tomas Marek 199bl, Margaret619 39bl, Martinmark 11t, Cameron Mcphail 316bl, Mehameleers 236, Galina Mikhalishina 110br, Luciano Mortula 110ca, Tomas Nevesely 24t, Nicunickie 212tr, Noppakun 303bl, Hrecheniuk Oleksii 239t, Gurkan Ozturk 322bl, Pascalou95 212 (Sand), 312c, Sean Pavone 45t, 56br, 244ca, 301b, Piotr Pawinski 8br (Boots), Ruth Peterkin 12tr, Pixattitude 74bc, 110cl, Pniesen 76br, Presse750 266tr, Andrej Privizer 220bl, Andreas Prott 204tr, Penchan Pumila 268br, Ricok 209bl, Ronniechua 63bl, Rudi1976 170, Sborisov 187bl, Scaliger 167, Seadam 337bl, Sergeychernov 282b, Serjedi / Sergio Bertino 110cr (temple), Alexander Shalamov 85bl, Volodymyr Shevchuk 210br, Ratchada Siwalaikul 312cl, Roman Slavik 24b, Jacek Sopotnicki 203tl, Ivan Soto 144t, Ron Sumners / Sumnersgraphicsinc 312c (Rock), Thanakorn Suppamethasawat 266bl, Takepicsforfun 263bl, Sergey Uryadnikov 271br, Roman Samokhin / Usensam2007 212ca, Vampy1 90tr, Kelly Vandellen 25tl, VanderWolfImages 217bl, Susan Vineyard 8bc, Vitalyedush 55tl, 312cr, Vitmark 75bl (boat), Gary Webber 327bl, Whitcomberd 128br, Wirestock 194br, 212tc (Kilimanjaro), Xantana 161, 192br

Ecoventura: Renato Granieri 88br
Getty Images: 117 Imagery 286tl, 4FR 27tl, Luis Acosta / AFP 89br, Peter Adams 215, Manuel Queimadelos Alonso 146bl, ANP 159bl, Shahar Azran 52tl, Gonzalo Azumendi 274b, Filippo Maria Bianchi 122tr, Mark Blinch 62bl, Bloomberg 320-321, Kitti Boonnitrod 288-289, Bill Boss / 500px 47tl, Marco Bottigelli 106t, 120b, Per

Breiehagen 81tl, Nancy Brown 298b, Nick Brundle Photography 235t, Simon M Bruty 135br, Nora Carol Photography 270br, Felix Cesare 315tl, Matteo Colombo 28t, 324br, 327t, Copyright by 8Creative.vn 285b, Sylvain Cordier / Gamma-Rapho 67tl, John Crux Photography 322t, Cultura 281b, Lauren DeCicca / Stringer 269tl, Michael DeMocker 35tl, Ibrahim Suha Derbent 229bl, Anthony Devlin 131tl, Denis Doyle Picasso Pablo, Guernica, 1937 © Succession Picasso / © DACS 2024 145tr, Michael Duff 219br, Harry Durrant 130br, Rafa Elias 145bl, Suliane Favennec 336bl, Franz Marc Frei 38br, 156tl, Susanne Fritzsche / Imagebroker 209tr, Geography Photos 68bl, Erika Goldring 34, Chris Gorman 128tl, Giuseppe Greco 188br, Jeff Greenberg 43br, Daniel Grill 46tl, R. Tyler Gross 230br, Marc Guitard 99tr, Leon Harris 123tr, Mike Hill 210tl, Phil Clarke Hill 82br, Matthew Horwood 148-149, Hiroyuki Ito 54tl, Thomas Janisch 341tr, Michael Lee 50tr, Zhenjin Li 291tr, Andrew Lichtenstein 84t, Cindy Liu / Stringer 281t, Jordan Lye 273t, Tim Macpherson 143bl, David Madison 86b, Maremagnum 307tr, Didier Marti 333, 335b, Charles McQuillan 115b, Maddie Meyer 56, Jeff J Mitchell 123bl, 125br, Roberto Moiola / Sysaworld 165tr, Terry Moore / Stocktrek Images 334br, Ken Murray / Icon Sportswire 33br, Nature, underwater and art photos / Narchuk.com 238tl, Dana Neibert 336tr, Richard T. Nowitz 33tl, James O'Neil 126tl, Simone Padovani 178tl, Ignacio Palacios 16br, Andrew Peacock 107tl, Anton Petrus 106b, Ingo Jezierski / Photodisc 244bc, Steve Woods Photography 280bl, Adrian Pope 248br, Byron Tanaphol Prukston 325br, Caroline Purser 19tr, John and Tina Reid 228bl, Vittorio Ricci - Italy 230tl, Ruben Earth 142bl, Saha Entertainment 300tl, San Francisco Chronicle / Hearst Newspapers 13tr, Anup Shah 232-233, J Shepherd 127tl, Khaichuin Sim 227br, Hugh Sitton 100t, Kevin Smith / Design Pics 12bl, Dmitry Smolyanitsky 500px 23tr, Pakin Songmor 259tr, Pintai Suchachaisri 95bl, Tetra Images 46br, The Asahi Shimbun 77, Achim Thomae 179, Jarry Tripelon 152, Santiago Urquijo 220tr, Usabin 186tr, VCG Visual China Group 293bl, Feng Wei Photography 15bl, 258b, Westend61 65bl, 81b, 243tr, 342tl, Nik Wheeler 14b, Lisa Wiltse 117tl, Zhangshuang 295tr

Getty Images / iStock: 1111IESPDJ 159tr, 400tmax 35br, 4FR 323bl, 4nadia 14t, a_Taiga 163tl, Oleg Albinsky 50bl, Aletheia97 168bl, Alxpin 158tr, Grant Ancevic 82tl, Anothersteph 312tl (Mackinnon Pass), Antagain 198bl, Aphotostory 4-5, 297, Roberto Armocida 70, AscentXmedia 65tr,

The rate that the world is changing is constantly keeping the DK travel team on our toes. Every effort has been made to ensure this book is accurate and up-to-date, but things can change in an instant. Festival dates move, attractions close their doors, and the natural world is influenced by so many variables. World events occur and policies change at a rapid pace, so it's important to check ahead of making your bucket list dreams a reality. The publisher cannot accept responsibility for any consequences arising from the use of this book. If you notice we've got something wrong, we want to hear from you. Please get in touch at travelguides@dk.co.uk

Senior Editor Zoë Rutland
Project Editor Tijana Todorinović
Designer maru studio G.K.
Editors Sarah Bailey, Michael Clark, Keith Drew, Rebecca Hallett, Alex Pathe, Molly Price, Alexander Rennie, Lucy Sara-Kelly, Danielle Watt
Senior US Editor Megan Douglass
Proofreader Stephanie Smith
Indexer Hilary Bird
Picture Researcher Claire Guest
Publishing Assistant Simona Velikova
Senior Executive Cartographic Editor James Macdonald
Jacket Illustrator and Illustrations Tanya Cooper
DTP Designer David Almond
Image Retouching Michelle Brier
Production Controller Kariss Ainsworth
Managing Editor Hollie Teague
Managing Art Editor Gemma Doyle
Art Director Maxine Pedliham
Publishing Director Georgina Dee

First American Edition, 2024
Published in the United States by DK Publishing,
a division of Penguin Random House LLC
1745 Broadway, 20th Floor, New York, NY 10019

This book was made with Forest Stewardship Council™ certified paper—one small step in DK's commitment to a sustainable future. Learn more at www.dk.com/uk/information/sustainability

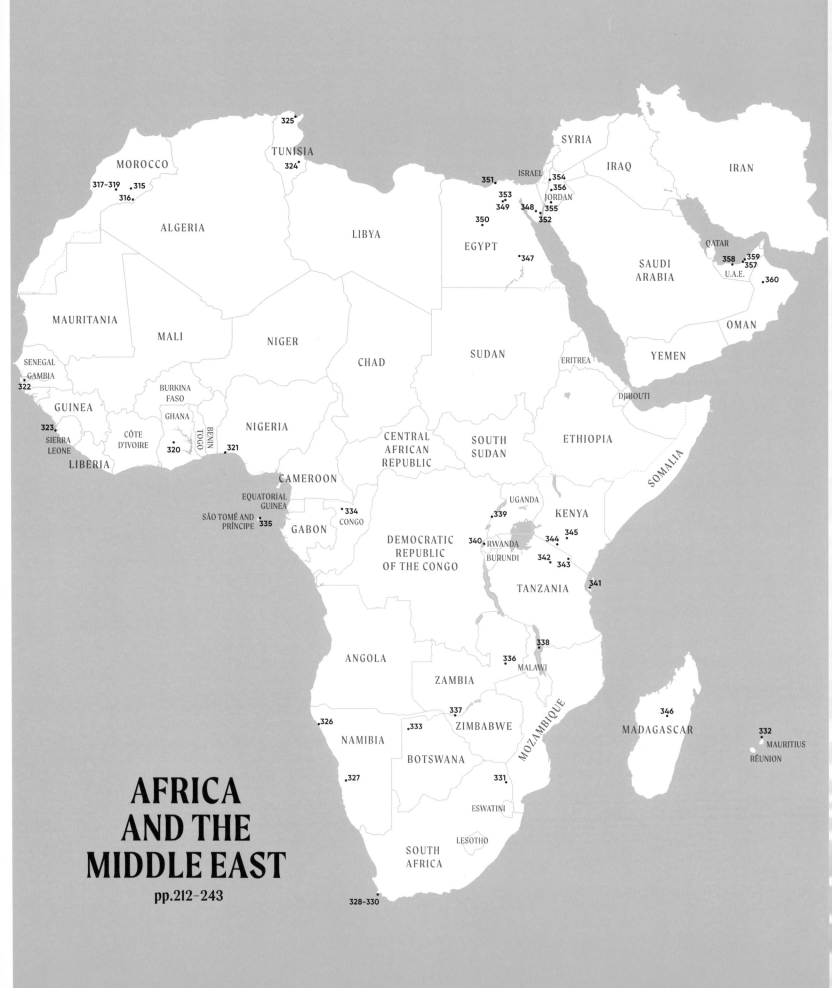

AFRICA
AND THE
MIDDLE EAST

pp.212–243

MOROCCO
• 325
TUNISIA
• 324
317–319 • • 315
316 •
ALGERIA
LIBYA
• 351
SYRIA
IRAQ
IRAN
ISRAEL
• 354
JORDAN • 356
• 353
349 • 348 • 355
350 • 352
EGYPT
SAUDI
ARABIA
QATAR
358 • • 359
• 357
U.A.E.
• 360
OMAN
• 347
MAURITANIA
MALI
NIGER
CHAD
SUDAN
ERITREA
YEMEN
DJIBOUTI
SENEGAL
GAMBIA
322 •
GUINEA
BURKINA
FASO
GHANA
BENIN
TOGO
NIGERIA
CENTRAL
AFRICAN
REPUBLIC
SOUTH
SUDAN
ETHIOPIA
SOMALIA
323 •
SIERRA
LEONE
CÔTE
D'IVOIRE
• 320
• 321
LIBERIA
CAMEROON
EQUATORIAL
GUINEA
SÃO TOMÉ AND
PRÍNCIPE • 335
GABON
• 334
CONGO
DEMOCRATIC
REPUBLIC
OF THE CONGO
UGANDA
• 339
KENYA
344 • • 345
340 • RWANDA
BURUNDI
342 • • 343
• 341
TANZANIA
ANGOLA
ZAMBIA
• 338
• 336
MALAWI
MADAGASCAR
• 346
• 332
MAURITIUS
RÉUNION
• 326
NAMIBIA
• 333
• 337
ZIMBABWE
BOTSWANA
MOZAMBIQUE
• 327
• 331
ESWATINI
LESOTHO
SOUTH
AFRICA
328–330 •